Crossing Digital Fronteras

Crossing Digital Fronteras

Rehumanizing Latinx Education and Digital Humanities

Edited by

Isabel Martínez, Irma Victoria Montelongo,
Nicholas Daniel Natividad, and Ángel David Nieves

Cover image: *Realidades y Suenos*. Alondra Aca García. Used with permission.

Published by State University of New York Press, Albany

© 2024 State University of New York

All rights reserved

Printed in the United States of America

No part of this book may be used or reproduced in any manner whatsoever without written permission. No part of this book may be stored in a retrieval system or transmitted in any form or by any means including electronic, electrostatic, magnetic tape, mechanical, photocopying, recording, or otherwise without the prior permission in writing of the publisher.

Links to third-party websites are provided as a convenience and for informational purposes only. They do not constitute an endorsement or an approval of any of the products, services, or opinions of the organization, companies, or individuals. SUNY Press bears no responsibility for the accuracy, legality, or content of a URL, the external website, or for that of subsequent websites.

For information, contact State University of New York Press, Albany, NY
www.sunypress.edu

Library of Congress Cataloging-in-Publication Data

Names: Martínez, Isabel, 1974– editor. | Montelongo, Irma Victoria, editor. | Natividad, Nicholas Daniel, 1977– editor. | Nieves, Ángel David, editor.
Title: Crossing digital fronteras : rehumanizing Latinx education and digital humanities / edited by Isabel Martínez, Irma Victoria Montelongo, Nicholas Daniel Natividad, and Ángel David Nieves.
Other titles: Rehumanizing Latinx education and digital humanities.
Description: Albany : State University of New York Press, [2024] | Includes bibliographical references and index.
Identifiers: LCCN 2023047291 | ISBN 9781438498072 (hardcover : alk. paper) | ISBN 9781438498089 (ebook)
Subjects: LCSH: Hispanic Americans—Study and teaching. | Latin Americans—Study and teaching. | Digital humanities. | Computer-assisted instruction.
Classification: LCC E184.S75 C76 2024 | DDC 371.829/68073—dc23/eng/20240327
LC record available at https://lccn.loc.gov/2023047291

Crossing Digital Fronteras

Rehumanizing Latinx Education and Digital Humanities

Edited by

Isabel Martínez, Irma Victoria Montelongo,
Nicholas Daniel Natividad, and Ángel David Nieves

Cover image: *Realidades y Suenos*. Alondra Aca García. Used with permission.

Published by State University of New York Press, Albany

© 2024 State University of New York

All rights reserved

Printed in the United States of America

No part of this book may be used or reproduced in any manner whatsoever without written permission. No part of this book may be stored in a retrieval system or transmitted in any form or by any means including electronic, electrostatic, magnetic tape, mechanical, photocopying, recording, or otherwise without the prior permission in writing of the publisher.

Links to third-party websites are provided as a convenience and for informational purposes only. They do not constitute an endorsement or an approval of any of the products, services, or opinions of the organization, companies, or individuals. SUNY Press bears no responsibility for the accuracy, legality, or content of a URL, the external website, or for that of subsequent websites.

For information, contact State University of New York Press, Albany, NY
www.sunypress.edu

Library of Congress Cataloging-in-Publication Data

Names: Martínez, Isabel, 1974– editor. | Montelongo, Irma Victoria, editor. | Natividad, Nicholas Daniel, 1977– editor. | Nieves, Ángel David, editor.
Title: Crossing digital fronteras : rehumanizing Latinx education and digital humanities / edited by Isabel Martínez, Irma Victoria Montelongo, Nicholas Daniel Natividad, and Ángel David Nieves.
Other titles: Rehumanizing Latinx education and digital humanities.
Description: Albany : State University of New York Press, [2024] | Includes bibliographical references and index.
Identifiers: LCCN 2023047291 | ISBN 9781438498072 (hardcover : alk. paper) | ISBN 9781438498089 (ebook)
Subjects: LCSH: Hispanic Americans—Study and teaching. | Latin Americans—Study and teaching. | Digital humanities. | Computer-assisted instruction.
Classification: LCC E184.S75 C76 2024 | DDC 371.829/68073—dc23/eng/20240327
LC record available at https://lccn.loc.gov/2023047291

Isabel Martínez:
To Angelo Lozada, who tirelessly supported my beliefs that
my students and I could achieve whatever we dreamed.
Love you forever.

Irma Victoria Montelongo:
To the women whose shoulders I stand on:
Gavina Vasquez, Eduarda Montelongo, Paz Ruiz, Yolanda Alvarado,
and especially my mom, Martha Elena Montelongo,
none of this is possible without your selfless examples
of what it means to be courageous yet fierce.

Nicholas Daniel Natividad:
To baby Eve and my forever coauthor in life, Osito.

Ángel David Nieves:
For Richard "Dick" Foote, the love of my life,
and the forever my "ride or die" in the struggle
for racial equality and social justice for almost three decades.
I know you and the ancestors are with me as we continue that "good fight."

Isabel, Irma, and Nicholas:
Our dear coeditor and friend, Ángel David Nieves,
unexpectedly died prior to this book's publication.
Always amidst laughter, he inspired and drove us to
push boundaries in this book. We also dedicate this book to him.

Contents

List of Illustrations ... ix

Acknowledgments ... xi

Introduction
Digital Divides, Borders, and Liberatory Edges: Latinx DH (Digital Humanities) *Finally* Comes of Age ... 1
    Isabel Martínez, Ángel David Nieves, and Cassie Tanks

Chapter 1
Toward a Rehumanizing Latinx Studies Curriculum ... 33
    Nicholas Daniel Natividad and Cynthia Wise

Chapter 2
Digital Pedagogy in a Multicultural Setting: Learning History and Connecting through Technology ... 49
    Lissette Acosta Corniel

Chapter 3
Latinx Spaces, Discourses, and Knowledges: Student Voices and the Rehumanization of Latinx Identity in the United States ... 75
    Isabel Martínez and Irma Victoria Montelongo

Chapter 4
Translanguaging and Multiple Literacies: Podcasting as a Linguistically and Culturally Sustaining Medium in a Multicultural Teacher Education Course ... 97
    Jen Stacy, Mildred Ramos, and Adriana Correa

CHAPTER 5
US Latinx Digital Humanities: Rehumanizing the Past through
Archival Digital Pedagogy   127
    *Gabriela Baeza Ventura, Lorena Gauthereau, and
    Carolina Villarroel*

CHAPTER 6
The Delis Negrón Digital Archive: A Pedagogical Approach to
Latinx Familial and Community Archives   145
    Sylvia Fernández Quintanilla and Annette Michelle Zapata

CHAPTER 7
Crossing Pedagogical Front|eras through Collaborative
World-Making and Digital Storytelling   163
    Jeanelle D. Horcasitas and Olivia Quintanilla

CHAPTER 8
Developing Action Research Projects for Latinx Students in a
Predominantly White Institution   183
    Gerardo Mancilla and Donna Vukelich-Selva

CONCLUSION
Reimagining Digital Pedagogies in Hispanic-Serving Institutions
and Beyond   219
    Isabel Martínez and Irma Victoria Montelongo

CONTRIBUTORS   235

INDEX   241

Illustrations

Figure 3.1 Group e-portfolio "Mujeres Fuertes Unidas" banner. 90

Figure 3.2 Group e-portfolio "Latinxs on the Rise" banner. 91

Figure 4.1 Interlocuters in podcast assignment. 110

Figure 7.1 Bird's-eye view of a story map. 173

Figure 8.1 Walking by the border wall. 197

Figure 8.2 Border wall. 198

Figure 8.3 An immigrant made this. 202

Figure 8.4 Families belong together poster. 203

Figure 8.5 What if I'm picked up by I.C.E.? 204

Acknowledgments

This book is over a decade in the making that began as a chance encounter at a First Year Experience conference. Over the decade, this group of editors saw numerous personal triumphs, tragedies, a global pandemic, and a rapidly shifting university landscape whose embrace of technology accelerated because of unforeseeable conditions. This book would have never come to fruition without the support of each other across these events as well as the encouragement of many individuals who supported the evolution of this book from what was merely an idea for a course to this collection of essays. First and foremost, we would like to thank the Inter-University Program for Latino Research (IUPLR) who provided generous financial support for our working group and several iterations of this project, and more specifically, Dr. Pamela Quiroz, Dr. Maira E. Alvarez, Dr. Marisela Moreno, Jessica Y. Thiam, Dr. Maria de los Angeles Torres, Olga Herrera, and others at IUPLR who championed our work over the past six years. At our respective institutions, we would also like to thank those who provided us with much appreciated intellectual, financial, curricular, and technological support including at John Jay College of Criminal Justice: the Department of Latin American and Latinx Studies, the Student Academic Success Program, and the Department of Information Technology, especially Chief Information Officer Joseph Laub, and lastly, the Office of the Advancement of Research and RF-CUNY; at New Mexico State University: Andreia Scarborough of the Department of Criminal Justice and Dr. Dulcinea Lara of the Department of Borderlands and Ethnic Studies; and at The University of Texas at El Paso: special thanks to Dr. Dorothy Ward and the Entering Students Program, Dr. Dennis Bixler-Marquez and Ms. Rosa Gomez in the Chicano Studies program, Pedro Espinoza and the staff at UTEP Technology Support, and the administration at UTEP for believing in this project. Lastly, we thank our research assistants who provided critical support at various stages of the project: Alondra Aca García and Vanessa Torres. Alondra Aca Garcia was also our cover artist and she diligently read all of the chapters and translated the authors' and editors' ideas into a visual masterpiece. Because she witnessed the project's evolution from idea to completion, we are grateful for her vision that encapsulates our work.

We are especially grateful for our acquisitions editor, Rebecca Colesworthy, who stuck with the project through partner losses, the ups and downs of the pandemic, and shifts in institutional affiliations. Our essayists have been such great colleagues throughout this process. Their patience and understanding with our many delays has been greatly appreciated. They are some of the very best scholar-activists in Latinx DH. We are so proud they agreed to be a part of this volume. We also want to thank the anonymous reviewers who carefully read our manuscript and provided detailed and thoughtful feedback. And of course, we give deep thanks to SUNY Press for being exceptional to work with in every way possible.

Isabel Martínez: My deepest appreciation is for my husband, Angelo Lozada, who supported my commitment to the education of Latinx youths every single day that we shared. He deeply believed in my work and was this project's biggest cheerleader and I know that he is continuing to cheer it on from the heavens. I also thank my coeditors and my squad, including Dr. Antonio (Jay) Pastrana and Dr. Crystal Jackson, who continuously inspire me to think critically about and advocate for Hispanic-Serving Institutions. I also give many thanks to Tique, David, Dick, and Murray, as well as Angelo's family and community for loving me and believing in my work in Angelo's absence. And lastly, many thanks to my role models, my mom and my dad, Belia Martínez and Ramiro S. Martínez, and my brother, Ramiro Martínez II, for providing unconditional love and support all of these years.

Irma Victoria Montelongo: For the last seventeen years, I have had the honor and privilege of working with the students at The University of Texas at El Paso. Their passion for life and learning and their ability to survive in a space defined by hyper-nationalism, razor-wired boundaries, and media misconceptions inspires me. They are the reason I wake up every day and do the work at hand. I am indebted to my coeditors, their resilience and brilliance never cease to amaze me. Special thanks to Dr. Josefina Carmona for the necessary conversations that keep me grounded in critical analysis of the many borders we traverse. Finally, I want to acknowledge the support and love I receive from my family: Mom, Sam, Alex, and Fred thank you for always being in my corner. Maggie, I miss you terribly . . .

Nicholas Daniel Natividad: I am especially grateful to my partner Michelle Wilson who has been a source of strength in challenging times. My parents Toby and Maria Natividad who taught me how to cross out the borders that cut through us. I would also like to thank my coauthor Dr. Cynthia Wise for her advocacy in the community and reminding me what rehumanizing praxis looks like.

Ángel David Nieves: I am saddened that my husband and partner, my soulmate, of twenty-nine years did not see this book completed. His diagnosis and passing, in just eight-months, from glioblastoma, has left irrevocable damage in its wake, and my heart will forever ache because of his absence. The work on this volume has helped me to begin healing. I am especially grateful to Isabel Martínez and Cassie Tanks for coauthoring the introductory essay with me as I dealt with my husband's health issues.

Lastly, we would like to thank our students who inspire us to develop courses and projects that integrate digital tools into our teaching, so that together we can engage in richer learning and humanizing experiences. This book is for them.

Introduction

Digital Divides, Borders, and Liberatory Edges: Latinx DH (Digital Humanities) *Finally* Comes of Age

Isabel Martínez, Ángel David Nieves, Cassie Tanks

This collection of essays is not about beginnings or endings, but about *crossings*, or the intellectual and praxis-based journeys that have been long underway before we came together to "make" this volume a reality. The volume brings into conversation Maria Cotera's concept of *encuentros* and Stefano Harney and Fred Moten's *undercommons* as we cross this critical moment in Latinx DH as it takes shape at the institutions represented by the authors in this volume. For the volume editors, *crossings* between Latinx Studies and Black Studies while remaining attentive to intersectional analyses and our own meaning-making with each other are only some of the benefits that the comparative critical ethnic studies frameworks found in this volume bring to the digital humanities.

"With our hearts in our hands, and our hands in the soil"[1]

Interstate 5 (colloquially known as the 5) stretches the entire length of the Pacific Coast of the United States. It is a multilane, high-speed concrete titan that runs from the rainy and verdant *frontera* with Vancouver, Canada, to the *sol dorado*-drenched *frontera* with Tijuana, Mexico. The path that this beast cuts through San Diego, California—a city that, save for the *frontera* between the US and Mexico, is essentially a megalopolis extension of her sister, Tijuana—is marked by enormous concrete pillars. Mythical indigenous Mesoamerican *Quinametzin* giants may have also roamed here, perhaps even along the same paths that the *5* now occupies in *Aztlán,* the sacred cultural homelands of the *Mexica* that encompass the lands from Mexico's *frontera* with Guatemala, parts of the Yucatán, up the Pacific Coast to Oregon, across Colorado, and east towards Texas. But unlike the *Quinametzin* who built sites of indigenous Mesoamerican ways of knowing, like *Pirámide de Cholula* and *Tenochtitlan,* the path of the *5* has been strategically used to destroy sites of Latinx knowing, making, and community.

In 1963, the *5* stomped through *Barrio Logan,* its giant concrete pillars and forty-foot retaining walls destroying large sections of the historically Mexican neighborhood nestled on the south side of downtown San Diego along the Pacific Ocean. In 1967, the *5* took more of *Barrio Logan* when an on-ramp to the Coronado Bridge began construction, connecting San Diego to Coronado, a small wealthy city with major military bases located on an isthmus just across the bay from the *barrio* and one of the most expensive and exclusionary zip codes in the county. Attempting to assuage the outrage of *Barrio Logan* residents, the city "promised" to build a park in the neighborhood underneath the interstate.

Two years later, in March 1969, local San Diego State College (SDSC)[2] students, alongside other Chicanx students from across the US Southwest, founded Movimiento Estudiantil Chicano de Aztlán (MEChA) at a student conference at the University of California at Santa Barbara.[3] Reconvened two months later by word of mouth and through flyers and news articles, the young Chicanx activists, led by Corky Gonzalez, drafted *El Plan Espiritual de Aztlán,* a rallying cry of unity that unflinchingly proclaimed that "with our hearts in our hands and our hands in the soil, we declare the liberation of our Mestizo nation."[4] SDSC students interpreted this as it pertained to their immediate surroundings and returned ready to fight for *Barrio Logan.* Upon learning that the City of San Diego had no intention of honoring its promise and instead was planning to build a California Highway Patrol station on what little land remained below the *5* in the heart of *Barrio Logan,* SDSC student, Chicano activist, and Brown Beret Mario Solis and other community members organized and agitated to protect their space. Chicana feminist Laura Rodriguez, the barrio's matriarch and a public-health activist who would soon save the local Neighborhood House health clinic, laid her body in the dirt in protest while others came together as a community to plant trees in the land of their *parque.*[5] By 1971, the City of San Diego conceded, signing into law the establishment of *Chicano*

Park.⁶ Plans to create an outdoor gallery of murals celebrating the history of the barrio, Mexican heritage, and Chicano futurity immediately went into motion. Painting began in 1973 and, in spite of the gender politics of the Chicano Movement spilling over into this project, many Chicano students and alumni from SDSC and San Diego City College contributed. Perhaps best known for her *Guadalupe Triptych*, which reimagines the iconic Virgen de Guadalupe as herself, her mother, and her grandmother asserting themselves while also uplifting working-class Mexican women, San Diego born Chicana artivist Yolanda Lopez, faced repeated rejection by the all-male steering committee to paint a mural in the park. Other local young women who collectively became known as Las Mujeres Muralistas including Julietta A. Garcia-Torres, Cecilia de la Torre, Rosa de la Torre, and Eva Craig, also encountered resistance for their mural proposals that spoke to their experiences as Chicanas.⁷ It took Lopez's determination to obtain approval, five years after other male painters were able to begin contributing to the park. In 1978, the women were finally "granted permission" to create *Chicanas/Escuela* on one of the pillars and they quickly began their project.⁸ These young women "understood exactly," Lopez recalled in a 2021 interview, "to them, it was, I think, too natural . . . it was like, We're ready to go! [laughs] They were ready to go."⁹

In New York City, Puerto Rican students were also joining African-American students in solidarity to protest discriminatory conditions in the city and its higher education system. By the mid-late 1960s, Puerto Rican and Black students were taking their places in campuses across the City University of New York (CUNY) and challenging the university system to revise policies and practices to increase admissions of and support the knowledge-building of their peoples via curriculum and engagement with the surrounding communities. This came to a head in April 1969, when students at Harlem-based City College led a campus-wide occupation and formed their own free university, the University of Harlem, for two weeks. Advertised by word of mouth and hand-sketched, mimeographed flyers, students were joined by their elders including Betty Shabazz and Adam Clayton Powell and sponsored a free breakfast program, held political education classes about anti-colonial efforts across the world, hosted free walk-in clinics, and more. Students also distributed typewritten flyers that laid out their Five Demands, which included the establishment of Black and Puerto Rican/Third World Studies. By the following year, Professor Federico Aquino-Bermúdez, along with other Puerto Rican educators, were tapped as faculty to staff this new department of Urban and Ethnic Studies (UES)

(Reed 2021). Efforts such as these were occurring across CUNY including at Brooklyn College where students in the Puerto Rican Alliance (PRA) and the Brooklyn League of Afro-American Collegians also presented a list of eighteen demands to the administration to transform the admissions policies and curriculum to support Puerto Rican and Black students.

Hostos-CUNY professor Inmaculada Lara-Bonilla points out, however, that Puerto Rican and Latinx activists consciously kept the unique needs of their communities separate, though were still supportive of, African-American specific needs in the movement.[10] The colonization of Puerto Rico, bilingual education, and need for "Latina/o interethnic inclusiveness" were concerns that bridged community, students, and higher education. This solidarity facilitated the establishment of Eugenio María de Hostos Community College (Hostos), the first fully bilingual college in the northeastern region of the United States that symbolized that culturally responsive and decolonialized higher education is not only a civil right, but a right of "(im)migrant communities."[11] In a very real sense, these Latinx students and faculty, with the many others across the United States, began, long before their designations, creating the frameworks for what Hispanic-Serving Institutions (HSIs) and Latinx Studies programs and departments could and should be.

¡Ya estábamos aquí!

These are just two examples of how, even before HSIs and Latinx Studies programs officially emerged, Latinx students and supportive educators combined media, scholarship, and activism to remain rooted to their history while working towards a more expansive future. Long before being recognized as best practices for first-generation Latinx students, these educational activists enacted liberating pedagogical and institutional principles while integrating interdisciplinary multimedia scholarship that were not yet labeled *digital humanities*. In doing so, however, Latinx students and educators have had to cross many *fronteras*, including digital ones of today, that, like the manufactured US-Mexico border, are social constructions that were instantiated and perpetuated by educational institutions to privilege whiteness and dehumanize Afro-, Indigenous, and Mestiza Latinx students.

These *fronteras*, however, are not fixed, and in many cases Latinx students and scholars have had to navigate constantly shifting borders that *cross them*. Pushed to the margins, Latinx students and scholars are oftentimes systematically denied the digital tools needed to realize their scholarly creativity and liberation. Ironically, however, Latinx students and scholars are disproportionately subject to weaponized technologies utilized to surveil them, at the US-Mexico border but also across all the other geopolitical spaces discussed in this volume. In spite of these violences, Latinx students and scholars have persisted against neoliberal forces, creating and curating radical knowledge-building in the face of the more palatable "multicultural" foci that are creeping into Ethnic Studies spaces.[12]

Crossing Digital Fronteras is concerned with challenging these shifting neoliberal borders aimed at weakening Latinx Studies and other studies of power and empowering students and scholars to take on digital humanities work that advances Latinx ways of knowing that explicitly disrupt these divides. This means thinking and even working outside the confines of existing structures of higher education in order to promote critical student self-empowerment at all grades through more sustainable, long-term strategies for self-discovery, and self-definition. The essayists in this volume provide us with pedagogical interventions, guidelines for new approaches, and pathways for working in ethically engaged practice within our own Latinx communities.

Digital Humanities?

What is digital humanities? Some authors dedicate entire sections of their essays to digital humanities, while others do not mention the term once. Yet, all of the *Crossing Digital Fronteras* essayists engage deeply *with,* and contribute *to,* the digital humanities. How is this so? Let's begin by unpacking the term and exploring the problems with *digital* before reviewing how HSIs and Latinx Studies programs are in a unique position to push the field forward.

Attempting to provide a definition for *digital humanities* has been, and remains, elusive and highly subjective. This debate remains relevant only because Latina/o or Latinx Studies in the United States, much as Afro-American Studies, African-American Studies, and Africana Studies, was resistant to digital humanities as a project of whiteness as originally conceived and defined until it was harnessed by coming from across critical ethnic studies in the 2010s. So much so, that it has become a comedic (for many) point of discussion amongst practitioners. Twitter account "DH Defined" is a bot that aggregates definitions of digital humanities and randomly tweets them out, at once complicating and making light of the difficulty of defining the field.[13] On March 18, 2009, digital humanists attempted to define it by organizing the first "Day in the Life of the Digital Humanities" (Day of DH), a social media event that invited scholars to share, in English, how they conceptualize digital humanities and how the projects they were working on with each other embody their definitions.[14] Growing from eighty-five participants to thousands, Day of DH has created the space (in Spanish and French versions as well) to (re)define and (re)imagine DH annually on social media. In 2014, Jason Heppler compiled the Day of DH responses into a spreadsheet and created What Is Digital Humanities?,[15] a website that randomly displays definitions scraped from Twitter. Responses range from the data driven "I see the digital humanities as a set of methods that apply information technologies to humanities problems. For me, DH presents a set of tools to use when collecting, analyzing, and visualizing data—whether that data is derived from text, images, code, sound, or any other medium."[16] To the humanities focused "A range of definitions (or rather, ways of understanding): humanities explored using a range of digital technologies for explanation, expression, reflection and knowledge production/creation."[17] To the future focused "Digital Humanities are the first step towards Future Humanities."[18] The range of these responses represents the evolution of digital humanities as both a subfield of the humanities and medium for expressing humanities knowledge. Rooted in what is called *humanities computing*, an academic pursuit that developed in tandem with the development of computers, DH first emerged during the mid-twentieth century when emerging computer companies like International Business Machines (IBM) were interested in digitizing literature in partnership with institutions of higher education. Over the decades, the computing company developed various machines for test taking, personalized education, and, of course, data processing. By 1964, IBM gathered together scholars interested in humanities computing at a conference to discuss ideas, possibilities, and problems to overcome.[19] Soon after, English and Western European literature were first digitized on punch cards that could be put into early computers and read on screens with hypertext capabilities utilized to make the digitized text more interactive. As digital media became more sophisticated—thanks to the evolution from punch cards, to floppy disks, to CD-ROMs—so too did the means of using the digital for academic inquiry.

During the late 1980s, scholars began developing markup languages that allowed a string of symbols, or tags, to be added to sections of digital text that indicated what that section of text was and its relationship to the text as a whole. A group of academics from the United States and Canada worked to create a standard for using markup languages for academic inquiry and, in 1994, the Text Encoding Initiative (TEI), which grew from humanities computing, published guidelines on systematically categorizing and defining sections of humanities text for scholars.[20] These guidelines are largely considered the beginning of as well as a point of division in contemporary digital humanities. Emphasizing hybridity, Susan Hockey argues that "humanities computing has had to embrace 'the two cultures,' to bring the rigor and systematic unambiguous procedural methodologies characteristic of the sciences to address problems within the humanities that had hitherto been most often treated in a serendipitous fashion."[21] The combination of "the two cultures" of computing and humanities establishes interdisciplinarity as a feature, but it also introduces assumptions that it is the *computing* aspect that made the pursuit rigorous, not humanities inquiry. Additionally, it establishes a primacy of the English language and cultural interpretations rooted in Western thought. Marking up digital text significantly affects how it is read, interpreted, processed, and interacted with—especially by students. Ernesto Priani Saisó and Ana María Guzmán Olmos, both scholars of philosophy, technology, and digital humanities at la Universidad Nacional Autónoma de México, argue,

> Pero lo más significativo de colocar una etiqueta en una palabra es que esa operación interpretativa queda registrada y es puesta a prueba con el procesamiento del texto. De cierta forma, con el marcado, hacemos algo muy parecido a lo que hacía la persona de la que hablábamos al principio: marcar significa hacer ese procedimiento de selección y de decisión sobre lo que sería deseable encontrar en un texto sin tener que leerlo todo detenidamente. Pero, a diferencia de marcar poniendo una línea o un color, lo que hacemos al usar TEI es utilizar palabras para etiquetar. Las palabras con las que marcamos tienen un sentido, no son formas o colores, sino conceptos que agrupan los objetos marcados adhiriéndose a ellos. Poner <name> a un objeto que también es una palabra, significa el surgimiento de un nuevo sentido que acontece en esa unión.[22]

(But the most significant thing about placing a label on a word is that this interpretive operation is recorded and is tested with the processing of the text. In a way, with marking, we do something very similar to what the person we were talking about at the beginning did: marking means carrying out that selection and decision procedure about what would be desirable to find in a text without having to read it all carefully. But, unlike marking by putting a line or a color, what we do when using TEI is put words to label. The words with which we mark have a meaning, they are not shapes or colors, but concepts that group the marked objects by adhering to them. Putting <name> to an object that is also a word, means the emergence of a new meaning that occurs in that union.)

Because using TEI text and standards does some of the "thinking" for students and allows them to skim text without deeply reading or engaging in a culturally informed heuristic process, variations "in the interpretation, selection and application of those codes by different groups, individuals and cultures" is minimized in favor of a "universalizing, Western-centric approach to the representation of cultural artifacts."[23]

Thanks to college teachers and scholars who continue to push against the racialized whiteness of the field, digital humanities has advanced beyond purely data-driven and computationally dependent investigation of the humanities. In recent years, DH has shifted its focus here in the US and is now changing its recent, largely Eurocentric text-based scholarship to begin to address racial injustice and anti-colonialism. That focus has propelled a radical shift in scholarship, and through an intersectional and feminist framework that examines factors of race, class, gender, and sexuality, has allowed humanists to research messier and more complex relationships between people, power, and the state across a whole range of scales and time periods. Digital humanities is increasingly a field that can be used to more fully explore the potentials of interdisciplinary academic inquiry, knowledge creation, pedagogy, and public engagement that the essayists detail in this volume. Multimedia storytelling, critical digital archiving, and podcasting are just a few examples of how the digital humanities are leveraged by faculty found in Hispanic-Serving Institutions and Latinx Studies programs and departments to enhance the cultural and linguistic experiences and learning of Latinx students specifically, and can improve outcomes for all BIPOC (Black, Indigenous, and people of color) students, generally.

Los problemas con "lo digital"

Digital humanities projects and pedagogy now receive much attention and accolades by colleges and universities (though much less appreciation when it relates to faculty tenure or advancement, an issue that is outside the scope of the volume but tangentially related). However, the emphasis on digital work and digital productions compounds the deep-rooted and structural problems with *the digital* in the United States. Dan Greene argues that the United States' emphasis on combating poverty by providing access to the digital and wedding the funding of organizations *to* this "access doctrine" is deeply neoliberal and forces traditional sites of information access, such a public libraries and schools, to massively reconfigure their organizations to attempt to reproduce the culture of tech start-ups.[24] This is "how the problem of poverty is transformed into a problem of technology" and "bootstrapping" in order to cross the "digital divide,"[25] inequalities that all worsened during the Trump administration and the COVID-19 lockdowns.

Latinx DH: Defining a Situatedness

As suggested earlier, SDSC and Hostos are just two examples of where we might begin the story of Latinx Studies, here in the US, on the West Coast and East Coast, respectively. Beginnings are by their very nature sites of contestation, most often politically, and in these spaces over the rights to claim ownership over new knowledge construction and field formation. The debates over What is DH? have filled volumes and made important contributions to our understanding of the needs for more accountability concerning power, privilege, and access, while also remaining particularly attentive to intersectional frameworks of analysis and community engaged methodologies but have remained relatively silent about DH's place in Hispanic-Serving Institutions and on Latinx issues. Situating the precise moment when and where Latinx DH began isn't the task at hand here, but instead we are focused on bringing to light the ways in which digital technologies have always been an important part of educational reform in our communities and have been reflexively built into the various sorts of activism we have undertaken to promote social change. Social movements tied to higher education reform, especially those in Chicana/o Studies, Puerto Rican Studies, Black Studies, and Dominican Studies have always included multimodal tools and multimedia forms of production including zines, use of photocopiers, mimeograph machines, large format printing, and other "technologies" that help expand our definition of digital humanities in relation to social justice. As Lorena Gauthereau has argued, a US Latinx Digital Humanities must consist of certain methods, and "Critical to work in this field is a methodology that prioritizes community narratives and puts into practice an ethics of care when dealing with data. Rather than create projects about or on the community, ethically conscious projects should approach history with and for the community. This means protecting data and the people represented by these data, as well as presenting material in ways that are accessible to the community they are meant to serve and represent."[26] Methodologically, we would agree with Gauthereau, but her definition is primarily focused on the ways in which Western scholarship has situated Latinx communities as static communities to be studied rather than the dynamic, autonomous communities that they are, subject to shifting border lines or colonial expansion. This is where the work of scholars like Vicki Ruiz, Fred Moten, Edward Soja, bell hooks, Mary Pat Brady, and la paperson begins to talk to one another and suggests that another way forward is possible (a third way?), and always has been, when we return to the methodologies of community engagement, social justice, and practices of care from which so much of our work originated before the neoliberal turn and the over professionalization (where we are only agents of accreditation) through the liberal arts, writ large. In other words, a Latinx DH that articulates a clear methodological framework that prioritizes community engagement, ethical practices, complex narratives, archival preservation, data protection, and community asset management all maintained by community organizations might actually move the much-needed conversations forward. The essays in this volume move us in that direction.

Several projects are however worth noting because they have historically been long-standing Latinx DH projects that have not received proper scholarly attention, or the kinds of resources that other more mainstream projects have garnered with less attention to community engagement. Maria Cotera's Chicana por mi Raza Digital Memory project, formerly at the University of Michigan, now at The University of Texas at Austin, is a project that brings together "researchers, educators, students, archivists and technologists dedicated to preserving imperiled Chicanx and Latinx histories of the long Civil Rights Era."[27] The CPMR has modeled how a digital history project can involve undergraduate students in high-level humanities-based research while also maintaining connections with community leaders and former activists across the country involved in the long multiethnic Civil Rights Movement. The archival collection maintains over seven thousand digital records and over five hundred video clips in what Cotero describes as *encuentro* and exchange of new knowledge(s). An earlier project that did receive NEH (National Endowment for the Humanities) support, the Bracero History Archive: Collaborative Documentation in the Digital Age, developed at George Mason University in 2007 by Roy Rosenzweig, Jack R. Censer, and Tom Scheinfeldt was one of the first collaborative, bilingual, online archives documenting the Bracero Program, which brought Mexican guest workers to the United States between 1942 and 1964. The Bracero History Archive brought critical attention to contemporary debates on immigration policy and made clear to many in Latino Studies, at the time, how understudied the Bracero Program had been in our understanding of border studies, masculinity studies, race relations, and transnational studies, more generally.

This volume was originally conceived only a few short months after the Trump administration was sworn in, when its insidious campaign of legislative policy decisions and social media attacks on Black and Brown communities across the US had not been yet fully rolled out. This was also years before this administration bungled responses to the double pandemic of COVID-19 and white supremacy reflected in the murder of George Floyd and the anti-Asian racism following the advent of the public health crisis.[28] Still only partially understood today, this campaign against minority communities persisted throughout the length of Trump's presidency, resurrecting and repurposing the earlier culture wars of the 1980s and 1990s. The culture wars of those decades had been coupled with a policy of Reaganomics and neoliberalism that disavowed progressive social policies and took aim squarely at communities of color. With the selection of Betsy DeVos as secretary of education and Ajit Pai as FCC chairman, President Trump was clearly signaling a return to a model of educational reforms that would be cash-strapped by design and would continue to downplay the need for access to resources and services that would help alleviate existing disparities and repair crumbling infrastructure—both physical and technological—in public schools across the country.[29] This neglect would be laid bare during the pandemic when the image of two Salinas City Elementary School District girls sitting on the pavement outside a local Taco Bell—huddled together, cross-legged on the short sidewalk outside the restaurant and using some low hedges as back support, with one nearby adult presumably supervising—while working on their homework assignments and attempting to access the restaurant's free Wi-Fi, circulated. In Salinas Valley of California, just south of the resource-rich home of tech start-ups, the Bay Area, the digital divide among Latinx communities couldn't have been made more apparent, as school districts there worked to provide access to free hot spots to families. The Salinas Valley—the social and political epicenter of the Latinx and Filipino civil rights movements for farm workers of the 1940s—remains one of the most culturally diverse areas in the US today, and here as well as elsewhere, Black and Hispanic[30] adults remain less likely than whites to say they own a traditional computer or have high-speed internet access at home. According to a Pew Research Center fact sheet, between 2019 and 2021, little progress was made to close the digital divide with Black and Latinx adults still lagging behind whites in terms of desktop or laptop computer ownership and home broadband access.[31] While Black adults increased their home broadband access from 66–71 percent during this time period, only 65 percent of Latinx adults reported possessing home broadband by 2021; 80 percent of white adults possessed home broadband in 2021, an increase of only one percent over the two-year period. In particular, access to digital technologies including higher-speed broadband service, cable, or fiber optics is most often found among those who are US-born Latinx, or in English-dominant households.

Additionally, the zero tolerance disciplinary policies—just one aspect of the school-to-prison pipeline—were reinforced by DeVos's own appointees, and helped to increase incidences of violence that further criminalized Black, Afro-Latinx, Indigenous Latinx, Native and Indigenous, and Southeast Asian children and youth.[32] However, this revival of culture and "Border Wars" of the 1990s and the reassertion of Republican right-wing rhetoric about Brown bodies across the southern border also suggest to us opportunities to understand the space of the *fronteras* as places where contestation and the liberatory and rehumanizing potential of the digital exist simultaneously. The interdisciplinarity of the digital humanities, and more broadly of BIPOC (Black, Indigenous, and people of color) ways of knowing that predate the field, make this field especially critical to this work.

Despite the digital humanities turn to embrace interdisciplinarity and "deep collaboration" as argued by Patrik Svensson in his 2011 essay "Beyond the Big Tent," it is BIPOC (Black, Indigenous, and people of color) faculty and students who often conduct this kind of digital work more regularly and expertly.[33] However, digital humanities in general has not been particularly attentive to Latinx communities or improving their outcomes, nor has it devoted energies to propose theories, methods, and practices for engaging in a Latinx DH.

For us personally, the emergence of the *Big Tent* as a metaphor for a bounded digital humanities also provided a certain amount of intellectual cover to the generation of students who had succeeded an earlier generation of students who, in turn, had openly rejected the institutionalizing of feminist theory and cultural and ethnic studies in academe—a topic

Martha Nell Smith has expounded upon elsewhere.[34] We would argue that this next generation of scholars also used the idea of the *Big Tent* to avoid engaging with discussions about race and racial inequalities in the field's history and ongoing exclusionary practices in faculty and staff mentoring, review, and funding. In the absence of race and any kind of racial analysis, or an implicit belief in the post-racial myth of America, DH has been working "to normalize racial inequity and deny that racism is dividing and devastating our society."[35] To borrow from colleague Ibram X. Kendi's essay in *The Atlantic*, "Our New Postracial Myth," DH scholars such as Dorothy Kim, David Golumbia, and others have similarly echoed this sentiment as they describe the systemic impact of "everyday whiteness" and entrenched color blindness.[36] Even in a field-changing volume such as Kim and Koh's *Alternative Historiographies of the Digital Humanities*, Latinx DH is only mentioned once and in relation to a 2018 special issue of *American Quarterly*.[37]

Today, it is no longer acceptable that a legacy of white supremacy and institutionalized color blindness persists—one that has erased from the history of digital humanities the contributions of BIPOC faculty, professional staff, and students across the academy. Scholars including Jessica Marie Johnson, Eduard Arriaga, Alex Gil, Lorena Gauthereau, and Lisette Acosta-Corniel— to name a few key researchers (who appear either as essayists or are mentioned in the pages of this volume)—have each made significant scholarly proposals as to the contours of a Latinx DH, its practice, its engagement, and its purpose for liberation and rehumanization of Latinx students not just at HSIs or enrolled in Latinx Studies, but across the United States.[38] At its center, as scholar Jessica Marie Johnson articulated in conversation with Melissa Dinsman,

> The digital—doing digital work—has created and facilitated insurgent and maroon knowledge creation within the ivory tower. It's imperfect and it's problematic—and we are all imperfect and problematic. But in that sense I think the digital humanities, or doing digital work period, has helped people create maroon— free, black, liberatory, radical—spaces in the academy. I feel like there is a tension between thinking about digital humanities as an academic construct and thinking about what people do with these tools and digital ways of thinking. DH has offered people the means and opportunity to create new communities. And this type of community building should not be overlooked; it has

literally saved lives as far as I'm concerned. People—those who have felt alone or maligned or those who have been marginalized or discriminated against or bullied—have used digital tools to survive and live. That's not academic. If there isn't a place for this type of work within what we are talking about as digital humanities, then I think we are having a faulty conversation.[39]

The tools, pedagogies, and methods used by the authors of this volume exemplify the importance of using the digital humanities to resist neoliberal *bootstrapping* and the *access doctrine*, both of which are entrenched in whiteness, especially at Hispanic-Serving Institutions and in Latinx Studies curriculum. A return to our pedagogical and methodological roots in community engagement and multiethnic organizing can inform a Latinx DH that centers on the historical narratives of our communities while also engaging in future social change.

Latinx-Serving Digital Humanities

According to leading HSI scholar Dr. Gina Ann Garcia, to move beyond the institutional definition of Hispanic-Serving that focuses solely on 25 percent Latinx student enrollment, to be *truly* Latinx-Serving, colleges and universities must exhibit both high levels of outcomes *and* high levels of cultural support for Latinx students. To do this, educators must embrace that Latinx students are, as expressed by cultural theorist Gloria Anzaldúa in her essay "La Conciencia de la Mestiza," caught between (at least) one culture and another while also being in all cultures at the same time.[40] This way of being, simultaneously between and among different worlds, captures the ways in which Latinx college-age students maneuver their complex racial and ethnic identities and their stratified socio-political standing in the two United States. Understanding better ways of engaging Latinx students in higher education requires a critically informed engagement with their origin stories and their current lived experiences, not just merely enrolling them in high numbers. Employing these methods can push digital humanities centers, Latinx Studies programs, and, ideally, entire campuses towards becoming a supportive, rather than ostracizing, third space for Latinx students. Significantly, their personal goals as they work to secure their degrees often means something very different from what their families and even traditional faculty, staff, and administrators might expect. Students are constantly crisscrossing borders, moving beyond those borders, and making new sites for exploring identity, shared experiences, nation, citizenship, labor, and humanity. Simply securing larger enrollments of Latinx students in higher education but failing to meet the specific needs of these students is unacceptable.

It is also in this *third space* that access to digital technologies remains as divided as access to innovative pedagogies in higher education. It is our belief, however, that here, Latinx digital humanities also possesses its most liberatory promise. By advocating for additional and distributing available resources in equitable and innovative ways, we can better ensure that all our students are exposed to justice and belonging and not only neoliberal policies of diversity, equity, and inclusion. The authors of *Crossing Digital Fronteras* are practitioners of pedagogy and theory that use the digital humanities to authentically and wholly serve their Latinx students by engaging with culturally informed ways of knowledge building that simultaneously improve the outcomes of their students and increase their confidence and critical engagement with the digital.

It is important to understand that in *Crossing Digital Fronteras,* we implicitly and explicitly include the Afro-Latinx in our use of Latinx DH for a more accurate, richer, and fuller historical and cultural understanding of Latinx DH (see chapter 3, for example). However, it is also important to keep it in an area separate and apart from this volume. There is currently ongoing important work by Jessica Marie Johnson, Alex Gil, Eduard Arriaga, Kaiama Glover, and others that provides a framework for a body of scholarship that looks critically at race and the Afro-Latinx diaspora. Such research in the US, Caribbean, and across Latin America deserves its own stand-alone volume of methods, theories, and practices given the silences and absences around Blackness across the Americas, the Caribbean, and elsewhere.

Latinx Studies

Students enrolled in English 1B piled into a classroom on the San Diego State campus during the fall 1968 semester. Sunlight likely streamed into the room, gently illuminating the undergraduate students as the professor introduced one of the semester-long assignments: to keep a daily journal reflecting their thoughts and experiences. One student, Arturo Casares, initially found the task difficult:

Wednesday, September 25, 1968

This is the first time I have had a class where the instructor has given a daily writing assignment. I have never been able to write everyday because there are too many other things to be done, besides I enjoy reading more.[41]

Arturo certainly had many things to do—he had recently moved to San Diego from Texas to gain an education, had a young son to care for, a mother and family in Long Beach, and he needed to balance work with school. On top of this, he was navigating higher education as a former field worker and a Mexican-American student. Arturo, like Latinx students across the United States, longed for community and joined the fight to establish Latinx Studies programs that were culturally and politically informed.

Tuesday, October 8, 1968

I went to the MAYA [Mexican American Youth Association] meeting today. I've signed up for three committees. We are trying to get a Mexican-American major established at SDSC. I think it is a good idea because a lot of people don't know too much about this very important minority group which is the largest in California. We also talked about the "huelga" and Cesar Chavez. Someone suggested that a committee be formed for the purpose of asking Hubert Humphrey if he supports the grape boycott when he comes here later in the month . . .

Saturday, October 12, 1968

Let's boycott California grapes now. It's not fair for farm workers to earn something like one-dollar forty cents an hour for six months and then live in camps like the ones in Tulare County for the next six months. No one likes to live in a shack made of two wooden rooms. The conditions are really bad for these people . . . **my people** because I'm a Mexican American. I remember when I was growing up in Texas and had to work in the fields. It's not very pleasant. The government has done a good job of keeping us down but now we have a good thing going. We need the support of the people. If we can try to raise standards, I am sure that the gap will be narrowed. I wonder how Lafferty ever got his job. I guess there are many conservative cats around that still follow the old ways.

Things have to change.

It was a nice day today. I had my son over and we played some Beatle albums. They are beautiful people.[42]

The more Arturo became involved with MAYA, the more dismayed he grew at the oppression and exclusion of Latinx history and triumphs—in all its indigeneity and complexity—from United States education.

Tuesday, October 15, 1968

Mexico has a pre-Hispanic culture that is fascinating. First I want to say that in all my years in school I had never been exposed to this [sic] indigenous cultures: Chichimeca, Toltec, Maya, Incan, Chimu, etc. They were so advanced in astronomy, architecture, and government. Of course I did learn all about Western civilizations. I think that the American system of education has completely ignored the Indian cultures of the Americas which is really sad. There is enough evidence in this field to create a specific area of studies. Just as we study particular phases of European history we should study the steps of development in the Indian cultures in the Americas.[43]

Arturo's journal is quoted extensively here because he articulates a yearning for what Nicholas Natividad and Cynthia Wise argue Latinx Studies provides beyond simply an education "about" Latinx-ness; it centers belonging, community, growth, activism, and a means for students who have been othered and dehumanized by the United States to reassert their humanity on their terms (see chapter 2). With their histories and thus, humanity, absent from textbooks, students conceived the dream of Latinx Studies in order to improve the conditions for their communities and students who came after them. It has always been student-centered, and it remains so. Nearly fifty-five years later, students like Arturo, who are caught between cultures, can explore their complexity and express their knowledge in Latinx Studies programs that critically engage with the digital. The digital pedagogy and practices of Latinx Digital Humanities (Latinx DH) detailed in this volume are tools for continuing this vital work.

A growing number of Latinx DH projects are receiving national attention but many remain invisible because of the limitations of funding and the peer-review system. Two such projects are Alex Gil and Kaiama Glover's the Caribbean Digital and their peer-reviewed journal *archipelago/a journal of Caribbean digital praxis*. These two projects that emerged from Columbia University and Barnard College helped make possible Glover's next project, In the Same Boats: Toward an Intellectual Cartography of the Afro-Atlantic, which traces the movements of intellectuals across the Atlantic world including Afro-Latinx cultural actors.[44] Most recently, the Andrew W. Mellon Foundation has provided support to the Caribbean Digital Scholarship Collective (CDSC) with a $5-million-dollar four-year grant.

Another effort, Roopika Risam and Alex Gil's Torn Apart/Separados project,[45] mapped the location of private juvenile detention facilities and ICE (Immigration and Customs Enforcement) facilities as volume I of their work. In the follow-up hackathon at the International DH Conference in Mexico City, they sought to rapidly prototype maps that would correlate information on money and ICE funding, but to also raise deeper questions about the role of DH and other humanistic work in the service of social justice.[46] The Detainee Allies project out of the Hispanic-Serving Institution San Diego State University (SDSU), along with the SDSU Digital Humanities Initiative and local grassroots activists, brought much-needed attention to the plight of Latinx, Latin American, LGBTQiA+, and many other immigrants being held at the border in deplorable conditions at the Otay Mesa Detention Center. Through a letter writing exchange between the detainees at Otay and students and local activists, the detainees told their stories while the students and activists worked to identify and code human rights violations within the written testimony. The letters provided important insight into the lives of asylum seekers and migrants both before and during detention in these for-profit US-run centers. As a result of this project and the mounting evidence found in these letters, the California State University System's Retirement Fund divested its holdings associated with the companies that profited from the maintenance, food preparation, and/or overall management of these detention centers.[47]

Lastly, the University of Houston's Latino cARTographies project features Houston's social and geographic landscape of visual Latino art, past and present. Under the leadership of Center of Mexican American Studies Director Dr. Pamela Ann Quiroz, this visual archive centers the artistic and cultural contributions of Houston's Latinx artists as well as the communities in which their art is and was created. At a time when museums' commitment to European art canons is changing at a glacial pace, this project, in bilingual, portable, digital boards, immerses users into a dynamic experience that challenges our understandings of art as well as how it is presented and accessed.

These projects all act to uncover as well as recover lost, ignored, and purposefully hidden Latinx histories. All addressing disparate segments of Latinx histories that have been neglected and even whitewashed, these projects are tangible examples of how social justice and a Latinx DH come together to make social change possible. In this volume, Mancilla and Vukelich-Selva and Baeza Ventura, Gauthereau, and Villarroel have each also leveraged the space of the academy as a place where forms of insurgent practices in Latinx Digital Humanities may take shape but also occur outside the classroom and within respective community partnerships. While Mancilla and Vukelich-Selva outline how partnerships with community-based organizations in the borderlands can deepen students' understandings of geopolitical spaces, Baeza Ventura, Gauthereau, and Villarroel describe the kind of scaffolding that has made the team at the Hispanic-Serving Institution, University of Houston, and Arte Público Press successful in their outreach efforts to other Latinx communities—communities that are themselves now employing meaningful archive-making and literary practices.[48]

Organization of *Crossing Digital Fronteras*

This volume is organized into three broad sections that a) illuminate the need for rehumanizing undergraduate curriculum at HSIs, b) connect and broaden Latinx student knowledges and pedagogies through technology, and c) challenge colonial narratives and centering projects that focus on recovering Latinx histories. To further characterize Latinx DH, a field that is as fast-evolving as the rest of DH—we frame the subsequent chapters in relation to their critical significance during yet another epoch of attempted minority disempowerment (see voting rights, abortion rights, attacks on DEI [diversity, equity, and inclusion] initiatives) across huge swaths of the US.

Firstly, the need for rehumanizing undergraduate curricula is critical, and Nicholas Natividad and Cynthia Wise (both of New Mexico State University) in chapter 1, "Toward a Rehumanizing Latinx Studies Curriculum," address what is broadly understood as *rehumanization*—contemporary attempts to counter long-standing and widespread historical and practices that dehumanized or objectified and exploited Latinx communities—with the caveat that illegitimate and marginalized peoples were subject to these same dehumanizing practices. Natividad and Wise argue that, as such, communities must understand themselves and others as minoritized beings. Natividad and Wise also understand Latinx Studies and Latinx DH as integral to disrupting processes of dehumanization by positioning resistance and promoting curricula of rehumanization beyond brick-and-mortar classrooms and through the use of digital tools and technologies. In digital spaces, these technologies facilitate learning that is decentralized and has the potential to be counter hegemonic. They assert that Latinx Studies provides an education that not only can move between ideological positionings to break the appearance of mutual exclusivity of oppositional practices of consciousness and social movements but is also decolonizing and healing.

Practice in DH and Latinx DH is critical to ensure that technology is made readily available, with hopes that Latinx student knowledges and pedagogies are connected and broadened. In chapter 2, "Digital Pedagogy in a Multicultural Setting: Learning History and Connecting through Technology," Lissette Acosta Corniel of CUNY's Borough of Manhattan Community College documents how she utilizes technology to "center student voices and identities" and, in doing so, students become "co-constructors of not only knowledge in the classroom, but also of assignments and policies." Acosta Corniel has been critical of historical as well as current social and political processes that have shaped Latinx experiences. As a corrective, resources used by Acosta Corniel include Google Docs, Blackboard discussion boards, and the First Black Americans archive. In particular, as a Caribbeanist she draws on experiences and history of the Afro-Latinx peoples of the Dominican Republic and then shares their analyses across technologies.

In chapter 3, "Latinx Spaces, Discourses, and Knowledges: Student Voices and the Rehumanization of Latinx Identity in the United States," authors Isabel Martínez, a former associate professor at John Jay College of Criminal Justice, CUNY, and Irma Montelongo, associate professor of instruction and the director of the Chicano Studies program at The University of Texas at El Paso—two professors separated by 1800 miles—recount how they connected two classrooms in HSIs located in two far-apart immigrant gateway communities, El Paso, Texas, and New York City. Joining the two classrooms are digital tools such as videoconferencing and shared digital platforms, where students and professors in these two classrooms learn, in depth, about the lived experiences of members of each other's classrooms. Practices include discussions with each other about the shared readings via videoconferencing and students from both campuses collaborating through shared digital spaces. Here, they bridge experiences as they share knowledges, and swap analyses of texts to produce new, hybrid knowledges that are rooted in two different Latinx geographic locales.

In chapter 4, "Translanguaging and Multiple Literacies: Podcasting as a Linguistically and Culturally Sustaining Medium in a Multicultural Teacher Education Course," Jen Stacy, Mildred Ramos, and Adriana Correa, all affiliated with Cal State University, Dominguez Hills, discuss the use of podcasting to promote translanguaging and the use of Latinx students' linguistic capital in academic settings, in a particular setting where bilingualism is not understood as the *full* mastery of two or more individual (separate) languages. The authors recount how two Latinx students approached their professor to expand the boundaries of their assignment to include their natural linguistic practices. Outside the constraints of typical classroom surveillance, translanguaging provides students with spaces to process concepts in their native languages. Conversely, it allows professors another opportunity to learn from their students. With nearly 30 percent of the US K–12 public school system identifying as Hispanic, this chapter provides insight into how popular and readily available digital tools can be used in teacher education programs to validate educators' bicultural and bilingual identities and those of their students as well.

The saying goes that we are condemned to repeat history if we remain ignorant of it, and so it is urgent that historically victimized communities contest colonial narratives and Latinx students must continue to recover Latinx histories. In chapter 5, "US Latinx Digital Humanities: Rehumanizing the Past through Archival Digital Pedagogy," authors Gabriela Baeza Ventura, Lorena Gauthereau, and Carolina Villarroel, throw a spotlight on the US Latino Digital Humanities program (USLDH) and its Recovering the US Hispanic Literary Heritage (Recovery Program) that is housed at the University of Houston. This archive challenges long-reproduced, unfailingly disparaging narratives about Latinxs. With students trained to use Omeka, an open-source web publishing platform, they create their own exhibits, maps, or other digital representations of underrepresented archives housed in the Recovery Program. In both the English and Spanish languages, these students at the University of Houston learn and also critically engage with Latinx histories. Grounded in an "ethics of care" they identify, excavate, curate, and then exhibit un/undertold Latinx stories and also develop, with guidance, their own processes to do so.

Delis Negrón, a transnational Puerto Rican newspaper editor, poet, translator, professor, and activist challenged national borders and fluidly moved and engaged across two nation-states, the United States and Mexico, during the first half of the twentieth century. In chapter 6, "The Delis Negrón Digital Archive: A Pedagogical Approach to Latinx Familial and Community Archives," Sylvia Fernández Quintanilla of The University of Texas at San Antonio and Annette Zapata of The University of Houston write of their efforts to create an open-access digital archive with Delis Negrón as subject. In the service of this archive, graduate students used Wix, a platform whose accessibility also extends beyond academic and national borders. The authors demonstrate how, in addition to recovering, preserving, and reinserting often forgotten figures and voices into historical memory, digital archival projects can be decolonial in nature.

In chapter 7, "Crossing Pedagogical Front/eras through Collaborative World-Making and Digital Storytelling," authors Jeanelle D. Horcasitas and Olivia Quintanilla, both affiliated with the University of California, San Diego, relate how they create *Front/eras*, a world-making project that allows students to imagine San Diego thirty years from now. They utilize various digital tools including the digital storytelling platform Twine and StoryMaps where students imagine and propose more equitable and just futures for Latinxs, especially those living on the US-Mexico border. Using multimodal, nonlinear, digital storytelling platforms and map makers, they instructed users to be critical of their surroundings, but to also create, imagine, and place themselves into just and equitable futures. Here, constructing speculative forms of knowledge acts as a kind of methodology for engaging with social justice issues.

In chapter 8, "Developing Action Research Projects for Latinx Students in a Predominantly White Institution," Gerardo Mancilla and Donna Vukelich-Selva of Edgewood College consider how a growing Latinx population at a small liberal arts college can find courses that address its academic and culturally specific needs grounded in community-based outreach methods and Latino critical theory (LatCrit). Initially, a program that started as advocacy for DACAmented students with ties to immigration in predominantly white institutions (PWIs)—first documenting counter-stories about immigration and the US-Mexico border—it also employed digital methods such as digital storytelling, hash-tagging, and website development, and naturally evolved into a leadership program, LIBRE or Leadership Institute for Borderland Research and Education.

In the conclusion, "Reimagining Digital Pedagogies in Hispanic-Serving Institutions and Beyond," Isabel Martínez and Irma Victoria Montelongo conclude that full digital citizenship for Latinx students is possible only when we counter dehumanizing epistemicide and re-center Latinx students as knowledge producers and theory makers. The siloed approaches of HSIs that regionalize and market their experiences to a very narrowly defined Latinx student, dependent only on the local geography, also tends to diminish the understanding of the much wider diversity that exists among our students. Martínez and Montelongo raise two important questions: "What happens if what we are doing (with digital technologies) isn't called DH?" and "Does that matter?" It matters, as they suggest, because BIPOC faculty, staff, and technologists are very often the key innovators at HSIs and elsewhere and their work goes unrecognized. Sadly, they are often left out of important conversations because they are not seen as a part of any mainstream knowledge communities. Even at an HSI, BIPOC faculty are so few in number—and so few people actually know about their work—that they remain outside discussions about new interdisciplinary and epistemological approaches or innovative curricular change.

La Futura

With this in mind, it has become critical that scholars already working in Latinx DH settle upon two immediate goals and begin building:

1. Cooperative research networks across different types of institutions to promote digital scholarship in Latinx Studies, including (but not limited to) R1s pairing with non-R 1 HSI universities and community colleges.

2. Academic communities with mutually agreed upon agendas that advocate for Latinx Digital Humanities within the academy and elsewhere.

Agendas that lead us towards a more robust Latinx Digital Humanities, as examined in the pages of this volume, may include:

1. Institutionalizing the opportunity for Latinx Digital Humanities practitioners, especially BIPOC faculty and staff, to regularly present their work at their home institutions, ideally at the university library, as part of a series of talks/ short form presentations to raise awareness of their innovative digital scholarship and pedagogical interventions; this

includes providing adequate resources (funding and course releases) for BIPOC faculty and staff and rewarding them to engage in and develop these projects during tenure and promotion decisions.

2. Organizing a yearly, campus-wide Latinx Digital Humanities Project Showcase (recall science fairs from back in the day) where faculty, staff, and students can present informally on their projects developed as part of their coursework.

3. Employing existing online networks such as H-Net, DHNow, or Humanities Commons as a means to coordinate local, city, or regional DH practitioners to begin showcasing, presenting, discussing common interests, project overlaps, etc. on projects specific to Latinx Digital Humanities.

4. Preserving the working papers, material objects, organizational records, etc., of nearby BIPOC community groups in the university or college library, as a working partnership between those groups and the university or college. These partnerships, between BIPOC community groups and university or college libraries have not been without controversy, risk, or challenges and require careful planning where power sharing or shifted power relations are adopted. Seeking out local area archivists and information workers who can simultaneously identify aspects of library and archival science practices that continue to be deeply racialized white while practicing preservation methods that fit the needs of stakeholders. Because the relationship between marginalized communities in the United States and institutional sites of information (including, but not limited to, libraries and archives affiliated with universities, colleges, and government) has been historically extractive and in service of whiteness, allies may come from different places. Identifying invested librarians and/or archivists in your institutions' libraries and special collections, reaching out to local area community archiving programs or initiatives, and seeking opportunities to fund your own preservation efforts are critical to preserving Latinx history in culturally informed ways.

The editors imagine the future of Latinx Digital Humanities to be experimental, dynamic, culturally significant, and a gateway to further study in Latinx Studies, Ethnic Studies, LGBTQiA+ Studies, Women's and Gender Studies, and the continued study of other BIPOC communities. The impact Latinx DH will have on teaching in Hispanic-Serving Institutions and Latinx Studies classrooms cannot be emphasized enough. We have explored the ever-changing technology landscape, tools, and ideas for rehumanizing higher education for Latinx students in different contexts, but especially at HSIs, where many challenges persist, and so strengthening the pedagogical and learning goals of students already enrolled at our institutions is critical and essential to achieving a just and equitable society. Acknowledging that many students are living in households with multigenerational families, are often caring for a range of relatives, and meeting varying family needs is necessary to provide them a safety net and ensure their academic success. Making clear to our students that both equal access to digital technologies and critical use of them will help advance not only their skills attainment but also how they interrogate the content and context of the materials they encounter in any classroom—e.g., asking humanistic questions in whatever field they enter—is critical. The kinds of questions and answers made possible through a Latinx DH at HSIs are examined in the subsequent pages of this volume, and these authors, in particular, applaud a Latinx DH of theoretical and methodological maturity, poised to explore *fronteras* of possible liberation.

Notes

1. Rodolfo Gonzales and Alberto Urista [Alaurista, pseud.], "El plan espiritual de Aztlan," *El grito del Norte* (Alburquerque, New Mexico), vol. II, no. 9 (July 6, 1969): 5. https://icaa.mfah.org/s/es/item/803398; http://www.insearchofaztlan.com/preamble.html.

2. Raymond G. Starr, *San Diego State University: A History in Word and Image* (San Diego, CA: San Diego State University Press, 1995), 187.

3. "Interview with Alurista" conducted in San Diego, California 2000. From San Diego State University, *The San Diego State University Library, Special Collections & University Archives*. Audio. The San Diego State University Library, Special Collections & University Archives.

4. Rodolfo Gonzales and Alberto Urista [Alaurista, pseud.], "El plan espiritual de Aztlan," *El grito del Norte* (Alburquerque, NM), vol. II, no. 9 (July 6, 1969): 5.

5. Kera N. Lovell, " 'Everyone Gets a Blister': Sexism, Gender Empowerment, and Race in the People's Park Movement," *Women's Studies Quarterly* 46, no. 3 & 4 (2018): 103–19. https://www.jstor.org/stable/26511334.

6. Kevin Delgado, "A Turning Point: The Conception and Realization of Chicano Park." *The Journal of San Diego History* 44, no. 1 (1998): 48–61. https://sandiegohistory.org/journal/1998/january/chicano-3/.

7. https://chicanohistory.sdsu.edu/chapter11/c11s03.html.

8. Image: https://library.ucsd.edu/dc/object/bb6829431n.

9. https://www.sfmoma.org/listen/yolanda-lopez-oral-history/.

10. Inmaculada, Lara-Bonilla, "Crafting a Latina/o Higher Education Rights Discourse in New York: The Founding and 'Saving' of Eugenio María de Hostos Community College," *New York History* 97, no. 2 (2016): 187–228.

11. Lara-Bonilla, 225–226.

12. Juan Gonzalez, "Latinos, Race, and Empire," Graduate Center, City University of New York. December 12, 2022. https://www.youtube.com/watch?v=oZhslVA4UFM.

13. @DHDefined. 2017. "A bot randomly tweeting definitions of the digital humanities from https://github.com/hepplerj/whatisdigitalhumanities. Every 4 hours. Sibling of @WordsDH." Twitter, https://twitter.com/DHDefined.

14. Geoffrey Rockwell, Peter Organisciak, Megan Meredith-Lobay, Kamal Ranaweera, Stan Ruecker, and Julianna Nyhan, "The Design of an International Social Media Event: A Day in the Life of the Digital Humanities," *Digital Humanities Quarterly* 6,no. 2 (2012). https://dhq-static.digitalhumanities.org/pdf/000123.pdf.

15. Jason A. Heppler, "What Is Digital Humanities?" What Is Digital Humanities. March 8, 2017. https://whatisdigitalhumanities.com/.

16. Amanda Licastro, *What Is Digital Humanities?*, 2015, distributed by GitHub Repository, https://github.com/hepplerj/whatisdigitalhumanities.

17. Nehal El-Hadi, *What Is Digital Humanities?*, 2015, distributed by GitHub Repository, https://github.com/hepplerj/whatisdigitalhumanities.

18. Davor, *What Is Digital Humanities?*, 2015, distributed by GitHub Repository, https://github.com/hepplerj/whatisdigitalhumanities.

19. Susan Hockey, 2004. "The History of Humanities Computing," in *Cover Image A Companion to Digital Humanities*, ed. Susan Schriebman, Ray Siemens, and John Unsworth (Oxford, England: Blackwell Publishing, 2004) https://companions.digitalhumanities.org/DH/.

20. Hockey, "The History of Humanities Computing." https://companions.digitalhumanities.org/DH/.

21. Hockey, "The History of Humanities Computing." https://companions.digitalhumanities.org/DH/.

22. Ernesto Priani Saisó and Ana María Guzmán Olmos, "TEI como una nueva práctica de lectura," in *Humanidades Digitales: desafíos, logros y perspectivas de futuro*, ed. Sagrario López Poza and Nieves Pena Sueiro, Janus [en línea], Anexo 1

(2014), 373–82, publicado el 11/04/2014, consultado el 29/05/2023. https://www.janusdigital.es/anexos/contribucion.htm?id=34.

23. Domenico Fiormonte, Desmond Schmidt, Paolo Monella, and Paolo Sordi, 2015, "The Politics of Code. How Digital Representations and Languages Shape Culture." https://infolet.it/files/2015/06/politics-of-code-fiormonte-et-al-def.pdf.

24. Dan Greene, *Promise of Access: Hope and Inequality in the Information Economy*. Cambridge, MA: The MIT Press, 16.

25. Greene, 5.

26. Reviews in DH Special Issue Latinx DH, https://reviewsindh.pubpub.org/latinox-studies

27. https://chicanapormiraza.org/about.

28. Brianna Starks, "The double pandemic: COVID-19 and White Supremacy," *Qualitative Social Work* 20, no. 1–2 (2021): 222.

29. Luis Urrieta and Eric Ruiz Bybee, "Policies and Politics: An Introduction," *Handbook of Latinos and Education*, ed. Enrique G. Murillo et al. (New York, NY: Routledge, 2021).

30. Hispanic is used here to match the data being referenced.

31. The editors of this volume owe a debt of gratitude to the Inter-University Program for Latino Research (IUPLR) for providing the initial seed funding and subsequent support that allowed us to meet in-person in El Paso and New York, and virtually during the COVID-19 pandemic.

32. Stacey Dutil, "Dismantling the School-to-Prison Pipeline: A Trauma-Informed, Critical Race Perspective on School Discipline," *Children & Schools* 42, no. 3 (July 2020): 172.

33. Patrik Svensson, "Beyond the Big Tent," *Debates in the Digital Humanities*, ed. Matthew K. Gold (Minneapolis: University of Minnesota Press, 2012).

34. Martha Nell Smith, "The Human Touch Software of the Highest Order: Revisiting Editing as Interpretation," *Textual Cultures* 2, no. 1 (2007): 1–15.

35. Ibram X. Xendi, "Our New Postracial Myth: The Postracial Idea Is the Most Sophisticated Racist Idea Ever Produced," *The Atlantic*, June 22, 2021.

36. David Golumbia and Dorothy Kim, "Digital Humanities and/as White Supremacy: A Conversation about Reckonings," *Alternative Historiographies of the Digital Humanities*, ed. Dorothy Kim and Adeline Koh (Santa Barbara, CA: Punctum Books, 2021), 69.

37. Lauren Tilton, Amy Earhart, Matt Delmont, Susan Garfinkel, Jesse P. Karlsberg, and Angel David Nieves, eds., "Special Issue: Toward a Critically Engaged Digital Practice: American Studies and the Digital Humanities," *American Quarterly* 70, no. 3 (2018): 361–70.

38. Roopika Risam, "Beyond the Margins: Intersectionality and the Digital Humanities," *Digital Humanities Quarterly (DHQ)* 9, no. 2 (2015). Available from http://www.digitalhumanities.org/dhq/vol/9/2/000208/000208.html.

39. Melissa Dinsman, "The Digital in the Humanities: An Interview with Jessica Marie Johnson," *Los Angeles Review of Books*, July 23, 2016.

40. Gloria Anzaldua, "La Conciencia de la Mestiza," *Borderlands/La Frontera: The New Mestiza* (San Francisco, CA: Aunt Lute Books, 1999), 78–79.

41. "English 1B Journal" by Arturo Casares, 1968, 0440_01_05_001, Arturo Casares Papers, Chicana and Chicano Community, Special Collections and University Archives, San Diego State University, San Diego, CA. http://hdl.handle.net/20.500.11929/sdsu:33488.

42. "English 1B Journal" by Arturo Casares, 1968, 0440_01_05_001, Arturo Casares Papers, Chicana and Chicano Community, Special Collections and University Archives, San Diego State University, San Diego, CA. http://hdl.handle.net/20.500.11929/sdsu:33488.

43. "English 1B Journal" by Arturo Casares, 1968, 0440_01_05_001, Arturo Casares Papers, Chicana and Chicano Community, Special Collections and University Archives, San Diego State University, San Diego, CA. http://hdl.handle.net/20.500.11929/sdsu:33488.

44. Kaiama L. Glover and Alex Gil, "On the Interpretation of Digital Caribbean Dreams," *The Digital Black Atlantic* (Minneapolis: University of Minnesota Press, 2021).

45. Roopika Risam and Alex Gil, "Torn Apart/Separados," https://xpmethod.columbia.edu/torn-apart/volume/1/.

46. Emily Dreyfuss, "'ICE Is Everywhere:' Using Library Science to Map the Separation Crisis," *Wired*, June 25, 2018. https://www.wired.com/story/ice-is-everywhere-using-library-science-to-map-child-separation/.

47. Lisa Peet, "SDSU Library Detainee Archive Details Migration, Asylum Stories," *Library Journal*, March 28, 2019, https://www.libraryjournal.com/?detailStory=SDSU-Library-Detainee-Archive-Details-Migration-Asylum-Stories; Liz Robbins, "'A Light for Me in the Darkness:' For Migrant Detainees, a Bond Forged by Letter," *New York Times*, February 28, 2019, https://www.nytimes.com/2019/02/07/us/immigrant-detainee-letters.html.

48. Gabriela Baeza Ventura, Lorena Gauthereau, and Carolina Villarroel, "Recovering the US Hispanic Literary Heritage: A Case Study on US Latina/o Archives and Digital Humanities," *Preservation Digital Technology & Culture* 48, no. 1 (2019): 17–27.

Bibliography

"About." About | Chicana por mi Raza. https://chicanapormiraza.org/about.

Anderson, Monica. "Mobile Technology and Home Broadband 2019." *Pew Research Center: Internet, Science & Tech*, June 13, 2019. https://www.pewresearch.org/internet/2019/06/13/mobile-technology-and-home-broadband-2019/.

Anzaldúa, Gloria. "La Conciencia de la Mestiza." *Borderlands/La Frontera: The New Mestiza*, 78–79. San Francisco: Aunt Lute Books, 1999.

Baeza Ventura, Gabriela, Lorena Gauthereau, and Carolina Villarroel. "Recovering the US Hispanic Literary Heritage: A Case Study on US Latina/o Archives and Digital Humanities." *Preservation Digital Technology & Culture* 48, no. 1 (2019): 17–27.

Casares, Arturo. "English 1B Journal." 0440_01_05_001, Arturo Casares Papers, Chicana and Chicano Community, Special Collections and University Archives, San Diego State University, 1968. http://hdl.handle.net/20.500.11929/sdsu:33488.

"Chapter 11: The Chicana and the Arts." Chapter 11.3: San Diego Chicano History. https://chicanohistory.sdsu.edu/chapter11/c11s03.html.

Delgado, Kevin. "A Turning Point: The Conception and Realization of Chicano Park." *The Journal of San Diego History*, 1998. https://sandiegohistory.org/journal/1998/january/chicano-3/.

Dinsman, Melissa. "The Digital in the Humanities: An Interview with Jessica Marie Johnson." *Los Angeles Review of Books*, July 23, 2016.

Dreyfuss, Emily. "'ICE Is Everywhere:' Using Library Science to Map the Separation Crisis." *Wired*, June 25, 2018. https://www.wired.com/story/ice-is-everywhere-using-library-science-to-map-child-separation/.

Dutil, Stacey. "Dismantling the School-to-Prison Pipeline: A Trauma-Informed, Critical Race Perspective on School Discipline." *Children & Schools* 42, no. 3 (July 2020): 172.

Fiormonte, Domenico, Desmond Schmidt, Paolo Monella, and Paolo Sordi. "The Politics of Code. How Digital Representations and Languages Shape Culture." 2015. https://infolet.it/files/2015/06/politics-of-code-fiormonte-et-al-def.pdf.

Glover, Kaiama L., and Alex Gil. "On the Interpretation of Digital Caribbean Dreams." *The Digital Black Atlantic*. Minneapolis: University of Minnesota Press, 2021.

Golumbia, David, and Dorothy Kim. "Digital Humanities and/as White Supremacy: A Conversation about Reckonings." In *Alternative Historiographies of the Digital Humanities*, edited by Dorothy Kim and Adeline Koh, 69. Santa Barbara, CA: Punctum Books, 2021.

Gonzales, Rodolfo, and Alberto Urista [Alaurista, pseud.] "El plan espiritual de Aztlan." *El grito del Norte*. vol. II, no. 9, 5. July 6, 1969. https://icaa.mfah.org/s/es/item/803398; http://www.insearchofaztlan.com/preamble.html.

Greene, Daniel. *The promise of Access: Hope and Inequality in the Information Economy*. Cambridge, MA: The MIT Press, 2021.

Heppler, Jason A. "What Is Digital Humanities?" What Is Digital Humanities. March 8, 2017. https://whatisdigitalhumanities.com/.

Hockey, Susan. "The History of Humanities Computing." In *Cover Image a Companion to Digital Humanities*, edited by Susan Schriebman, Ray Siemens, and John Unsworth. Oxford, England: Blackwell Publishing, 2004. https://companions.digitalhumanities.org/DH/.

"Interview with Alurista." conducted in San Diego, California 2000. San Diego State University, *The San Diego State University Library, Special Collections & University Archives*. Audio. San Diego State University Library, Special Collections & University Archives.

Kendi, Ibram X. "Our New Postracial Myth: The Postracial Idea Is the Most Sophisticated Racist Idea Ever Produced." *The Atlantic*, June 22, 2021.

Lara-Bonilla, Inmaculada. "Crafting a Latina/o Higher Education Rights Discourse in New York: The Founding and 'Saving' of Eugenio María de Hostos Community College." 197, Ithaca, NY: Cornell University Press, 2016.

"Latino/x Studies Reviews in Digital Humanities." Reviews in Digital Humanities. https://reviewsindh.pubpub.org/latinox-studies.

López, Yolanda M. *Chicanas/Escuelas. Library Digital Collections*. UC San Diego Library, 2021. https://library.ucsd.edu/dc/object/bb6829431n.

Lovell, Kera N. "'Everyone Gets a Blister': Sexism, Gender Empowerment, and Race in the People's Park Movement." *Women's Studies Quarterly* 46, no. 3 & 4 (2018): 103–19. https://www.jstor.org/stable/26511334.

Peet, Lisa. "SDSU Library Detainee Archive Details Migration, Asylum Stories." *Library Journal*, March 28, 2019. https://www.libraryjournal.com/?detailStory=SDSU-Library-Detainee-Archive-Details-Migration-Asylum-Stories.

Priani Saisó, Ernesto, and Ana María Guzmá Olmos. "TEI como una nueva práctica de lectura." In *Humanidades Digitales: desafíos, logros y perspectivas de futuro*, edited by Sagrario López Poza and Nieves Pena Sueiro, no. 1 (April 11, 2014): 373–82. https://www.janusdigital.es/anexos/contribucion.htm?id=34.

Reed, Conor Tomás. "The Evolution of Puerto Rican Studies at City College." *Puerto Rican Studies in the City University of New York*, edited by María Elizabeth Pérez and Virginia Sánchez Korrol. New York: CENTRO, 2021.

Risam, Roopika. "Beyond the Margins: Intersectionality and the Digital Humanities." *Digital Humanities Quarterly* 9, no. 2 (2015).

Robbins, Liz. "'A Light for Me in the Darkness': For Migrant Detainees, a Bond Forged by Letter." *New York Times*, February 28, 2019. https://www.nytimes.com/2019/02/07/us/immigrant-detainee-letters.html.

Rockwell, Geoffrey, Peter Organisciak, Megan Meredith-Lobay, Kamal Ranaweera, Stan Ruecker, and Julianna Nyhan. "The Design of an International Social Media Event: A Day in the Life of the Digital Humanities." *Digital Humanities Quarterly*, 2012. https://dhq-static.digitalhumanities.org/pdf/000123.pdf.

Smith, Martha Nell. "The Human Touch Software of the Highest Order: Revisiting Editing as Interpretation." *Textual Cultures* 2, no. 1 (2007): 1–15.

Starr, Raymond G. *San Diego State University: A History in Word and Image*, 187. San Diego, CA: San Diego State University Press, 1995.

Svensson, Patrik. "Beyond the Big Tent." *Debates in the Digital Humanities*, edited by Matthew K. Gold. Minneapolis: University of Minnesota Press, 2012.

Tilton, Lauren, Amy Earhart, Matt Delmont, Susan Garfinkel, Jesse P. Karlsberg, and Angel David Nieves. "Special Issue: Toward a Critically Engaged Digital Practice: American Studies and the Digital Humanities," *American Quarterly* 70, no. 3 (2018).

Urrieta, Luis, and Eric Ruiz Bybee. "Policies and Politics: An Introduction." *Handbook of Latinos and Education*. New York, NY: Routledge, 2021.

"Yolanda López Oral History." Proyecto Mission Murals, March 31, 2021. https://www.sfmoma.org/listen/yolanda-lopez-oral-history/.

Chapter 1

Toward a Rehumanizing Latinx Studies Curriculum

Nicholas Daniel Natividad and Cynthia Wise

Introduction

Caminante, no hay puentes, se hace puentes al andar. [Voyager, there are no bridges, one builds them as one walks.]

—Gloria Anzaldúa, Borderlands/La Frontera

Gloria Anzaldúa in *Borderlands/La Frontera* reminds us that borders are always meant to create the *other*.[1] What occurs during the process of bordering are efforts to dehumanize and render others as *illegitimate* members of society. To understand how we can begin to advance a rehumanizing curriculum we must first understand the role, significance, and impact dehumanization has on rendering others as subaltern members. Dehumanization is based almost exclusively as a tool of racism, which "has historically been a banner to justify the enterprises of expansion, conquest, colonization and domination and has walked hand in hand with intolerance, injustice and violence."[2] The practice of dehumanization has been found to be polarizing and, in the extreme, a precursor to genocide.[3] It is at the crossroads of these multiple and intersecting oppressions that we can begin to deconstruct dehumanizing agendas to fully understand how social change can occur to break down processes of *othering*.

Leo R. Chavez in his book *The Latino Threat: Constructing Immigrants, Citizens, and the Nation* outlines the ways laws, policies, media, and academic scholarship contribute to dehumanizing processes of Latinx in the US. Chavez explores how the constructed discourse of illegality and illegal immigration frames Latinx, and particularly Mexicans, as the quintessential *illegal alien* (and thus anti-American) destroying the American way of life.[4] This socially constructed threat narrative attempts to render Latinx as illegitimate members of society undeserving of social benefits, rights, and citizenship. The Latinx threat narrative has had its antecedents in US history and has included other groups like Japanese and Chinese immigrants, Catholics immigrants, and German-language immigrant threats. Each threat has served as an alarmist discourse to target a particular group and their children with the goal of allocating resources favorable to one group over another and justifying it through dehumanizing laws, policies, and practices. Thus, despite Latinx integrating into US social and economic culture and life, as Chavez points out, a "Latino Threat Narrative" continues to cast Latinx as different from other ethnic or immigrant threat narratives from the past. This can be seen in recent years as immigration laws and policies have been at the center of national conversation.

However, what makes the "Latino Threat Narrative" so important is not only what it tells us about how Latinx social identity has been constructed in the US, but also what it reveals about the meaning of community membership and the permeability of national borders. Chavez argues the real reason the threat narrative has existed historically and has intensified to this day, is suggestive of the contemporary crisis in the meaning of citizenship that has resulted from a complex global society. Latinx vary greatly in terms of historical heritage, culture, language, and background, yet threat narratives of Latinx in the US are consistent in conveying the message that Latinx are changing the moral fabric and culture of the US. Such stereotypes ignore historical immigration patterns that demonstrate the ebb and flow of human migration as part of the land, long before any nation-state was established. However, when immigrant-related events or issues arise in the US, anti-immigrant activists immediately target Latinx as part of the ongoing devolution of American values, not knowing what is really being revealed is a social conflict over the meaning of membership, citizenship, and belonging. What is meant by *citizen* has always been up to debate in the US, from the early iteration of it in US history, which did not include slaves, women, white males without property, and others. The meaning of *citizen* and who belongs and does not belong has been at the center of national conversation since the founding of the nation. This debate dovetails logics of race in the US and rather than reveal an inherent crisis on the meaning of citizenship, produces dehumanizing practices to further define membership and allocate who *deserves* social benefits and rights and who does not.

What Latinx have experienced in the US as the *perpetual immigrant* or the social other, positions Latinx to respond to, understand deeply, and unite with other *illegitimate* members of society throughout the world who are struggling with other crises in the meaning of membership and belonging in unique and different ways. Given recent developments in technology that have propelled globalization to new levels, this chapter examines the ways Latinx Studies can address dehumanizing practices and processes to advance a rehumanization curriculum. Latinx Studies is the story of movement and migration that moves beyond nationally constructed identities. It is a large part of a Global Studies movement that provides new meanings to belonging and citizenship. Therefore, what does it mean to place in dialogue Latinx Studies with Brexit, the Malawi and Tanzania border dispute, Israeli-Palestinian conflict, and other social conflicts worldwide? Chela Sandoval would remind us that we must build coalitions that are capable of recognizing varying struggles and relations between struggles.[5] This chapter questions whether Latinx Studies is providing an education that can move between ideological positionings and break the appearance of mutual exclusivity of oppositional practices of consciousness and social movement and instead allow for the positioning of resistance. Furthermore, it examines how Latinx Studies can move towards shared reality with other *illegitimate* members of society that are being rendered throughout the world. It asserts that the future of Latinx education must disrupt processes of dehumanization by pushing the boundaries of Latinx Studies identities (with the use of technology) coming from nation-states versus from within. For this, a new theoretical lens is proposed that can view the process of borders and bordering differently as a result of the digital age and be able to bridge the future of digital Latinx studies with a rehumanizing agenda.

Rehumanization

The term *rehumanization* has been used in multiple disciplines from psychosocial rehabilitation in psychotherapy to transitional justice instruments in international human rights law.[6] Most scholarship on rehumanization has focused on the role empathy plays in creating a shared understanding on the meaning of human dignity and equality.[7] Rehumanization is usually referenced in relation to group-based conflict in which dehumanization by one group denies full humanity of others in order to justify any violence and suffering inflicted on the group. What follows after dehumanization are processes to restore human dignity and wholeness to individuals or groups that have gone through the process of being othered for socio-political reasons.[8] Relatedly, scholarship on the systematic theoretical basis for the concept of dehumanization has focused on conditions of social conflict that have led to extreme violence like genocide.[9] Other models on dehumanization have argued that its manifestation emerges not only in conditions of extreme conflict but also as an everyday social phenomenon in which denial of another's humanity will justify prejudiced and discriminatory laws, policies, and procedures that lead to violence and suffering.[10] What follows after dehumanization is reconciliation between perpetrators and victims/survivors to rehabilitate perceptions toward one another.[11] Because most processes of rehumanization take place after fractured relationships between groups or individuals, scholarship focuses on repairing relationships between and amongst groups. However, for this book we offer the definition of rehumanization that centers not only rehabilitating relationships between people, but also restoring relations that have been fragmented due to intersecting processes of dehumanization. Therefore, rehumanization is the process of restoring people to their full humanity after historical violation, oppression, and trauma. This includes restoring and redefining relationships to themselves, one another, and to the land. People targeted by the many forms of prejudice and related acts of violence are then able to heal wounds in restorative social environments that can include physical, psychological, and spiritual aspects to the healing process. Rehumanization in this instance not only includes processes to redefine the other and restore human dignity, but also to allow a person after experiencing trauma to redefine themselves and their relationship to the land. This working definition provides for a more wholistic perspective toward humanity and the processes for rehumanization.

Academic scholarship has helped reframe understandings of humanity and the role education can play in creating a shared understanding of human dignity and life. Latinx scholars have been at the forefront of helping mold these understandings beyond traditional Western models of humanity. Most notably, radical feminist theory has articulated how coalitional praxis can assist in moving between ideological positionings and allow for new understandings of solidarity located in what Gloria Anzaldúa would call the "crossroads" of subjectivities.[12] Chela Sandoval in her five-location topography of oppositional consciousness further elaborates how working upon other modes of consciousness allows for the transfiguration of meanings so that a differential consciousness no longer accepts artificially constructed explanations of the world that have been created to serve forms of power.[13] Sandoval reminds us that the practice of mediation from a subaltern position as a form of oppositional consciousness can intervene in power for marginalized groups. This work has assisted in creating bridges amongst and between subjectivities and has helped us understand why oppositional ideologies do not register within the inventories of current structures and institutions.

Similarly, critical race theorists have reshaped the ways we understand history by using different techniques such as counter-storytelling as analytical frameworks to shift narrative change and magnify experiences, stories, and narratives of silenced and marginalized groups.[14] Critical race theory (CRT) has united legal scholars and activists to deconstruct the complexities of how race and racism is deeply embedded in everyday social institutions and structures of power.[15] This includes the multifaceted way law is used as an instrument in constructing and solidifying social prejudices that, along with other social constructions, has created a set of interpretive codes and racial meanings that operate in the everyday interactions of people.[16] Counter-storytelling has been used to tell the narrative of silenced experiences and challenge stories from the dominant discourse in order to, amongst other things, build community at the margins of society, transform belief systems and realities, and unveil the politics behind the production of knowledge in education.[17] It has helped unearth alternative ways to think of race by directly challenging the "pre-suppositions, perceived wisdoms, and shared cultural understandings persons in the dominant race bring to the discussion of race" to offer a new reality of those living at the margins of society.[18]

Each contribution has helped us understand how rehumanization and processes associated with rehumanization are complex requiring reformulation of the self, others, and new definitions of resistance, humanity, empathy, and shifts in consciousness. They have challenged institutions by revealing how racism is about institutional power and particularly how educational institutions have the potential to oppress and marginalize as well as the ability to emancipate and empower. However, as institutions have shifted and changed due to globalization and advancements in technology, so have innovative ways to connect and form community outside traditional community membership changed. Each movement, from bridging resistance to decolonial practices and counter-storytelling, has confronted processes of dehumanization and allowed resistance movements to adapt to changing cultural environments and new power dynamics. But the changing political economy of globalization has brought more technological advancements and, with it, new challenges with increased growing inequalities and environmental degradation on a level the world has never witnessed prior. With such changes, living in the digital age brings with it new ways to conceive of identity. But also new ways to conceive of humanity and rehumanization. For these reasons, we need a theoretical framework that can encompass past frameworks and that can center rehumanization for the digital age. A framework that can push the boundaries of Latinx Studies identities beyond old identity politics of the civil rights era in the US. With new and innovative connectedness through technology today, a starting point can be examining scholarship that complicates borders and the boundaries of identities and interrelatedness between communities.

Rehumanization in the Digital Age

In order for education to center rehumanization, we must first let go of historical notions that education is limited to brick-and-mortar structures, organized classrooms, and textbooks. For students of the digital age (1980 and beyond), learning and knowledge construction occurs 24–7 and most likely occurs through the use of digital tools and technology. While it is unlikely Dewey could have conceived of the vast technological developments of the twentieth century, his argument that learning is socially constructed and something that is done collectively rather than as an abstract concept still holds true.[19] Likewise, Vygotsky argued that a person's community influences how they make meaning or co-construct what they experience and see, and the messages they receive.[20] The explosion of digital opportunities has provided students with the platforms to challenge traditional education, which Althusser described as an ideological state apparatus (ISA), used to reproduce existing patterns of colonization and oppression, especially among marginalized populations.[21] Ruiz et al. agree, asserting that education is primarily "designed for the intentional colonization of marginalized populations."[22] As Kellner and Kim posited, "If a society hinders individuals from obtaining voluntary and critical human agency, it dehumanizes individuals by perpetuating a dehumanizing environment."[23]

At the same time, we must also free ourselves from traditional concepts of citizenship. As suggested by Kymlicka, "We are all just human beings who find themselves in a particular place at a particular moment."[24] Global migration patterns would suggest this is increasingly the case as the number of people living in a country other than their countries of birth has tripled in the last fifty years. It is imperative, Kymlicka argues, that we must begin to "think in a critical and ethnically responsible way about the diversity of people who belong in society, and the diversity of ways in which they legitimately express that belonging."[25] Traditionally, the main aim of schools and universities was to "develop citizens who internalized national values . . . and accepted glorified versions of national histories."[26] In the twenty-first century, however, those concepts have been eroded and the concept of traditional assimilationist education has been unmasked. Starkey argues that education should foster a cosmopolitan citizenship that allows students to see themselves as connected to the global community.[27]

While the COVID-19 pandemic put a spotlight on the global digital divide, for those that do have access to digital devices and high-speed internet, digital tools and social media have provided the means to decentralize the hegemonic flow of information both inside and outside the classroom, allowing for the creation of new and more authentic forms of knowledge. This is especially true for millennial and Gen Z students of color. Where existing textbooks portray some populations through a negative or deficit lens (if at all), digital tools create a bridge so that students can become producers of a more democratic view of reality limited only by the digital divide. Through internet-based sites students can "empower themselves in relation to dominant media and culture."[28] As Freire suggested, this can help oppressed and marginalized populations "truly transform reality."[29] Statistics show that social media usage is at an all-time high with the average user spending more than three hours a day surfing sites like YouTube, TikTok, Instagram, and Facebook.[30] As noted earlier, in order to better meet the needs of Latinx students, it is imperative that universities, especially Hispanic-Serving Institutions, reimagine their practices to better reflect the lived experiences of their students.[31]

Online sites like TikTok create the opportunity for peoples to rebut the dominant narrative. As examples, @Nava_jo, a self-described mother, educator and ShíDiné content producer on November 25, 2020, challenged the portrayal of a young Native girl on the cover of the children's book *Sing Down the Moon*.[32] The book tells the story of a young Navajo girl, but the cover art depicts a young girl in traditional Plains attire. @Nava_jo created an alternative cover with a photo of someone dressed in traditionally Diné apparel to distribute to her students. In another TikTok post, content producer

James Jones, whose channel @notoriouscree has 3.1 million followers, posted a video regarding the message created via Native drum songs.[33] During the COVID-19 pandemic, New Mexico State University's American Indian and Chicano programs began going live with presentations on multiple platforms. Michael Ray, director of NMSU's American Indian Programs, says the sites allow them to archive content and reach more people in the long run than previous in-person presentations ever allowed.[34]

Social media sites have also been instrumental in bringing people together to transform their sociopolitical condition. For students of the digital age, the internet has changed the way people interact. Where once we were isolated by physical and financial limitations—people from one side of the globe to another can now connect with the touch of a button allowing people to view themselves beyond the nation-state.[35] Facebook specifically is credited with mobilizing Arab youth in January 2011 for events throughout Egypt that ultimately brought down President Hosni Mubarak.[36] At the same time, where numerous textbooks have recounted atrocities and genocide at so called Indian boarding schools throughout the Western hemisphere in the nineteenth and twentieth centuries, it took only hours for the spread of information via social media sites like Twitter regarding the discovery of the remains of hundreds of First Nations children at the site of former residential schools in British Columbia, Canada, to prompt Interior Secretary Deb Haaland to call for an investigation of federal boarding schools in the United States.[37]

"To speak of education in the 2000s is inevitably to speak of cultural identity."[38] Exactly how people construct a reimagined and rehumanized knowledge of their cultural identity is multifaceted and "determined by the experiences of the learner."[39] A person's sense of self is formed early in life, from messages they receive from their parents and friends, in the classroom, and from media in its varied forms. In the first stage of Banks's six stages of cultural identity, "the individual internalizes the negative societal beliefs about his or her culture."[40] This knowledge does not have to exist in the reality of the real world, it is based strictly on perceptions.[41] A person's sense of self as it relates to their cultural identity "has proven to be an important aspect of adolescents' developmental experiences, as it has been related to their psychological well-being."[42]

The use of technology helped students participating in a curriculum writing workshop at New Mexico State University to dig into counter-stories about their Hispanic identity. Students investigated online archives detailing the story of Carmelita Torres, a teenage girl who sparked a multiday protest over chemical baths used to delouse migrant laborers at the US-Mexico border. The lesson showed the historic dehumanization of Mexican workers in the US, but also showed the strength of a single teenager who forced the discontinuation of the practice. Another lesson from the project involved the Empire Zinc Mining strike near Silver City, New Mexico. Rather than using a deficit model to portray workers in a negative light, the lesson showed the strength and resilience of women of Mexican ancestry in standing up to a corporation that discriminated against their husbands and families. Utilizing digital storytelling techniques, they used an interview with an elder from the community to provide a firsthand account of the events.[43]

The use of technology alongside art has helped make others aware of ongoing human rights violations taking place at the US-Mexico border. Refugees fleeing poverty, extreme violence, and natural disasters due to climate change have been met at the US-Mexico border with restrictive immigration policies that have resulted in the detention of tens of thousands of migrants, including unaccompanied minors. In an effort to address the psychological well-being of those children, a virtual and traveling exhibit, *Uncaged Art*, was created to show both the resiliency and talents of children held at the Tornillo, Texas, detention center.[44] As noted by Déa, art is often the first expression of resistance, "becom(ing) a crucial and fundamental way of conveying demands, struggles, and collective identities."[45] Whether that art comes in the form of graffiti, murals, or more formal museum exhibits, art allows for a counter-story to the dominant narrative. In 1990, the coauthor was active in calling for changes at the El Paso Art Museum in order to be more reflective of the city's Latinx heritage.[46] Since then, museums have increasingly worked to become more reflective of the communities they serve in an attempt to become more inclusive, and have used the internet to help foster that inclusivity. For instance, Pearson identified several online exhibits focusing on social justice and environmental issues.[47] Among them is an online exhibit on antiracism and activism at the Museum of New Zealand.[48]

The reimagining of education that occurred during the pandemic also gave birth to the *Pluriversity Imagination Collective* on YouTube. Created by a group of professors from New Mexico State University, the pluriversity was intended to open spaces through online discussions to begin imagining a pluriversity in our lives and these borderlands. By decolonizing university institutions, pluriversities shape "a process of knowledge production that is open to epistemic diversity."[49] Included in the *Pluriversity* series was a discussion of colonization and healing.

Conclusion

In conclusion, the future of Latinx Studies must center rehumanization and use digital tools to reconfigure and rethink categories of belonging and membership, which will allow for positioning of resistance and solidarity in new and innovative ways. This chapter looked at how Latinx social identity has been constructed in the United States, in terms of the "Latino Threat Narrative," and what that identity means about the meaning of membership. In order to counter those constructed identities, the chapter turned to rehumanization as a means of restoring human dignity to those who have been othered and viewed as perpetual immigrants even at universities that profess to be Hispanic-Serving Institutions. The chapter explored the use of academic scholarship to reframe understandings of humanity and the role education can play in creating a shared understanding of human dignity. The chapter then looked at examples at how digital tools like social media can be used to rehumanize Latinx populations, allowing them to embrace their historical heritage, culture, language, and background. Using technology in creative ways and dovetailing it with a rehumanizing curriculum allows Latinx Studies to expand the meanings of membership and belonging beyond a simple state-centric lens and instead toward intentional bridge building thus no longer reinforcing efforts that render others as illegitimate members. This allows for curriculum that can be built on radical inclusivity. Furthermore, by moving beyond traditional boundaries and concepts of education and curriculum we can enhance students' understanding of Latinx knowledges in all its complexity and wholeness.

Notes

1. Gloria Anzaldúa, *Borderlands/La Frontera*, 1987.
2. Rigoberta Menchu, *The Problem of Racism*, 1996.
3. Johanna Vollhardt et al., "Deconstructing Hate Speech in the DRC," 2007.
4. Leo R. Chavez, *The Latino Threat*, 2013.
5. Chela Sandoval, *Methodology of the Oppressed*, 2000.
6. Mary E. Wheeler and Susan T. Fiske, "Controlling Racial Prejudice," 2005; Sylvia Karl, "Rehumanizing the Disappeared," 2014.
7. Jodi Halpern and Harvey M. Weinstein, "Rehumanizing the Other," 2004.
8. David L. Smith, *On Inhumanity*, 2020.
9. Smith, 2020.

10. Nick Haslam, "Dehumanization," 2006.
11. Priscilla B. Hayner, *Unspeakable Truths*, 2011.
12. Gloria Anzaldúa, *Borderlands/La Frontera*, 1987; Pedro J. DiPietro, Jennifer McWeeny, and Shireen Roshanravan, *Speaking Face to Face*, 2019; Andrea J. Pitts, Mariana Ortega, and José Medina, *Theories of the Flesh*, 2020.
13. Chela Sandoval, *Methodology of the Oppressed*, 2000.
14. Richard Delgado, "Storytelling for Oppositionists and Others," 1989.
15. Kimberle Crenshaw et al., *Critical Race Theory*, 1995; Richard Delgado, *Critical Race Theory*, 1995.
16. Ian Haney-López, *White by Law*, 2006.
17. Daniel G. Solorzano and Tara J. Yosso, "Critical Race and LatCrit Theory and Method," 2001.
18. Richard Delgado and Jean Stefancic, "Critical Race Theory," 462.
19. John Dewey, *Experience and Education*, 1938.
20. Lev S. Vygotsky, *Mind in Society*, 1978.
21. Louis Althusser, "Ideology and Ideological State Apparatus," 1971.
22. Marisol Ruiz, Dulcinea Lara, and Dana Greene, "Mirrored Repressions," 1.
23. Douglas Kellner and Gooyong Kim, "YouTube, Critical Pedagogy, and Media Activism," 12.
24. Will Kymlicka, Foreword to *Citizenship Education and Global Migration*, xxi.
25. Kymlicka, xxiv.
26. James A. Banks, "Introduction," xvii.
27. Hugh Starkey, "Globalization and Education," 2017.
28. Douglas Kellner, *Media Culture*, 2.
29. Paulo Freire, *Pedagogy of the Oppressed*, 100.
30. Brent Barnhart, "Social Media's Demographics," 2021.
31. (Garcia 2016, Contreras et al. 2018).
32. @Nava_jo, "New Cover Photo," 2020.
33. James Jones (@notoriouscree), "Let's Educate Spread the Message in a Good Way," 2020.
34. M. Ray, personal communication, June 11, 2020.
35. Hugh Starkey, "Globalization and Education," 2017.
36. Killian Clark and Korhan Koçak, "Eight Years after Egypt's Revolution," 2019; Jon Nordenson, *Online Activism in the Middle East*, 2017.
37. K. Tsianina Lomawaima and Teresa L. McCarty, *"To Remain an Indian,"* 2006; Andrew Woolford, *This Benevolent Experiment*, 2015; Christine Hauser and Isabella Grullón Paz, "U.S. to Search for Former Native American Schools," 2021.
38. Cornel Pewewardy and Patricia C. Hammer, *Culturally Responsive Teaching*, 70.
39. Stephen N. Elliott et al., *Educational Psychology*, 256.
40. James A. Banks, "Cultural Identity, Stages of," 38.
41. Marcy P. Driscoll, *Psychology of Learning for Instruction*, 2000.

42. Adriana J. Umaña-Taylor, Ruchi Bhanot, and Nana Shin, "Ethnic Identity Formation during Adolescence," 390.

43. Dulcinea Lara and C. Bell, "Carmelita and the Bath Riots of 1917," 2022.

44. For a brief description and account of the exhibit see UC Staff, "UTEP Exhibit Gives Voice to Tornillo's Silenced Teens," *UTEP Campus Newsfeed* online, April 1, 2019, https://www.utep.edu/newsfeed/campus/UTEP-Exhibit-Gives-Voice-to-Tornillos-Silenced-Teens.html.

45. Ariane D. Déa, "Representation of Resistance," 5.

46. David Crowder, "Art Museum Lags," 1990.

47. Stephanie Pearson, "Why 2021 Will Be Momentous," 2021.

48. See "Antiracism and Activism: Articles on Protest, Decolonisation, and Antiracism from Our Experts and across the Web," *Te Papa Collections* Online, Museum of New Zealand Te Papa Tongarewa, 2021. https://www.tepapa.govt.nz/discover-collections/read-watch-play/antiracism-and-activism.

49. Achille Mbembe, "Decolonizing Knowledge," 15.

Bibliography

@Nava_jo. "New cover photo #native #navajo #utah #singdownthemoon #booktalk #librariansoftiktok #greenscreen #greenscreensticker." TikTok video, November 25, 2020. https://www.tiktok.com/@nava_jo/video/6899180613266410757?lang=en.

Althusser, Louis. "Ideology and Ideological State Apparatus." In *Lenin and Philosophy and Other Essays*, 85–126. London, England: New Left Books, 1971.

Anzaldúa, Gloria. *Borderlands/La Frontera: The New Mestiza*. San Francisco, CA: Aunt Lute Books, 1987.

Banks, James A. "Cultural Identity, Stages of." In *Encyclopedia of Diversity in Education*, edited by James A. Banks, 38. Thousand Oaks, CA: SAGE Publications, 2012.

Banks, James A. "Introduction: Global Migration and Citizenship Education." In *Citizenship Education and Global Migration: Implications for Theory, Research, and Teaching*, edited by James A. Banks, xvii. Washington: American Educational Research Association, 2017.

Barnhart, Brent. "Social Media's Demographics to Inform Your Brand's Strategy in 2021." Sprout Social, March 9, 2021. https://sproutsocial.com/insights/new-social-media-demographics/.

Chavez, Leo R. *The Latino Threat: Constructing Immigrants, Citizens, and the Nation*, 2nd ed. Stanford, CA: Stanford University Press, 2013.

Clark, Killian, and Korhan Koçak. "Eight Years after Egypt's Revolution, Here's What We've Learned about Social Media and Protests." *Washington Post*. January 25, 2019. https://www.washingtonpost.com/news/monkey-cage/wp/2019/01/25/eight-years-after-egypts-revolution-heres-what-weve-learned-about-social-media-and-protest/.

Contreras, Frances E., Lindsey E. Malcom, and Estels M. Bensimon. "Hispanic Serving Institutions: Closeted Identity and the Production of Equitable Outcomes for Latino/a Students." In *Interdisciplinary Approaches to Understanding Minority Serving Institutions*, edited by Marybeth Gasman, Benjamin Baez, and Caroline S. Turner, 71–90. Albany: State University of New York Press, 2008.

Crenshaw, Kimberle, Neil Gotanda, Gary Peller, and Kendall Thomas. *Critical Race Theory: The Key Writings that Formed the Movement*. New York, NY: New Press, 1995.

Crowder, David. "Art Museum Lags Behind Other Cities, Report Says." *El Paso Times*, April 24, 1990, 1–2B.

Déa, Ariane D. "Representation of Resistance in Latin American Art." *Latin American Perspectives* 39, no. 3 (2012): 5.

Delgado, Richard. *Critical Race Theory: The Cutting Edge*. Philadelphia, PA: Temple University Press, 1995.

Delgado, Richard. "Storytelling for Oppositionists and Others: A Plea for Narrative." *Michigan Law Review* 87 (1989): 2411–41.

Delgado, Richard, and Jean Stefancic. "Critical Race Theory: An Annotated Bibliography." *Virginia Law Review* 79 (1993): 462.

Dewey, John. *Experience and Education*. New York, NY: Collier Books, 1938.

DiPietro, Pedro J., Jennifer McWeeny, and Shireen Roshanravan. *Speaking Face to Face: The Visionary Philosophy of Maria Lugones*. Albany: State University of New York Press, 2019.

Driscoll, Marcy P. *Psychology of Learning for Instruction*. Boston: Allyn & Bacon, 2000.

Elliott, Stephen N., Thomas R. Kratochwill, Joan Littlefield Cook, and John Travers. *Educational Psychology: Effective Teaching, Effective Learning*, 3rd ed. Boston, MA: McGraw-Hill College, 2000.

Freire, Paulo. *Pedagogy of the Oppressed*. New York, NY: Continuum, 1970.

Garcia, Gina Ann. *Becoming Hispanic-Serving Institutions: Opportunities for Colleges and Universities*. Baltimore, MD: Johns Hopkins University Press, 2019.

Gómez, Santiago Castro. *Crítica de La Razón Latinoamericana*. Bogotá, Colombia: Editorial Pontificia Universidad Javeriana, 2015. https://www.perlego.com/book/1928083/crtica-de-la-razn-latinoamericana-pdf.

Halpern, Jodi, and Harvey M. Weinstein. "Rehumanizing the Other: Empathy and Reconciliation." *Human Rights Quarterly* 26, no. 3 (2004): 561–83. http://www.jstor.org/stable/20069745.

Haney-López, Ian. *White by Law: The Legal Construction of Race*. New York: New York University Press, 1996/2006.

Haslam, Nick. "Dehumanization: An Integrative Review." *Personality and Social Psychology Review* 10, no. 3 (2006): 252–64. https://doi.org/10.1207/s15327957pspr1003_4.

Hauser, Christine, and Isabella Grullón Paz. "U.S. to Search for Former Native American Schools for Children's Remains." *New York Times* online. June 23,

2021. https://www.nytimes.com/2021/06/23/us/indigenous-children-indian-civilization-act-1819.html.

Hayner, Priscilla B. *Unspeakable Truths: Transitional Justice and the Challenge of Truth Commissions*, 2nd ed. New York, NY: Routledge, 2011.

Jacobs, Bette. "Indigenous Identity: Summary and Future Directions." *Statistical Journal of the IAOS 35,* no. 1 (2019): 147–57. https://doi.org/10.3233/SJI-190496.

James Jones (@notoriouscree). "Let's Educate Spread the Message in a Good Way #indigenous #dance #native." TikTok video, December 4, 2020. https://www.tiktok.com/@notoriouscree/video/6902220227229076738?lang=en.

Karl, Sylvia. "Rehumanizing the Disappeared: Spaces of Memory in Mexico and the Liminality of Transitional Justice." *American Quarterly* 66, no. 3 (2014): 727–48. https://doi.org/10.1353/aq.2014.0050.

Kellner, Douglas. *Media Culture: Cultural Studies, Identity and Politics between the Modern and the Postmodern.* New York, NY: Routledge, 1995.

Kellner, Douglas, and Gooyong Kim. "YouTube, Critical Pedagogy, and Media Activism." *Review of Education, Pedagogy, & Cultural Studies* 32, no. 1 (2010): 3–36.

Kratochwill, Thomas, Joan Littlefield Cook, and John F. Travers. *Educational Psychology: Effective Teaching, Effective Learning.* Boston, MA: McGraw-Hill College, 2000.

Krogstad, Jens Manuel, and Gustavo Lopez. "Roughly Half of Hispanics Have Experienced Discrimination." Pew Research Center. June 29, 2016. https://www.pewresearch.org/fact-tank/2016/06/29/roughly-half-of-hispanics-have-experienced-discrimination/.

Kymlicka, Will. Foreword to *Citizenship Education and Global Migration: Implications for Theory, Research, and Teaching, xix–xxv.* Edited by James A. Banks. Washington, DC: American Educational Research Association, 2017.

Lara, Dulcinea, and C. Bell. "Carmelita Torres and the Bath Riots of 1917." [Conference Presentation]. Re(visioning) Social Studies Showcase. Las Cruces, NM.

Lomawaima, K. Tsianina, and Teresa L. McCarty. *"To Remain an Indian": Lessons in Democracy from a Century of Native American Education.* New York, NY: Teachers College Press, 2006.

Mbembe, Achille. "Decolonizing Knowledge and the Question of the Archive." Lecture in *Wits Institute for Social and Economic Research (WISER),* Johannesburg, South Africa: University of Witwatersrand, 2015: 15. https://wiser.wits.ac.za/system/files/Achille%20Mbembe%20-%20Decolonizing%20Knowledge%20and%20the%20Question%20of%20the%20Archive.pdf.

Menchu, Rigoberta. "The Problem of Racism on the Threshold of the 21st Century." Letter, Sixth Lascasianas Symposium at Iowa State University, May 21, 1996. https://awpc.cattcenter.iastate.edu/2017/03/21/the-problem-of-racism-on-the-threshold-of-the-21st-century-may-21-1996/.

Mitchell, Christopher. *Western Hemisphere Immigration and United States Foreign Policy.* University Park: Penn State University Press, 1994.

Nordenson, Jon. *Online Activism in the Middle East: Political Power and Authoritarian Governments from Egypt to Kuwait.* London, England: I.B. Tauris, 2017.

Ntigurirwa, Hyppolite. "The Dilemma of Affirmative Rehumanization: Words Are just the Beginning." *Yale Journal of International Affairs*, 2021. https://www.yalejournal.org/publications/the-dilemma-of-affirmative-rehumanization-words-are-just-the-beginning.

Pearson, Stephanie. "Why 2021 Will Be Momentous for Social Justice in Museums." *MuseumNext*, January 26, 2021. https://www.museumnext.com/article/why-2021-will-be-momentous-for-social-justice-in-museums/.

Pewewardy, Cornel, and Patricia C. Hammer. *Culturally Responsive Teaching for American Indian Students.* Charleston, SC: Eric Publication, 2003.

Pitts, Andrea J., Mariana Ortega, and José Medina. *Theories of the Flesh: Latinx and Latin American Feminisms, Transformation, and Resistance.* New York, NY: Oxford University Press, 2020.

Ruiz, Marisol, Dulcinea Lara, and Dana Greene. "Mirrored Repressions: Students and Inmates in a Colonial Landscape." *Critical Education* 9, no. 7 (2018): 1–23. http://ojs.library.ubc.ca/index.php/criticaled/article/view/186120.

Sandoval, Chela. *Methodology of the Oppressed.* Minneapolis: University of Minnesota Press, 2000.

Smith, David L. *On Inhumanity: Dehumanization and How to Resist It.* New York, NY: Oxford University Press, 2020.

Solorzano, Daniel G., and Tara J. Yosso. "Critical Race and LatCrit Theory and Method: Counter-Storytelling." *International Journal of Qualitative Studies in Education* 14, no. 4 (2001): 471–95. https://doi.org/10.1080/09518390110063365.

Starkey, Hugh. "Globalization and Education for Cosmopolitan Citizenship." In *Citizenship Education and Global Migration: Implications for Theory, Research, and Teaching*, edited by James A. Banks. Washington, DC: American Educational Research Association, 2017, 41–64.

Umaña-Taylor, Adriana J., Ruchi Bhanot, and Nana Shin. "Ethnic Identity Formation during Adolescence: The Critical Role of Families." *Journal of Family Issues* 27, no. 3 (2006): 390. https://doi.org/10.1177/0192513X05282960.

Vollhardt, Johanna R., Marie Coutin, Ervin Staub, George Weiss, and Johan Deflander. "Deconstructing Hate Speech in the DRC: A Psychological Media Sensitization Campaign." *Journal of Hate Studies* 5, no. 1 (2007): 15–35.

Vygotsky, Lev S. *Mind in Society: The Development of Higher Psychological Processes.* Cambridge, MA: Harvard University Press, 1978.

Wheeler, Mary E., and Susan T. Fiske. "Controlling Racial Prejudice: Social-Cognitive Goals Affect Amygdala and Stereotype Activation." *Psychological Science* 16, no. 1 (2005): 56–63. https://doi.org/10.1111/j.0956-7976.2005.00780.x.

Woolford, Andrew. *This Benevolent Experiment: Indigenous Boarding Schools, Genocide, and Redress in Canada and the United States.* Lincoln: University of Nebraska Press, 2015.

Chapter 2

Digital Pedagogy in a Multicultural Setting
Learning History and Connecting through Technology

Lissette Acosta Corniel[1]

Introduction

Latinx Studies has been around for decades as an area of study in the United States with the creation of programs, majors, departments, centers, and institutes that focus on a particular region, culture, and/or country.[2] However, several institutions have begun to broaden their interest from a general history on Latinxs to a more focused lens and specifically include Indigenous and Afro-Latinx Studies. This is the case at the CUNY Dominican Studies Institute in the City College of New York (CUNY DSI).[3] While much had been documented about free and enslaved Blacks in Spain and Brazil, there existed a gap about the contributions of Blacks in Santo Domingo, today, the Dominican Republic, the seed of the Americas. As a result, and to fix the problem, historian Anthony Stevens-Acevedo produced the First Blacks in the Americas database where I had the role of research associate cocurating sixteenth century documents for the exhibit *Sixteenth-Century La Española: Glimpses of the First Blacks of the Early Colonial Americas*. The exhibit would serve as the preamble to the First Blacks in the Americas database, a pioneering tool in Latinx Digital Humanities. The documents in the database allow users to learn about the early years of slavery in the Americas, the beginnings of the transatlantic slave trade, and the experiences of free and enslaved Blacks. First Blacks is also an open educational resource that can be used in the classroom. As educators, we often struggle to find sound free resources and tools that enhance our teaching and learning, and First Blacks fills that gap for Afro-Latinx students and educators.

As educators, we hope that our students engage with the assignments in ways that break the cultural and psychological barriers that often leave Latinx students feeling on the outside of academic work. This chapter discusses the process, implementation, and results of three interactive assignments using digital technology in a classroom of predominantly Latinx students in two separate Ethnic Studies courses, "The History of the Dominican Republic," (Class A)[4] and "The Latino Experience in the US," (Class B).[5] In each assignment, students had to relate their work to the course topic and their daily lives. The latter was not limited to lived experiences, but included knowledge of the subject learned through class material or outside of the classroom. Through these assignments, this chapter demonstrates how Latinx students learn about the history of their sending countries and the US.

One of the courses' learning objectives is to increase student participation and engagement. This is done not in an effort to increase the number of students who raise their hands or complete the assignments, but in an effort to increase participation with meaning and critical input. The end results prove that with these assignments students do both. They participate by completing the assignment and engage by continuing the conversation and making references in future discussions whether private or public.

Equally important, the goal of these pedagogical practices is to allow students to participate emotionally, intellectually, and physically by being exposed to material that they are familiar with and/or that they can relate to as well as make critical analyses on how the material and students relate to past and current events. In the process, students not only learn history but are also exposed to universal human values that they learn from each other or simply have the opportunity to develop. Here, I follow Eugenio María de Hostos's teaching philosophy of teaching to build students' intellect while they are in touch with their emotions and develop a will to learn and be global citizens. In other words, teach the material, and make an effort so that the students make a personal and societal connection while they develop the will to do.[6] I also build on bell hooks's philosophy of adding excitement to critical thinking in the classroom. hooks explains that while she was going to school, her professors "often used the classroom to enact rituals of control that were about domination and the unjust exercise of power. In this setting, I learned a lot about the kind of teacher I did not want to become."[7] Befittingly, I believe that shared authority in the classroom between the instructor and the students is important and may lead to increased student interest, individual and/or collective participation, and intellectual harmony where both the instructor and the student learn from each other. I often ask, "What do you propose that we do?" Take for instance the exams my students take. I do not create those exams. They do. They are assigned to submit two questions with their respective answers that they believe should be part of the exam. I later curate the questions adding some questions of my own. They earn a class participation grade for submitting the questions and their exam grade. This is fun teaching and sometimes may help professors learn which questions/topics/themes their students deem important. It also pushes the students to study because they must go back to the discussions to create their questions.

Excitement in the classroom should not only be experienced in the early grades or in discipline-specific classes where students make slime, go on a nature walk to identify sounds, visit a museum, or have the opportunity to meet someone who has made important contributions to our society. bell hooks adds that while she was going to school "excitement in higher education was viewed as potentially disruptive of the atmosphere of seriousness assumed to be essential to the learning process."[8] The author elaborates and shares that "critical reflection on [her] experience as a student in unexciting classrooms enabled [her] not only to imagine that the classroom could be exciting but that this excitement could co-exist with and even stimulate serious intellectual and/or academic engagement."[9] hooks's reflection better explains the reasoning behind another one of my classroom activities. We play academic bingo. In face-to-face classes we play bingo using peanuts, grapes, M&Ms, and Skittles, keeping in mind food allergies. In distance learning, we play virtual bingo.[10] Imagine learning about the United Fruit Company's impact in Latin America as a migration push factor for Latinxs while you play bingo. According to hooks, "Neither [Paulo] Freire's work nor feminist pedagogy examined the notion of pleasure in the classroom."[11] And thus, I aim to create assignments that are both fun and challenging.

In Class A, the assignment was: 1) First Blacks: students were tasked to visit the research database Firstblacks.org, complete a research report that answered the questions how, when, and why about the archival document they chose, and relate their research to today's social events in Dominican society, the United States, and their respective country of origin and/or families.

In Class B, the two assignments were: 1) Space and Place:[12] students were asked to provide a photograph (digital or print) that they felt a connection to in order to discuss space and place, place attachment, and memory.[13] This assignment was inspired by the novel assigned as the class text in lieu of a history book, *The Tattooed Soldier* by Hector Tobar, where Antonio, the main character, finds a photograph on two separate occasions. There were no restrictions on the type of photograph as long as it was appropriate. The photograph could be of themselves, another person, a place, or an object. 2) Immigrant Obituary:[14] the class was asked to write a poem titled "Immigrant Obituary" based on Pedro Pietri's poem "Puerto Rican Obituary," which we cover in class when discussing Puerto Ricans. Students could also contribute to the poem in their native language as a reference to *The Tattooed Soldier* where Antonio says, "In Spanish, I sound like the intelligent person I really am. In English, I am a bus boy."[15]

The assignments were very well-received by the students in large part because they provoked a strong emotional response and the opportunity for them to be included in the creation and assessment of the final project. For example, for the poem assignment there was nothing to edit in terms of content because we mainly addressed the grammar. The content was only addressed when we noticed inaccuracies and students helped each other to correct that. An example of this would be citing a wrong date, which we would discuss together. In the process, students felt included. The authority of the classroom was shared between the instructor and students honoring their human intellect and experience. Also, asking students to answer questions such as how Antonio's experience (from *Tattooed Soldier*) relates to the Latino experience in the US, which is the course topic, invites them to read the novel as a requirement, but most importantly, it invites students to read the novel and respond to the question from a personal perspective and the same can apply to immigrant students. For example, for me, it is important that a Pakistani student or descendant of Pakistani parents, who registers for one of my classes is able to relate and engage in our discussions. And often, we engage when we can relate.

While digital literacy is not a fundamental learning objective in these courses, it is used as a fun learning enrichment strategy. Students can use their phones, tablets, laptops, and computers to create videos, participate in class discussion chat groups, and complete an assignment. However, this approach may prove challenging for both the instructor and the students when many lack access to updated technology devices such as smartphones and/or the Internet. This proved exceedingly challenging during the COVID-19 pandemic when many students expressed not having computers and/or internet at home and only having access to such items when they were in school. In this case, I was left with the only option of sharing information about the limited resources offered by the school and by the city. But most importantly, the most sensible thing to do was to be flexible regarding quality and deadlines. I remember allowing one student to take a picture of their handwritten work and submit it until they had access to a better device because they said it was very difficult to complete the work on their phone. Clearly, this may not work for everyone. But I invite you to be a little flexible both mentally and physically. For instance, when was the last time you graded a handwritten assignment? And believe me, not everything is perfect in my teaching and learning world.

The courses "The Latino Experience in the US" and "History of the Dominican Republic" are introductory level courses that students may take as electives. Each course fulfills the US Experience in its Diversity and World Cultures and Global Issues requirement, respectively, necessary for the completion of the Associate Degree of Liberal Arts. The classes are taught at the Borough of Manhattan Community College (BMCC), a CUNY college located in the Manhattan neighborhood of Tribeca, where 40.8 percent of the student population is Latinx.[16] As such, with its high Latinx enrollment BMCC is a Hispanic-Serving Institution (HSI) with a general student population of over 26,000 students with 65 percent attending full time and over 50 percent being first generation to attend college. As of the spring of 2016, 89.8 percent of BMCC students came from New York City. Also, 46.4 percent of the first-time freshman population is Latinx.[17] The student population represents 163 countries with the majority coming from or being descendants of Dominican Republic, China, Bangladesh, Jamaica, Guyana, Haiti, Ecuador, Mexico, South Korea, and Trinidad and Tobago. It is important to note that in my courses, while the majority of the students were Latinx, some students were from other ethnic backgrounds. For this reason, while the assignments were created to focus on the Latinx experience given the topic of the courses and the classroom population, the exercises allowed students from other backgrounds to relate to the assignments while also learning about other cultures.

Methodology

The strategies used to develop, implement, and complete the three assignments primarily included students' input. The aim was to produce assignments that were not necessarily totally created by the instructor, that students could have input in the process of creating and/or fine-tuning the assignments. The digital tools and/or programs used like Google Docs and Discussion

Board on Blackboard, were selected because they seemed to be readily available and easy to use. Google Docs allowed us to work on the poem independently and simultaneously.

Discussion Board through Blackboard was used because Blackboard is the distance-learning platform at our institution. Discussion Board allows students to upload photos, videos, and links as well as create and respond to posts. However, the assignment can be equally effective using other online learning platforms such as Moodle or any other platform that allows for media sharing and peer interaction.

Of course, not everything was perfect, and with that comes the learning process for future implementations of the assignments. With Google Docs, one of the obstacles encountered by both the students and me was the fact that not every student has a Gmail account. And while our institution allows access to the Google apps, I soon realized that I had to walk students through this process. As a note to self, I now create short two- to three-minute tutorials explaining a particular tool or assignment, followed by a live demonstration in class. Overall, when the students were limited or felt limited to participate for a number of reasons—e.g., did not have Internet or a smartphone, had to share a computer with siblings, did not have photographs in digital form, or were shy to publicly participate—modifications were made privately without affecting the end result and without revealing their issues. In addition to taking into consideration students' limited access to technology, the methodology also considered other variables such as students' availability given that many of them had two jobs while being full-time students. The assignments were given with one- to two-month completion deadlines, with a weekly check-in for those due within one month and a biweekly check-in for the assignments due within two months. Extended time and flexibility were the only solutions I could think of to address the digital divide that affects Latinx students. Students were also presented with a series of digital resources such as websites and databases in addition to the course discussions and readings.[18] Exposure to these resources added to their knowledge and motivated Latinx and other students to complete the assignments.

However, while I was able to focus on solutions and not the problem, access to technology cannot be the barrier to learning any longer given the relative availability of hardware. Research shows that whites and Asians and Asian Americans have more access to technology than Latinx and Black students.[19] Paul Gorski and Christine Clark explain that the "divide" has referred to the difference in physical access rates among groups and that

Black and Latinx people are in the lower rates.[20] Teachers and students alone should not be expected to come up with solutions, especially at HSIs where the class ratio tends to be higher and students are more likely to possess lower financial means. Government officials and college administrators should deliver on their responsibilities and assist in lowering the tech divide for Black and Brown students allowing both educators and students to do a better job. Community colleges and aid providers need to realign their priorities to not only incorporate more digital literacies but also invest in the equipment that would allow professors to do so.

First Blacks in the Americas Research Assignment[21]

Digital tool used: First Blacks in the Americas Internet database and Spanish Paleography Digital Teaching and Learning Tool[22]

Method: Introduce the database and its tabs, focusing on the "Resources" and the "Archival Sources" subsection. Discuss the language challenge because the documents are written in sixteenth-century Castilian Spanish. Students are introduced to Spanish paleography through the Spanish Paleography Digital Teaching and Learning Tool as a way to ease them into the difficult task of deciphering ancient writing. Then, explain each part within a First Blacks database resource document: manuscript, transcription, translation, and commentary. Students have the option to select a document of their choice by reading the descriptive digital card attached to each document.

Learning objectives:

1. Recognize early colonial documents written in Castilian Spanish

2. Analyze historical content

3. Compare sixteenth-century events to current Dominican society

Assessment: Class discussion and written report

Through this assignment Latinx students were introduced to a wealth of information about the arrival of the first enslaved Black Africans, who today can be traced in the culture, spiritual practices, and language of many Afro-Latinx communities and in US society. While many students have read books, book chapters, and scholarly articles on the topic of slavery, this assignment allowed them to see, examine, and analyze the documents many authors study to produce such academic material. Most importantly, at the time of this publication, First Blacks is the only searchable database dedicated to the history of free and enslaved Blacks in Santo Domingo after the European invasion of 1492. In this process, students are exposed to documents that tell the history of the foundation of the Americas. Also, Afro-Latinx students can trace the roots of their ancestors to Santo Domingo, the first port of entry for the transatlantic slave trade. In addition, in the process, students are exposed to Spanish language skills by using the Spanish Paleography Digital Teaching and Learning Tool and by comparing the Spanish transcriptions with present day Spanish. But one of the most important takeaways of this exercise is students' ability to make important observations and connections that link the history found in First Blacks to current events. Other important databases such Gwendolyn Midlo Hall's slavebiographies.org and slavevoyages.org offer information on enslaved Blacks from the point of capture to the point of arrival.[23] However, First Blacks is the only and first database to focus on the very early years of the Atlantic slave trade providing a tool for both recovery and research, and also serving as a pedagogical tool. Latinx students made critical analyses of the documents they selected by drawing important conclusions that may serve as windows to look into what life was like for some free Blacks in 1575. Equally important, they were able to make connections between life back then and today, as they juxtaposed what they learned about Blacks in the colonial period with the lives of Blacks today. Most interesting were the students' critical views on family and migration as major components of society then and today.

How this Project Rehumanizes Latinx Education

When I first conceived this assignment, I debated how I could make it about the students because the assignment involved researching a database of sixteenth-century colonial manuscripts about the beginnings of slavery in Santo Domingo, Dominican Republic, the initial port entry of the transatlantic slave trade.[24] In an effort to best use the database to help students identify with the assignment, after I introduced the topic I asked what were some things they were interested in. Most students reported that they wanted to learn about how Black people were treated and how they lived in the initial years of slavery. Once they mentioned people, the assignment took its own course. It became a short research project involving Spanish paleography and discovering how the history of slavery in the Americas is also part of the history of Latinx people.

Latinx students must be included in what we teach and how we teach in order to rehumanize Latinx education. While we may not always succeed at this, it is important to know that it is OK to ask for help. In the case of this assignment, the students' input shaped how it was going to be conducted. The partial sample of this assignment shared below allows me to discuss the word *connection*, which is included in the chapter's title. While the two previous assignments discussed how students had the opportunity to express emotional connection through personal experience and often related to emotions, First Blacks allowed students to connect to the content in other ways. For example, the following excerpt from one of the students' assignments can best illustrate how the exercise served as a time machine between twenty-first-century students and sixteenth-century Castilian colonial manuscripts:

> I chose manuscript No. 006 because I am interested in the role agriculture has played and continues to play in the world economy, as well as understanding the human rights issues that are frequently tied to it. . . . This theme is important today as the Dominican Republic fights for greater individual freedoms and immigrants are continually exploited in agricultural and factory settings. While researching this topic, I found that the foundation of exploitation, marginalization, slavery, and maltreatment of fellow humans still underpin immigration issues in the country today.[25]

The author of the piece above found an academic and a possible career connection between herself and the manuscript she selected, while also connecting with the historical content discussed in class in relation to immigration, low-wage jobs, and exploitation. This student, who remained anonymous, made a personal connection with the manuscript she examined.[26] She explains that she chose manuscript 69 from the database because it made her think about her family. The manuscript that another student, Leslie, selected discusses the travel petition by María, a formerly enslaved woman born in Santo Domingo, residing in Seville, Spain, at the time of the petition (1575), and wanting to move to Perú. At the time of the petition, María had a daughter whom she also planned to take to Perú. Of all the invaded colonies, Mexico and Perú were the thriving places at the time. Leslie explained that as a mother, she would have wanted the best for her daughter too.

Assessment for this assignment included student feedback through class discussion and a written report of what they took away from the assignment. For example, Mary Kate Doherty wrote,

> The First Blacks assignment allowed me to gain a more detailed history of the Caribbean and what shaped its demographics. I knew that Africans had been brought to the area in the 15th century, but aside from that my knowledge on the topic was vague. I was introduced to new material in the form of the archival documents and I learned about the specific racial hierarchy. With clear instructions, I was able to gain a broader view of history in the DR. I particularly enjoyed learning about prominent Black women in La Española, as the history I've studied before does not always center their stories. Although I'm not of Dominican background, I felt I could connect the events of the assignment to current events now. As a white woman and a feminist, something I regularly think about is intersectionality. Historically, women have always been oppressed, but because of whiteness, there remains to be an understood racial hierarchy within that oppression.[27]

Future Possibilities for Teaching This Project

The "First Blacks in the Americas" short research project can take many forms. It can grow from an undergraduate thesis, to a PhD dissertation, to a book. The project also allows for the production of digital material using the archival resources available in the database. For example, students can use the digital tool Mapillary to record specific places connected to the history of slavery in Latin America and the US. This, too, can be organized as a multi-campus assignment allowing students from different places to record images within their assigned or chosen spaces. An additional tool, starting from the information on the First Blacks website, is to produce a picture story of places utilizing Google Earth. Being able to examine one sixteenth-century document about the first one hundred years of slavery in Santo Domingo and the beginnings of the development of the transatlantic slave trade may lead to students' interest in Afro-Latin American studies. Finally, this assignment can contribute to the increase of scholars in the area of Dominican Studies, a much-neglected field in the study of the history of Latin America.

Space and Place, Memory, and Place Attachment Assignment (photo)

Digital tool used: Google Slides and Blackboard Discussion Board

Method: Photograph submission with a description to create a class collage, to be discussed in class and shared publicly.

Learning objectives:

1. Explain why the two scenes with the photographs in *The Tattooed Soldier* are important
2. Discuss how they relate to the Latino/immigrant experience in the US

Assessment: Written and oral discussion of the assignment

This assignment was conceived after reading sections of the text being used in the class, *The Tattooed Soldier*, where the main character, Antonio, encounters old photographs. Antonio is an undocumented immigrant from Guatemala living in Los Angeles during the LA Uprising, who left his homeland to escape the Civil War after his wife and child were murdered by the government for their activism against corruption. At the beginning of the novel, Antonio finds a photograph of his wife and son and expresses how he feels about it. Toward the end of the novel, Antonio finds another photograph of his wife and son. The second photograph is a photo of their grave. The digital tools to submit the photos included email at first and Google Slides later for the in-classroom version of the assignment where students had the opportunity to talk about their photos. Google Slides was effective because students could simply copy their pictures into the slide and write why they chose each photo and what it meant to them. Also, I have been teaching this class online since before the COVID-19 pandemic; we used Blackboard Discussion Board for photo and comment submission, and this too has proven to be effective.

Assignment chart (original assignment in a classroom setting):

1. Students read about the first photograph at the very beginning of the novel.
2. Students read about the second photograph when Antonio finds the photograph at the end of the novel.
3. Students submit a photo with a short paragraph discussing why this photograph is important to them in the context of space and place and also explaining how the picture relates to the course topic "Latino Experience in the US" and/or immigrant experience in the US that is later discussed in class.
4. Students visit the board across from my office where all of the pictures they submitted are displayed along with blank leaflets of paper and pen to optionally write something and pin it to another photograph they connected with. It turns out that many students and passersby did write on the board.

Modified assignment for online class:

1. Students read about the first photograph.
2. Students read about the second when Antonio finds the second photograph at the end of the novel.
3. Students submit a photo with a short paragraph discussing why this photograph is important to them in the context of space and place and also explaining how the picture relates to the course topic "Latino Experience in the US" and/or immigrant experience in the US.
4. Students respond to posts discussing the photographs shared and engage with their classmates' responses about how the assignment relates to the two scenes in *The Tattooed Soldier*.

In both the face-to-face class and online, students who wanted to share a photo but felt that it was too personal to share with the entire class and/or have their names included on the space and place board, were given the option to send the photograph to me and I would post it on the picture board and title it "anonymous." Those in the online class had the option to send me the photograph and I would post it to the Blackboard Discussion Board on their behalf. This shared authority between students and the professor invites Latinx students to participate rather than feel intimidated. It allows them to trust their professor and come to a better understanding of how their participation might change the institution. The presence of their stories means better representation and more access.

During the discussion of the assignment, students expressed, both in the classroom and online, that what they enjoyed the most was seeing other people's photographs and reading/learning about their stories. In their words, "it felt like therapy." According to their feedback, they saw themselves in other photographs and stories too.

How This Project Rehumanizes Latinx Education

In this exercise where students were asked to submit a photo they felt connected to, a student submitted a photo of his neighborhood in Pakistan and wrote and discussed how he and the part of the family that resides in the US have not been able to go back because of civil unrest. Other students asked how that made them feel. A Chinese student shared a picture of the first building she lived in when she arrived in Queens, New York. She explained that although her family moved to a different neighborhood after her arrival, she will always remember that place and her experiences there. As a class and related to the description of the two photos previously shared, the students discussed arrival and the built environment. There were many tissue moments, but one stands out. A student submitted a photograph of an airplane wing, like those you take while sitting inside the plane.

When looking at the picture of "The Wing," as I have been calling the photograph, I imagined a story. Before hearing the student's version of why they felt connected to this picture, I imagined a tale of transnationalism of a foreign-born immigrant who returns to their country to visit their family when on vacation from school. There is no explanation as to why that was my first thought, but it was perhaps the fact they were a documented college student contributed to my imagined story. Other students confessed to having thought the same thing, and we apologized. The student who owned the picture of "The Wing," shared that they felt connected to that picture because it was the day that they left their country five year ago in 2018 and had not been able to go back to see their mother. There was a brief silence in the classroom. Students realized that "not having papers" is not the only reason why immigrants cannot return to their countries. We discussed migration's pull and push factors. During the discussion, we found that the reasons for migration for people around the world varied substantially and that financial stability might be the ultimate goal for those leaving Latin America, but not the direct reason why they leave.

For example, a study conducted in 1979 Britain indicated higher wages as the pull and push factor for internal migration. Revolutionary and post-revolutionary Guatemalan immigrants cannot say the same. While internal migration took place during the United Fruit Company takeover of Guatemala, the main reason for this internal migration by peasants and supporters of the working class was safety; this reason also extended to many Guatemalans who left to live abroad.

After discussing the many reasons for leaving their country, students also came up with a list of reasons why many immigrants cannot return to their homeland. They shared that most people think the main reason for immigrants not being able to return to their country to visit family is because they are undocumented, not imagining that there are several reasons beyond "not having papers." Their list included various forms of violence such as local and national governmental violence from the military and counter-revolutionary groups for not acquiescing, domestic violence, intrafamilial violence and/or sexual abuse, gang violence, drug cartels-related violence, civil unrest related to government corruption, as well as the financial costs associated with returning home.

About financial costs, the students explained that it is hard to save money to return to their countries and visit. The logistics of taking time off are challenging for many. It is even a bigger burden for the entire family to travel if it is a family of three or four. Returning to your home country for a visit is not just about bringing yourself to hug and be hugged by your loved ones. It also includes bringing multiple suitcases of goods requested or gifts to satisfy the needs of your family members. In their responses, the students shared that it could take years to save money for flights, to cover the costs of an unpaid week's vacation (if you are only given one), and to save for the goods you have to buy.

Finally, Latinx students saw something of themselves in Antonio from *The Tattooed Soldier*. Non-Latinx students also made some connections with the world issues discussed in the novel, like language, homelessness, family, violence, rage, education, and happiness. Most importantly, they thought of the assignment as a type of therapy, one that allowed them to connect to themselves and to places. Also, the assignment allowed them to reflect, ask questions, and share how it made them feel and how it made feel about others. The picture board began to be called "the therapy board."

A student explained that looking at all of the pictures on the "Space and Place" board was like looking at "interesting slices of life frozen in time."[28] Their peer said that "I chose a picture of Holland Bamboo in Jamaica because it reminded me of my childhood days when my mom used to take me to visit my aunt who was living in that neighborhood."[29] And, Emmanuel Paulino wrote

> I took away a lot from the assignment, as I mentioned before, it helped me get a lot closer to my own understanding of my past even though it was one I had shut out for a long time. Even though it wasn't something I was looking forward to sharing at first, it helped me feel a lot better later on. When I saw other people's pictures of their own "Spaces and Places," it helped me realize that we come from a lot of unique backgrounds and some of us can end up sharing those backgrounds with a few individuals while maybe not so much with others. I remember there were a lot of beautiful unique locations people had as their Spaces and Places and it was pretty cool seeing something or someplace that could mean essentially nothing to me, might mean the world to someone else.[30]

Future Possibilities for Teaching This Project

This assignment can be redesigned to be done using the digital tools Flipgrid or Zoom, which would allow the creation of a virtual collage that can be saved to be shared only among class members or made public in one or many of the social media outlets. Through Zoom, students have the option to create a photo collage or a video collage. With Flipgrid, students can record themselves and comment on each other's videos. If done and edited correctly, the video stories can be aligned to create a story that unfolds different themes. Another advantage of Flipgrid is that if students would like to have some type of anonymity, they can record themselves successfully completing the assignment part without sharing their personal information.

Immigrant Obituary, Poem Assignment

Digital tool used: Google Docs

Method: Provide an open Google Doc document where students can contribute independently by adding their words, phrases, abbreviations, and/or verses to the poem. They had all semester to contribute, until the last two weeks of school, and they could contribute as much as they wanted.

Learning objective/s:

1. Compare the Latino experience in the US from 1970 to the present

2. Relate the assignment to the course text *The Tattooed Soldier*

3. Relate the assignment to the Latino experience in the US

Assessment: Class discussion

It is already challenging to produce inclusive learning activities that do not require a digital component. Nonetheless, those who see education as a right for all students and strive to make sure that all students partake in the learning process aim to develop student-centered teaching strategies. Emily Smith, an elementary school teacher in Texas, teamed with her aide to make sure that students being pulled out of the classroom for enrichment programs spent an adequate amount of time with technology in the classroom, as much as her full-time students.[31]

Her strategy allowed the students being pulled out to have the same experience and develop the same digital literacy skills as the rest of the students. Like Emily Smith, this assignment attempted to give Latinx students an equal opportunity to succeed in an exercise that apparently required them to do something they thought they were not capable of or were not interested in.

The following semester, after seeing students' positive responses about the Space and Place assignment and after a class reading of Pedro Pietri's "Puerto Rican Obituary," I asked students what they thought about writing a poem. Their immediate response was a combination of "hell, no!," "are you crazy?," and "no way, altogether." They were then presented with the idea of writing the poem together as a class. Still, many students resisted the idea because they said they were not poets. Nonetheless, we proceeded to discuss my proposal and expectations, and their response was one hundred percent positive. Students were instructed to express themselves in the Google Doc and follow the instructions provided:

Instructions:

1. You are a poet.

2. Write anything: a word, phrase, name, verse, abbreviation, etc.

3. You can contribute to the document as many times as you want.

4. You can write in your native language.

5. Please do not erase anything after you contribute. Kindly use the strikethrough key allowing the text to remain for collective class review. You might not like what you wrote, but others might think it is brilliant.

6. If you are not an immigrant or a descendant of immigrants, use the resources provided throughout the course and contextualize it in your contribution. You may also write about experiences you have had with fellow immigrant friends, coworkers, and/or classmates.

7. We will review the document as a class every two weeks.

8. Add your initials to the input, or you can be anonymous.

9. We will edit the poem as a class upon reaching the deadline for input.

10. The poem will be printed in large font and displayed on the board at the Center for Ethnic Studies.

The result of their efforts cannot be underestimated. When the class reviewed what they had written so far, students gasped, with the phrases: "we did that?," "what that says, it's true," "who wrote that?," and "I want to cry!" The class was given ten minutes to read the poem in silence. They then read it aloud starting with the first row and ending with the last. Below you can read excerpts from the work of these poets.

Banana seeds
Blood on leaves
Remembered today
Forgotten tomorrow . . .[32]

One sentiment remains the same in my story
In Miguel's story
In María's story
In Manuel's story
In Marco's story . . .[33]

Allá we have rights Aquí we have duties
Allá we know our neighbors
Aquí each person lives their own life . . .[34]

They bring the culture . . .
Contribute to the melting pot
Expand our communities
Raise the GDP
Not the real criminals . . .[35]

How This Project Rehumanizes Latinx Education

Puerto Rican poet Pedro Pietri wrote "Puerto Rican Obituary" in 1973 to echo the struggles of the Puerto Rican community on the mainland. Although the title of poem claimed a specific geographic location, it resonated with the experience of the entire marginalized Latinx community. The assignment to write a poem titled "Immigrant Obituary" was an effort to allow Latinx students to replace Pietri's Puerto Rico and Puerto Ricans with their own country and people. The same applied to the rest of the immigrant students. Reading and teaching "Puerto Rican Obituary" already rehumanizes Latinx education. However, asking the students to write their own version of the poem provides the opportunity for creativity and personal connection. Pietri's Juan, Miguel, Milagros, Olga, and Manuel are replaced with the names of people students know and Puerto Rico becomes bigger than Gran Colombia, with emotional allies that extend to other continents.[36] Students are also able to provide a comparative historical analysis of Pietri's 1973 masterpiece and their own poems, at the same time that they ask critical questions such as what lies behind Pietri's verse, "all died yesterday today and will die again tomorrow passing their bill collectors on to the next of kin." Through their writing, Latinx students concluded that the answer to the previous question is the product of systemic inequality imposed on their sending countries and the immigrant communities in the US. One of the authors tries to better explain it as follow: "you can fight for this country you can slave for this country you can work for this country you can pay taxes for this country you can have kids in this country but you cannot receive benefits in this country live in this country, get an education in this country and you most definitely cannot be a citizen in this country."[37] Finally, how much more human can it get when a student contributes to the poem in their native language:

Afrique lhedi andi
Hin bheybhin no dogoudhe tchounhi maghe nhin Fhi
    mayeughol ka desert thon,
Nene bhe bouye wouli, Afrique lhedi andi.[38]
Moemoeā ki te haere atu
He whakamā matou.[39]

من خلال المشقة والدم والعرق والدموع ، خاضت عائلاتنا معركة من أجل تحسين مستقبلنا. لقد تم إخراجنا من بلادنا والآن نحن بحاجة لبدء حياة جديدة في بلد آخر كمهاجرين[40]

Están en busca del sueño americano. Vinieron de su país buscando oportunidades que el imperialismo les ha quitado. Se levantan temprano y trabajan duro. Pero no tienen tiempo para disfrutar con los que aman.
    Un ciclo sin fin.[41]

The students' response about being able to contribute to the poem in their native language is best summarized by Paola Durán who explained that "this assignment made me go back in time to my family's own struggles as immigrants in this country, and how we are all still fighting to achieve the American Dream.

I also love the format of this assignment because it allows me to contribute authentically from the bottom of my heart and soul, and the fact that I can use my first language to express things the exact way I think is priceless."[42]

Future Opportunities for Teaching This Project

Although it may sound mind-blowing, "Immigrant Obituary" can be developed into a collaborative activity among several classrooms and universities state or nationwide. The results can become a publication or publications of various forms and disciplines. The development of such an endeavor may require more time and effort than what was invested in the original assignment. Nonetheless, with willing collaborators, several grant options may be explored to craft a fine product where Latinx students feel represented and proud of their contribution to the project. A successful example is the four-campus digital project focused on the work of Walt Whitman titled "Looking for Whitman: The Poetry of Place in the Life and Work of Walt Whitman," which received funding from the National Endowment for the Humanities Digital Division.[43] Unlike the Walt Whitman project, the scope of "Immigrant Obituary" can be local, national, and/or global. "Looking for Whitman" focused on Whitman's work in the four cities where he lived. With 60 million Latinx in the US and 44.8 million immigrants (Latinx immigrants included) this potentially could be a lengthy poem.[44] Another successful example is The University of Texas at El Paso, and John Jay Global Learning Community project discussed in chapter four and created by Isabel Martínez and Irma Montelongo. The two professors made the program possible despite the 2,184-mile distance.[45] In the project, students from John Jay College of Criminal Justice, CUNY, and The University of Texas at El Paso, worked together using iMovie, Microsoft Moviemaker, web-based applications, and Digication, a digital e-portfolio platform hosted by John Jay College. While there were challenges during the process, such as finding compatible technology and scheduling given the different time zones, the program succeeded because of the Martínez's and Montelongo's commitment and the students' interest to learn about their cultures.[46]

Conclusion

With the Latinx population projected to reach 106 million by 2050 in the US, it is imperative that we continue to think of inclusive teaching strategies and materials that represent Latinx students.[47] The exercises "Space and Place," "Immigrant Obituary," and "First Blacks" rehumanize Latinx education because students feel connected. The Latinx students are able to contextualize the historical information they learn while doing assignments that allow them to see themselves and talk and write about things that relate to them and/or family members at home or abroad. Their connection was such that many times students not only wrote about the past or the present, but they also wrote about the future. They imagined their future as Latinx students in US society by mapping their life based on history and experience. Equally important, the exercises humanized education in the classroom through their interaction not only with each other but also with students from different backgrounds.

Latinx students make up the majority at the Borough of Manhattan Community College and are joined by students from various countries. Other studies show that assignments that promote the opportunity of self-awareness and awareness about others enhance students' learning. For example, according to Kristian Stewart and Daniela Gachago, "by facilitating dialogue and the sharing of digital stories by means of a closed Facebook group, instructors were able to investigate students' critical awareness and social consciousness regarding notions of 'self' and 'other' across continents."[48]

Also, Nadjwa E. L. Norton and Courtney C. Bentley explain that "home(land) pedagogies are the lessons people learn and are taught as a result of the connections they have to their homeland of birth. These pedagogies also connect to the (un)seen forces of the homeland in which they presently reside, their native and current languages, and their families that may live in both homelands and speak either and/or all of these languages."[49] "Home(land)" connected assignments should be deemed essential in Latinx classrooms as a way to rehumanize education, allow students to take part in designing their intellectual growth, and make it exciting. In the words of another student,

> the assignment Space and Place gave us the ability to connect with a specific picture, your memories from that day, what happened or if there was an important event that day that makes this picture special. Through a picture, we got to see how different things were back then and how much has changed . . . the assignment was important to me because not only it helped me learn about space and place, but it also allowed me to remember memories of my childhood in my native country, the Dominican Republic.[50]

Notes

1. I would like to thank the anonymous reviewers for their generous comments as well as Isabel and Ángel for their feedback. I also want to thank Pedro L. Martinez, Edward Palumbo, Emily Stauffer-Keenan, and Elizabeth Zimmer for reading and commenting on the early drafts. Most importantly, I want to thank my students for teaching me.

2. This includes Latino/a, Hispanic, Latin American, and area studies such as Mexican, Puerto Rican, Cuban, Dominican, and Central American studies, before the term Latinx began to be used.

3. Selected efforts at highlighting Afro-Latinx studies include the Afro-Latin American Research Institute at Harvard University, the first research institution in the United States devoted to the history and culture of peoples of African descent in Latin America and the Caribbean; the Graduate Certificate in Afro-Latin American Studies, Florida International University; and Afro-Latin American and Afro-Latino Studies Initiative, University of Pittsburgh.

4. "Class A" from this point forward.

5. "Class B" from this point forward.

6. Eugenio María de Hostos, *Moral Social*, 154. "Before anything, the teacher should be an educator of the child and adolescent mind; more than anything, school is a basis for principles. If you educate the intellect, it should be so that it develops according to nature and so that it accomplishes its goals, which is exclusively to interrogate and love the truth; if you teach feelings, is because they are the instrument of universal attraction among [humans]; if you teach will, it should be to guide it to know good as the only essence and the best in practice to drive any activity; in sum, if you teach what you should and how you should, it should be with the supreme objective of educating the mind to build minds . . ."

7. bell hooks, *Teaching to Transgress*, 5.

8. hooks, 7.

9. hooks, 7.

10. See *Aprendiendo—Latino Experience in the US*, Virtual Bingo Card, mfbc.us/m/zmz4nn. When playing in-classroom bingo, the cards are printed and distributed to students. Literature shows the use of digital tools may be used to improve and/or incite learning in Latinx classrooms. See for example Leona Kwon and Cati V. de los Ríos, "'See, Click, Fix,'" 2019; Martha E. Castañeda, Xiang Shen, and Esther M. Claros Berlioz, "This Is My Story," 2018; Megan Jeanette Myers, "The classroom, the Campus, and Beyond," 2019.

11. hooks, *Teaching to Transgress*, 7.

12. This assignment was first given in the fall of 2018.

13. See Dolores Hayden, *The Power of Place*, 16–18.

14. This assignment was first given in the fall of 2019.

15. Hector Tobar, *The Tattooed Soldier*, 4–5.

16. Borough of Manhattan Community College, *Enrollment, Retention, and Completion Report*, 8.

17. See the college's website, "More Facts and Statistics" section, https://www.bmcc.cuny.edu/about-bmcc/.

18. See for example "AfroLatin@Project"; "First Blacks in the Americas"; "CUNY Dominican Studies Institute"; "Smithsonian"; "Hispanics/Latinos"; "Advancing Latino Studies at Notre Dame"; "Bracero History Archive"; "Unaccompanied Latin American Minor Project"; "CUNY Mexican Studies Institute"; "Centropr Australia."

19. Paul Gorski and Christine Clark, "Turning the Tide of the Digital Divide," 29.

20. Gorski and Clark, 29.

21. Students were assigned to visit the www.firstblacks.org website to complete the assignment. More details on the assignment are included in the methodology section.

22. "First Blacks in the Americas."

23. "Slave Biographies"; "SlaveVoyages."

24. The first enslaved Blacks were taken to Santo Domingo in 1503 upon request of Governor Nicolás de Ovando, who requested the enslaved Blacks to work the gold mines. See www.firstblacks.org.

25. Anonymous student, History of the Dominican Republic, LAT 131–1000, fall 2019.

26. Leslie Marroquín, History of the Dominican Republic, LAT 131–1000, fall 2019.

27. Mary Kate Doherty, LAT 131–1000, spring 2019.

28. Anonymous student, LAT 150–1100, fall 2019.

29. Anonymous student, LAT 150–1302, fall 2018.

30. Emmanuel Paulino, LAT 150–1601, fall 2018.

31. Detra Price-Dennis, Kathlene A. Holmes, and Emily Smith, "Exploring Digital Literacy Practices," 196.

32. Xavier Souffront, The Latino Experience in the U.S., LAT 150–1100, fall 2019.

33. Kiarra Severino, The Latino Experience in the U.S., LAT 150–1100, fall 2019.

34. Lady Bravo, The Latino Experience in the U.S., LAT 150–0900, fall 2019.

35. Brittany Sanchez, The Latino Experience in the U.S., LAT 150–0900, fall 2019.

36. Gran Colombia was the result of the independent movement of former Spanish colonies from Spain, led by Simon Bolivar. Gran Colombia included the countries or parts of Brazil, Colombia, Ecuador, Guyana, Panama, Peru, and Venezuela. The Spanish Caribbean was also inspired by the independence movements that led to Gran Colombia, but none of what was planned materialized.

37. Nyia Outlaw, The Latino Experience in the U.S., LAT 150—1100, fall 2019.

38. Contribution to "Immigrant Obituary" written in Fulani using the French alphabet by Aissata Diallo, LAT 150–1201, fall 2020. Africa my Africa, People are fleeing their homes, only to die in the desert alone. And countless mothers have wept. Africa my Africa.

39. Maraea Dougall Mahanon, LAT 150–1000, fall 2021, expressed herself in Maori. Dreams to go further. We are made to feel inferior.

40. Muna Nassir, LAT 150–1200, fall 2021, from Yemen, wrote in Arabic. Through hardship, blood, sweat, and tears our families have gone through a battle in order to better our future. We were pushed out of our countries and now we need to start a new life in another country as immigrants. The footnote number appears in the beginning given the formatting for the language.

41. George K. Canarte, LAT 150–1000, fall 2021, wrote in Spanish. They're searching for the American Dream. They came from their country looking for the opportunities that imperialism has taken from them. They wake up early and work hard. But they don't have time to enjoy with their loved one. An unending cycle.

42. Paola Durán, LAT 150–1201, fall 2020.

43. Matthew K. Gold, "Looking for Whitman," 152.

44. Luis Noe-Bustamante and Antonio Flores, "Facts on Latinos in the U.S.," 2019.

45. Isabel Martínez and Irma Victoria Montelongo. "Latinx Spaces, Discourses, and Knowledges," 6.

46. Martínez and Montelongo, 6–7.

47. Jens Manuel Krogstad, "With Fewer New Arrivals," 2014.

48. Kristian Stewart and Daniela Gachago, "Being Human Today," 528.

49. Nadjwa E. L. Norton and Courtney C. Bentley, "Making the Connection," 53.

50. Arashel Vargas, LAT 150, Fall 2018.

Digital Materials

"Advancing Latino Studies at Notre Dame." University of Notre Dame: Institute for Latino Studies. https://latinostudies.nd.edu.

"AfroLatin@Project." Digital Repository. https://afrolatinoproject.org.

Aprendiendo—Latino Experience in the U.S. Virtual Bingo Card. mfbc.us/m/zmz4nn.

"Bracero History Archive." The University of Texas at El Paso, 2021. https://braceroarchive.org.

"Centropr Australia." https://www.centropr.org.

"CUNY Dominican Studies Institute." City College of New York. https://www.ccny.cuny.edu/dsi.

"CUNY Mexican Studies Institute." CUNY Lehman College. https://www.lehman.cuny.edu/cuny-mexican-studies-institute/.

"First Blacks in the Americas: The African Presence in the Dominican Republic." CUNY Dominican Studies Institute. Digital Platform. http://www.firstblacks.org/en/.
"Hispanics/Latinos." Pew Research Center. https://www.pewresearch.org/topic/race-ethnicity/racial-ethnic-groups/hispanics-latinos/.
Martínez, Isabel. "Unaccompanied Latin American Minor Project." 2022. http://ulamp.weebly.com.
"Slave Biographies: The Atlantic Database Network." Michigan State University, 2022. http://slavebiographies.org.
"SlaveVoyages." Rice University, 2021. https://www.slavevoyages.org.
"Smithsonian." Smithsonian Institute. https://www.si.edu.

Bibliography

Borough of Manhattan Community College. Enrollment, Retention, and Completion Report. New York: BMCC Office of Institutional Effectiveness and Analytics, 2019. https://success.bmcc.cuny.edu/Data%20and%20Resources%20Public/Enrollment%20Retention%20and%20Completion%20Report.pdf.
Castañeda, Martha E., Xiang Shen, and Esther M. Claros Berlioz. "This Is My Story: Latinx Learners Create Digital Stories during a Summer Literacy Camp." *Tesol Journal* 9, no. 4 (2018): 1–14. https://doi.org/10.1002/tesj.378.
Gold, Matthew K. "Looking for Whitman: A Multi-Campus Experiment in Digital Pedagogy." In *Digital Humanities Practices, Principles and Politics*, edited by Brett D. Hirsch, 151–76. Cambridge, United Kingdom: Open Book Publishers, 2012.
Gorski, Paul, and Christine Clark. "Turning the Tide of the Digital Divide: Multicultural Education and Politics of Surfing." *Multicultural Perspectives* 5, no. 1 (2009): 29–32.
Hayden, Dolores. *The Power of Place: Urban Landscapes as Public History*. Boston, MA: MIT Press, 1997.
hooks, bell. *Teaching to Transgress: Education as the Practice of Freedom*. New York, NY: Routledge, 1994.
Hostos, Eugenio María de. "Moral Social." *Alicante: Biblioteca Virtual Miguel de Cervantes*, 2010. http://www.cervantesvirtual.com/obra/moral-social--0/.
Krogstad, Jens Manuel. "With Fewer New Arrivals, Census Lowers Hispanic Population Projections." Hispanic/Latino Demographics. Pew Research Center, December 16, 2014. https://www.pewresearch.org/fact-tank/2014/12/16/with-fewer-new-arrivals-census-lowers-hispanic-population-projections-2/.
Kwon, Leona, and Cati V. de los Ríos. " 'See, Click, Fix': Civic Interrogation and Digital Tools in a Ninth-Grade Ethnic Studies Course," *Equity & Excellence in Education* 52, no. 2–3 (2019): 154–66. DOI: 10.1080/10665684.2019.1647809.

Martínez, Isabel, and Irma Victoria Montelongo. "Latinx Spaces, Discourses, and Knowledges: Student Voices and the Rehumanization of Latinx Identity in the U.S." In *Crossing Digital Fronteras*, edited by Isabel Martínez, Irma Victoria Montelongo, Nicholas Daniel Natividad, and Ángel David Nieves. Albany: State University of New York Press, 2022.

Myers, Megan Jeanette. "The Classroom, the Campus, and Beyond: Using Twitter to Connect in #Latinxstudies Courses." *Latino Studies* 17 (2019): 257–68. https://doi.org/10.1057/s41276-019-00175-1.

Noe-Bustamante, Luis, and Antonio Flores. "Facts on Latinos in the U.S." Research Topics. Pew Research Center, September 16, 2019. https://www.pewresearch.org/hispanic/fact-sheet/latinos-in-the-u-s-fact-sheet/#:~:text=There%20were%20nearly%252%20060%20million,of%20the%20total%20U.S.%20population.

Norton, Nadjwa E. L., and Courtney C. Bentley. "Making the Connection: Extending Culturally Responsive Teaching through Home(land) Pedagogies." *Feminist Teacher* 17, no. 1 (2006): 52–70. https://www.jstor.org/stable/40546002.

Price-Dennis, Detra, Kathlene A. Holmes, and Emily Smith. "Exploring Digital Literacy Practices in an Inclusive Classroom." *The Reading Teacher* 69, no. 2 (2015): 195–205. https://doi.org/10.1002/trtr.1398.

Stewart, Kristian, and Daniela Gachago. "Being Human Today: A Digital Storytelling Pedagogy for Transcontinental Border Crossing." *British Journal of Educational Technology* 47, no. 3 (2016): 528–42. DOI:10.1111/bjet.12450.

Tobar, Hector. *The Tattooed Soldier*. New York, NY: Picador, 1998.

Chapter 3

Latinx Spaces, Discourses, and Knowledges
Student Voices and the Rehumanization of Latinx Identity in the United States

Isabel Martínez and Irma Victoria Montelongo

Introduction

It began in a crowded conference room in Atlanta, Georgia. A chance meeting between two Chicana faculty members, both from Texas, both faculty at Hispanic-Serving Institutions (HSIs). The passion to serve our respective communities through our teaching was obvious and the spirit of collaboration was instant. Before we knew it, we had developed our first Global Learning Community with first-year students at John Jay College of Criminal Justice-CUNY and The University of Texas at El Paso. At this time, we had no idea that we would continue to collaborate and that our first-year course would evolve into an upper-level course that would more intentionally focus on Latinx identity formation. By academic year 2015–2016, we were creating a cross-campus global classroom designed for upper-division juniors and seniors. Entitled Brown Tide Rising: Interrogating Latinx Identity in the 21st Century, the course, first delivered in fall 2016, focused on Latinx identity/ies and its/their constructions nationally, as well as in New York City and El Paso, Texas. In 2018, we would teach this course again, renaming it Latinx Identity in the 21st Century.

The course was designed in a way that facilitated student learning about "cultures, life experiences, and worldviews that might be similar yet different than their own," as well as exploration of " 'difficult differences' such as racial, ethnic, and gender inequalities." Our learning objectives encouraged students to move beyond regional myopia and to develop and demonstrate an understanding of heterogeneity among and across Latinxs; to identify how historical and contemporary social, economic, and political conditions shape contemporary Latinx identity formation across the United States; and to analyze and articulate how intersectionality, or race, class, gender, sexuality, etc., shape Latinx identity formation in the United States. Our ultimate joint objectives, however, were to encourage students to effectively share diverse viewpoints, develop new knowledges, and collaborate with people of similar yet diverse backgrounds.

In order to meet these objectives, we framed the course around what Chicana historian Emma Pérez refers to as a *sitio and a lengua* (a site and a language).[1] Pérez argues that when people of color speak, their voices emerge from specific spaces that reject colonial ideology. Both the space and the language, according to Pérez, are rooted in both the words and the silences of people of color who create a place apart from traditional, imperialistic, and patriarchal sites. Our *sitio*, the virtual piece of our collaboration, made up of young Latinx and Chicanx students, located on opposite ends of the country, is what gives life to *las lenguas*, the voices, of our students.

Our pedagogical framework became more significant as the semester proceeded. Fall 2016 saw a major blow to the illusory post-racial unity the Obama Administration purported to achieve and in fact shed light on the real racial tensions that plagued the United States. Marked months earlier by his official campaign announcement where he denounced Mexicans as "criminals and rapists," Donald J. Trump's opportunistic dehumanization of the Latinx community would be amplified during the campaign months and solidified after he was elected. As a result, the delivery of a Latinx Studies course that squarely focused on interrogating the aforementioned diversity took on another explicit purpose, to challenge these dehumanizing tropes rooted in colonial and imperial hegemony. We did this by exposing the lie of Latinx homogeneity and highlighting *regional myopia*. Regional myopia refers to more narrow historical and contemporary outlooks firmly rooted in our respective regions and cultures.[2] For example, when a Chicanx person from the El Paso-Ciudad Juárez region is asked to define Latinidad, they think of themselves and their culture, their cuisine, their music, their region. They do not immediately think of themselves as part of a larger landscape that includes an assortment of Latinx peoples and cultures. Instead, their connection to their physical space is strong and they see their Latinidad from a regional perspective. Regional myopia is not necessarily a bad thing. It disrupts the myth of Latinx homogeneity and exposes the many different, beautiful, proud, strong Latinx enclaves that exist from one end of the United States to the other. And yet, regional myopia also works to keep Latinx communities apart because of the ethnic/cultural, class, and other metaphorical borders that we place between ourselves. This exactly was our objective, to break down those borders, these regional myopias, and to create a safe and enriching space, a *sitio*, where Latinx students could trust and feel comfortable with their professors and peers and where they could begin to see the heterogeneity of their Latinx identity with pride. A *sitio* where they could begin to rehumanize Latinidad with their own stories, with their own *lenguas*. We learned early on that the only way this could be achieved was within a context guided by pedagogies of trust between professors and students and students and students. Challenging current scripts that feed on everyday Latinx dehumanization, we and the students engaged in learning from positions of love, humility, mutual respect, and social justice where, even when conflict occurred, rehumanization could bloom.

Designing a Rehumanizing Course across Two Hispanic-Serving Institutions

The University of Texas at El Paso, located on the US-Mexico border, as well as in the tri-state region of Texas, New Mexico, and Chihuahua, is ideally situated for this type of learning experience because the diversity of Latinx identities that exist in this border region offers a unique space for comparing and contrasting Latinx experiences in other parts of the country. While El Paso itself is an immigrant gateway city, it is also a city that is historically situated in Chicana/o history. Founded in the late nineteenth century, it is a space inextricably linked with the growth of American capitalism. The rise of American industrialization in the latter half of the century set the stage for the arrival of thousands of Mexicans in the region whose stories of resistance and negotiation continue to define, inform, and inspire their descendants. These histories and characteristics make El Paso a desirable city for a University like UTEP, and for a project like the UTEP-John Jay Global Learning Community. For one, it is a Hispanic-Serving Institution. At UTEP, 76 percent of students are Hispanic and the majority is of Mexican-descent. Heterogeneity also exists here as approximately 10 percent of the ethnic Mexican student population includes international students who commute from Ciudad Juárez Chihuahua, El Paso's sister city, and from further destinations in Mexico. Many students are first-generation Mexican immigrants, second-generation Mexican Americans, and even students whose ancestry predates Texas's 1848 inclusion in the union. Most of UTEP's students hail from economically depressed El Paso County. With over 83 percent residing in the area, most are first-generation college students, most meet the eligibility requirements for Pell Grants and other forms of federal financial aid, and over 81 percent of the student body is employed, both part-time and full-time, in at least one job. Under these circumstances UTEP truly meets its local needs by providing access to education and invaluable training for the local labor market.

Long known as an immigrant gateway city, New York City is historically regarded as the main US destination city for Puerto Rican migrants and Dominican immigrants. Within the last thirty years, other Latina/o groups such as Mexicans, Colombians, and Ecuadorians have arrived in New York City and are redefining Latinidad in the city. Whereas in 1950, only 3 percent of the New York City population was Latinx of which 84 percent was Puerto Rican, sixty years later in 2020, nearly 29 percent of the city's population was Latinx, with Dominicans surpassing Puerto Ricans as the largest Latinx ethnic group, followed by Mexicans.

Over time, John Jay College of Criminal Justice, in both its admissions policies and curricular orientations has also reflected the city's growing Latinx demographics. Established in 1970, the first site of the Centro de Estudios Puertorriqueños, or the Center for Puerto Rican Studies, was located at John Jay College of Criminal Justice. By 1986, 25 percent of the John Jay student population was Latinx. By 2000, shifts in city demographics, as well as national trends to rename national-origins departments moved the department to reflect the city and the school's growing Latina/o heterogeneity in name as well as staffing. Renamed first the Department of Puerto Rican and Latin American Studies and then in 2006, the Department of Latin American and Latina/o Studies, this academic unit also reflects a variety of regional and ethnic expertise including Puerto Rican, Cuban, Mexican, Dominican, and others. As the second largest Hispanic-Serving Institution in the Northeast, John Jay College now possesses a total student population that is over 50 percent Latina/o, but, unlike at the inception of the city's first Department of Puerto Rican Studies, the vast majority of students are no longer Puerto Rican.[3] Simply reflecting the timing of migration, births and coming of age of Dominicans in New York City, it appears as if the majority of Latinx students are first- and second-generation Dominican students, followed by growing Mexican, Ecuadorian, and Colombian student populations. Predominantly low and moderate income, approximately 76 percent of the John Jay student population received federal student aid and 63 percent report working full- or part-time. Like The University of Texas at El Paso, John Jay College is a commuter campus, with 70 percent of the first-year students reporting spending over six hours a week commuting to campus. It was precisely these similarities and differences that prompted us to develop this collaboration that bridged these two similar yet disparate campuses with digital tools.

Digital Humanities and Digital Tools

The digital humanities continue to evolve leading to multiple definitions of what it means to be a practitioner of the field. Perhaps the most common way of defining the field is "an intersection between the humanities and information technologies."[4] For our collaboration we expanded that definition to reflect an intersection between the humanities and the social sciences, and information technologies. Ever evolving technologies make it possible for Latinx professors, teaching in interdisciplinary departments and programs, to incorporate free mobile and desktop applications and other digital tools into their courses. Digital tools allow Latinx professors to rethink not only the way they deliver courses but also how they design assessments. With digital tools, Latinx professors can create learning spaces and assignments that reject exclusive Western models of education that dictate rather than coproduce and instead provide students with new technologies that allow them to research and creatively express their own stories. In our particular case, digital tools also allow students to connect and collaborate across thousands of miles and experience the real diversity of Latinx communities.

Our classes met on a face-to-face basis at our respective campuses but then they also met and collaborated on assignments, across 2,184 miles, using live videoconferencing equipment, digital storytelling software such as iMovie and Microsoft Moviemaker, web-based applications, and Digication, a digital e-portfolio platform hosted by John Jay College. One of the cornerstones of a successful collaboration is the ability to communicate ideas with one another, share thoughts and research, and collaborate on projects in a welcoming and productive space. Videoconferencing is a useful digital tool for establishing communication, collaboration, and trust between various entities. According to Carter, "one of the primary motivations for using videoconferencing to communicate with the world is to increase the sense of social presence and social richness. Social presence refers to the extent to which the interaction between individuals is perceived as warm, sensitive, personal, or intimate while social richness describes the varying degrees of eye contact, intimacy of conversation, amount of smiling, or other behaviors that enhance levels of intimacy."[5] For social presence and social richness to be authentic, however, we also strove to establish trust in our classrooms. Videoconferencing involves either peer-to-peer applications such as Skype or FaceTime or applications that use centralized servers that provide both voice and video to the conference and allow several individuals to be present at the meeting. For our collaboration we used the latter. We scheduled videoconference meetings held at our respective campuses in classrooms equipped with videoconference equipment. This was not an easy feat.

First, we live in different time zones, so we had to schedule our classes around a two-hour time difference. Additionally, our class times did not align perfectly so students at John Jay often came into their class early or stayed late to accommodate the videoconference meeting times. Second, the two videoconferencing systems must be compatible with one another in order for the video and voice features to work. In the case of our collaboration, John Jay and UTEP had two different systems that did not always communicate in a smooth and effective manner; therefore, we had to ensure that for the videoconference meetings we had technical specialists present to handle any interruptions that could and did occur. It is equally important to keep in mind that videoconferencing is not always a practical tool. It requires all participants to be present at the same time and in the same place. It requires that colleges and universities have the necessary equipment, and even if they do, the equipment may not be compatible with the collaborating partner's equipment.

We followed our initial videoconference meetings with the first of two digital storytelling exercises. Patricia McGee, an authority in the pedagogical application of digital tools and resources that support learning, reminds us that in 1934, Ruth Benedict argued that stories are a part of a culture's larger identity and therefore reveal norms, values, and beliefs of the culture in which the story is situated. And yet we continue to reinforce colonizing curricula that actively erases the languages, cultural practices, traditions, and ways of knowing of racialized minorities. Instead, we continue to hold up racialized hierarchies of power and knowledge production and dissemination.

In the twenty-first century, digital stories provide the capacity to learn about culture across the globe, as well for individuals or organizations to express cultural identity in an increasingly inter-cultural world.[6] Using storytelling as an instructional method is a way for Latinx professors to rethink their methods and tools for teaching, it helps to dismantle regional myopia, and it helps to close the digital divide. There is a never-ending parade of new apps and digital tools that support learning, and it is important to choose those tools that will not only support learning but that will also prepare students for their professional lives.

After assessing the tools that were available at our institutions, we introduced the use of Digication, an e-portfolio tool for students to share their work online with their teachers, fellow students, and potential employers. Students create a professional portfolio that allows them to present themselves to potential employers, scholarship reviewers, and grad school committees in a way that is more personal than a resume.

Our students' portfolios consisted of their digital stories as well as written assignments as samples of their critical thinking skills. In the twenty-first century, it behooves Latinx professors to explore digital tools for the rehumanization of higher education in Hispanic-Serving Institutions.

The Need for Rehumanization in Hispanic-Serving and Latinx Studies Classrooms

But why do we need digital tools to engage in rehumanization? By the time Latinx students arrive to Hispanic-Serving Institutions, many have long been subject to dehumanizing practices that rely on subtractive schooling and messaging that considers their home language and culture deficient.[7] By the time they reach college, a decreasing but significant number of Latinx and Black youths have already ended their formal schooling and those who remain have done so in spite of efforts to deem their existences inferior.[8] Arguably, if these students arrive to a Latinx Studies classroom, they may suffer from internal colonization and either "act gringo" or even raceless, and/or even question their *capacidad* or ability to be successful college students.[9]

We developed this Global Learning Community to challenge just that. The young people whom we teach are undeserving of the dehumanizing education that, while beginning in K-12, too often extends to higher education.[10] To undo this violence, we recognize our students' "unique potentiality" or willingness and actualization of potential.[11] This can only occur, however, when students are vulnerable and willing to take risks, or in contexts where students are lifted up as knowledge producers, and their prior knowledges are championed as assets and held sacred. Enacting humanizing pedagogies that offset cultural deficit models in classrooms is critical and socially just; Latinx Studies courses are *the* sitios where this can occur.[12]

In her review of empirical research examining humanizing pedagogies in educational settings, Salazar identified ten specific principles and practices that promote rehumanization.[13] Drawing from data collected from pre- and post-course surveys as well as the students' e-portfolios, we found that, albeit to different levels, of the ten principles, technology and digital tools enabled us to emphasize and expand our course's humanizing scope, especially in achieving the following three principles developed by Salazar: a) cultivating trusting and caring relationships to advance humanization, b) centering and developing our students' critical consciousness, and c) building upon students' own knowledges with new learning. The following sections outline how we centered these three principles by embedding technology and digital tools into our classrooms and our students' realization of them.

Developing a Culture of *confianza* and Care within and across Latinx Studies Classrooms

In order to achieve transformative learning grounded in rehumanization, classrooms must be grounded in a culture of *confianza*, or sustained mutual respect and reciprocal trust.[14] Without it, Ybarra argues, students refrain from seeking help from professors or peers and may encounter obstacles to their learning.[15] Because deeper learning involves vulnerability and risk-taking, students who find themselves in classrooms where this culture has been intentionally fostered find themselves unfettered to thrive; students who do not find themselves in a culture of confianza are more likely to do poorly, fail, or drop out.

It is up to professors to establish a culture of confianza, but for many Latinx professors this can be difficult because they themselves are often left out and subjected to dehumanizing practices in an all-too-common manner. Like their students, many struggle with imposter syndrome fostered by race, gender, and pay inequity. The fact that many Latinx and Chicanx Studies units are programs and not departments or that they are tucked away under the umbrella of Ethnic Studies or that others are being dismantled underscores these disparities. Nevertheless, we created a safe space that countered and negotiated the varied and layered practices intended to dismiss our and our student's contributions. As professors, we established a culture of confianza by bringing our own relationships of trust and care into the courses and as such, signaled to the students that even across two thousand miles, two Xicana PhDs can collaborate and develop a rapport rooted in admiration, *respeto mutua*, and trust that is both academic and also personal. This speaks to the idea that as professors, we entered our classroom as whole individuals, not as imposters, and we modeled this. Establishing this was essential prior to and during the first videoconference where students hear the pride each of us has for the other and her academic as well as sociopolitical, academic, and personal accomplishments. In short, we plant the seed that you can also trust the other professor as well. Once the students meet and share with us, these seeds grow.

Our first videoconference was designed with the purpose of modeling the aforementioned social presence, social richness, and trust, as well as the type of relationships we wanted the students to develop. We wanted them to learn about each other as human beings before and as they engaged in critical intellectual debates across two thousand miles. This was the primary way in which the use of digital tools is essential. There is no way we could achieve this without videoconferencing platforms and digital stories that rendered the two thousand miles between our classrooms irrelevant. Without this element, students could have more easily remained tribal, unwilling to become vulnerable to sharing and then unraveling preconceived notions students in each geographic location may have held about each other. It was important for our students to interact in real time albeit at a significant distance. In doing so they experienced the complexity and diversity of Latinidad while forming connections based on inherent similarities.

In the first step towards trust-building and overcoming the physical space between our classroom, we held a first videoconference solely for student introductions. In this videoconference, students shared their names, majors, ethnic identities, neighborhoods they are from and what they hoped for in the course. Students alternated in speaking, with one student from John Jay introducing themselves followed by a student from The University of Texas at El Paso. Banking on the belief that each group of students has received messages about each other's spaces in the media and have developed ideas based on these messages, we use the remaining time for students to ask each other questions rooted in simply their own curiosities. With El Paso students hearing that New York is expensive, El Paso students have asked questions about housing and rental prices as well as commute times. John

Jay students begin to share stories of New York City's rapid gentrification and the accelerating pricing out of themselves and their working-class families from the housing market, an issue that surprises the UTEP students. John Jay students, alternately, have received more sinister messages about the US-Mexico border. Although trying to be polite, questions eventually turn to the prevalence of violence on the border and in El Paso. UTEP students are quick to dispel that myth, pointing to the city's ranking as one of the country's safest cities in the United States, a fact that is rarely emphasized. It is at this point that the students begin to "formulate, discover and test, through dialogue" preconceived/prior knowledges that they have held and begin the process of "transforming their knowledges, self, and others" or developing a critical consciousness.[16] Again, however, this becomes possible by making the classroom culture of confianza live via videoconferencing. Because the professors have already signaled that they trust each other and that this course was designed to create a space of intellectual inquiry based in mutual respect, the students are more relaxed and less offended with these lines of questioning. This allows for greater honesty and authenticity, and frankly, deeper learning once we turn to more intellectual interrogations of our geographic spaces and Latinx identities.

Across the course of the semester and the five videoconferences, we observed just how comfortable the students, both within the class and across the classes, became with each other. They actively and maturely began to dismantle the regional myopia that leads most of us to see ourselves through a prism of exclusivity based on region, stereotypes, particular forms of oppression, etc., rather than through a prism of inclusivity where all ethnic Latinxs, regardless of geography, are united in histories of colonization and oppression but have developed resistances and resilience, all contributing to a colorful, brilliant, talented, and strong tapestry of Latinidad. The developing critical consciousness we witnessed was due to the lively discussions about the readings and films the students engaged in during videoconferences. Other times, it was the shared experience of witnessing the technical difficulties associated with delivering a course like this and arguably, their professors' commitment to the ideal of developing deep understandings that go beyond reading texts and building community across space. In any case, students began to develop shared experiences that they could refer to, which in turn were the foundation of an "insider" culture that transcended our classroom borders and was inclusive of all our students.

According to Halpern and Weinstein, "imagining and seeking to understand the perspective of another person" is essential in developing a sense of community.[17] In order to do this, we created another opportunity for trust-building via the "Community Digital Stories" assignment where individual students developed digital stories highlighting the material spaces that were most important to them (neighborhoods, campuses, churches, student club offices, etc.). Students are then placed on cross-campus peer review teams and asked to note similarities as well as differences in their geographies. By virtue of the assignments, students are asked to share parts of their lives with their classmates as well as invite them into their worlds, acts that also require trust and vulnerability. These community digital stories allow students who are thousands of miles apart to see, through the eyes of their classmates, the perspectives associated with living in hyper-capitalist global cities.

Trust is an essential element of rehumanization and rehumanizing education. Highlighted in essays about reconciliation between previously warring groups, Halpern and Weinstein point to the necessity for individuals, not only policies, to engage in individual level interactions where exploration of and acknowledgement of the past occurs.[18] We engage in this exploration and acknowledgement through our collective, across space, in our review of Latinx history and the structural conditions that have allowed stereotypes to flourish, even intra-ethnically. While we assign texts that reveal these, it is through our individual conversations and assignments and the critical processing that occurs through these with the assistance of digital tools that allows for the disruption necessitated for reconciliation, internal and external.

Of course, the success of this assignment is predicated on the wish and ability of classmates to be vulnerable with each other and feeling safe enough to reveal intimate details of their lives, namely, the physical spaces and places that mean most to them and why. One student felt safe enough to share a physical space that was important to her and her girlfriend. In presenting her community digital story, she also shared, with the classes, her story of coming out to her family, something she had not shared before in public, and in this moment, she decided to share it with her classmates, both those who were immediate as well as those she had not physically met and were thousands of miles away. By the time students were placed in cross-campus groups to view and comment on each other's My Space digital stories, or videos that introduced classmates to the spaces that students spent the most time in and/or that were most important to them, students were growing more comfortable with each other. It is this vulnerability and comfort, enabled by digital tools, that allowed students to become less shy in asking each other questions about their spaces and lives, but would also establish a tone to engage in respectful intellectual debates via videoconferencing as well as in cyberspace in order to develop critical consciousness.

Prioritizing and Facilitating Critical Consciousness

Another central element of humanizing pedagogies is the development of critical consciousness, or a critical reading of the world. Critical consciousness challenges the traditional methods of *banking* or instances in which educators may teach subject matter in detached, two-dimensional ways that focus only on the reading and memorizing of texts and not the application or testing out of the texts' ideas.[19] Our class challenged this method by ensuring that students could interpret the readings in dialogue with each other while including their own lived experiences into the analyses. While we framed all of our course themes in this two-tiered approach, two themes in particular benefitted from these thorough evaluations: the role of geography in shaping Latinx identity and recognizing the impacts of colonialism on Latinx identity construction.

In the case of geography, we dedicated no less than a month to readings on both New York City and the US-Mexico border and scheduled two videoconferences during this time, one to discuss each space. In these meetings, we positioned students as experts who could teach not only their student peers but also their professors about the spaces they lived in. It was essential to allow students to interpret the ways that the social forces and experiences put forward in the written texts were shaping their own everyday experiences as well as how they were challenging them. In the 2018 course, students examined the US-Mexico border by reading excerpts from the controversial text *The Line Becomes a River*.[20] A former border patrol agent, the author explains the racist, nativist policies and practices that, in spite of his misgivings, he was upholding on the US-Mexico border including hyper-militarization. In videoconferences, UTEP students spoke personally about how this hyper-militarization impacted their everyday lives, with Mexican national students discussing how their everyday border crossing from Ciudad Juárez to El Paso just to attend school oftentimes took hours because of these policies and other students discussing the difficulties it had imposed on families who, for generations, have been spread across borders.

But undocumented students in New York City also taught us during these meetings. A number of undocumented students whose own families as well as themselves had crossed this same *line* that Cantú sometimes romantically recalled took offense at his characterizations and passionately challenged his employment with US Customs and Border Patrol, a position he argued he joined for his own academic edification, even if he later realized its personal toll on immigrants as well as on himself. Rather, these students did not possess this privilege and instead provided an additional authentic representation of the violent militarization of the border that challenged the version provided by a white-passing Latinx male who would never experience its dehumanization.

Despite the state-sanctioned violence imposed on the US-Mexico border by brutal state policies, students also suggested that the US-Mexico border was a site of possibilities. In fact, for many of the UTEP students the *line* is nebulous. They know it's there because of the barriers and heavy presence of law enforcement, yet it is a fluid conduit that they traverse on a daily basis in search of those possibilities. When asked in the post-course survey if the course changed their ideas about the US-Mexico border, all students, including the ones who reside on the border, answered affirmatively, with some students understanding it as a site of liberation. One student responded the following: "I believe that this class helped to clear my understanding of the US-Mexico border. Prior to this class, all I really knew about the border was things that I have fed all of my life by the media. In my opinion, after taking this course, I believe that the border symbolizes opportunity."

With students representing different nationalities, citizenship, and immigrant generations, an emphasis on the US-Mexico border also prompted discussions about the ways in which the *legal* and *illegal* immigration binary is constructed, who has access to which, and how that shapes Latinx identities. A student discussed learning about heterogeneity in the flow of immigrants across the border. According to this student, "the news always tends to spin that the border is full of illegals trying to jump the walls and it fails to show how many people travel with their visas and work in the US to help their families." The student continued to note how inequities in permission to immigrate also impact Latinx identity construction by stating "this is important to Latinx identity formation because it shows the struggles that some families go through. Not every family is able to have the money necessary to get a visa to work or has a stable job in their own country." More importantly, these discussions and critical thinking assessments compel students to be more introspective about their own prejudicial notions of *illegal* immigration.

Several students in New York City were shocked to learn how nativism existed even among people of Mexican-descent living on the border. Echoing his classmate, one student "learned that discrimination happens among the Mexican immigrants, the recent people who arrive from Mexico and settled along the US-Mexico border with the Mexican-American population. I was surprised it happened within the same race group." Realizing that this nativism, as well as other -isms played out in New York City as well, a student from El Paso revealed "I had never really thought about how Latinx New York is not really united before. We discussed this in some of the early videoconferences."

Development of critical consciousness about the US-Mexico border accompanied the realization that intra-ethnic hierarchies and divisions exist among Latinxs. In her discussions of the conflicts and social distancing that emerged between Dominicans and African Americans during the 2020 marches protesting the deaths of George Floyd, Brionna Taylor, and Tony McDade, García-Peña argues that in spite of being colonized by the United States, Latin Americans, and more specifically Dominicans, forget that they too have been oppressed by the US and distance themselves from other oppressed groups, especially African Americans.[21] This argument can be extended to explain intra-ethnic hierarchies with the Latinx population as well.[22] It is no secret that "super-diversity" has created a new class of factors such as race, immigration laws, etc., that have resulted in certain Latinx groups enjoying greater privileges and statuses than others, with many immigrant groups forgetting that United States imperialism and colonization, on top of Spanish colonization, caused many conditions that resulted in their movements, whether they are from Cuba or Honduras, whether they are first-generation or third.[23]

Through videoconferences, the community digital stories, and their Quien Soy Yo/Who Am I papers, which are uploaded onto their e-portfolios so that they may be read, peer-reviewed, and commented on in cross-campus groups, students in our course began to recognize intra-ethnic tension and also expressed desires to rectify this across the miles. When asked how the digital tools supported their learning, one student shared that "I hope that we learned to see each other as equals and not as rivals. I don't like that there is tension between us, for example, Mexicans vs. Puerto Ricans vs. Cubans vs. Dominican (Republicans). I think we need to unite and have one another's back and this includes our Afro-Latinx brothers and sisters. They face a lot of racism here in the U.S. and in Latin America and we need to nip that in the bud."

It became evident that our students had internalized these hierarchies but realized that in a nation that has dehumanized anyone brown, they shared commonalities. In a post-course survey response, one student shared that "(This course) made me reflect how similar I am to other Latinxs across the country. I used to think that I was really different from Chicanos living along the US-Mexico border because their families have already been living in the United States for generations. I realized that we are different in terms of our families' immigration status and education levels. However, we are the same in the sense that we still face similar issues such as being seen as foreigners regardless of our history."

With Latinx panethnicity and its utility and authenticity long debated, our students interrogated and reflected upon this but also probed the manufactured divisions that maintain white supremacy and how they play out in Latinx lives. Deconstructed and then reconstructed through critical conversations that occurred in videoconferences, video blogs, and digital peer reviews, our students named these ideologies and material realities as a first step towards critical consciousness. This realization of how colonization and imperialism shaped social hierarchies across the Latinx community was the first step in developing critical consciousness about intra-Latinx solidarity and divisions.

Building Upon the Students' Own Knowledges with New Learning

The third principle that we emphasized in our classroom is building upon the students' own knowledges with new learning. Otherwise regarded as transformative learning, this occurs when students take risks and are willing to migrate from their own understandings of their relationships with themselves and that which they are studying to develop new knowledges and frankly, become someone new. Although we exercise transformative learning throughout the semester, students are provided with one last opportunity in their final assignment. For this assignment, we placed our students on cross-campus teams with the final objective of creating a shared definition of Latinidad that takes each team member's understandings of Latinx identity into account. Each student was tasked with posting their own definitions onto their shared e-portfolio and once collated, the team collectively debated to create one master definition that included elements of the individual definitions. This definition would be the anchor of their group e-portfolio, which they would then collectively adorn with Latinx iconography to reflect their group understanding of Latinidad.

Throughout this final project, students are asked to draw upon the learning that they have engaged in, with each other, throughout the semester. For the final project, students arrive to their groups with their own knowledges, but, using digital tools, together engage in one last dialogue to create new, co-constructed knowledge. Drawing from their own individual definitions posted on the group e-portfolio, students use a variety of digital tools including texts, emails, Skype and even Rabb.it, to engage in this dialogue and ultimately create their group definition that accompanied the individual ones. Using these tools, students argued about whether or not the Spanish language, Catholicism, slavery, mestizaje and other factors comprise Latinidad to come to one conclusion. Group final definitions included colonization, Daisy Hernandez's contention that Latinidad includes "living with loving and hating where you came from" and Elizabeth Acevedo's characterization of Latinxs as being composed of a "beautiful tragic mixture" of European, African, and Indigenous cultures.[24] Factors such as pride, hard work, liberation, and unity were also valued in their shared new definitions.

But perhaps the most telling of the students' transformation, as well as the two aforementioned principles is best evidenced in the groups' names. Final e-portfolios and groups were named the following: Mujeres Fuertes Unidas (United Strong Women), Breaking Borders, Latinxs on the Rise, New Paso Group, and Ageless. Accompanying photos exemplified the newfound solidarity constructed with the use of digital tools across classrooms (see figures 3.1 and 3.2).

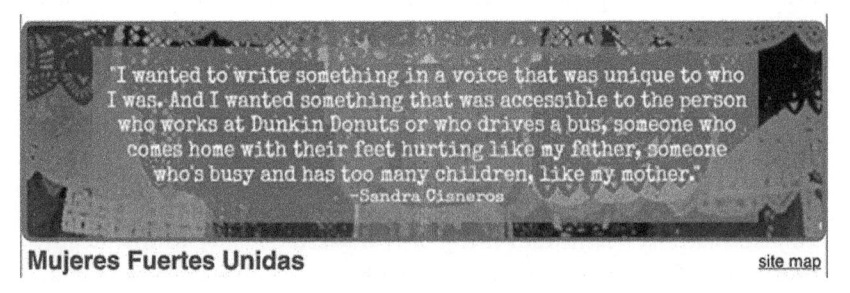

Figure 3.1. Group e-portfolio "Mujeres Fuertes Unidas" banner, created by Magdalena Oropeza (2016).

Figure 3.2. Group e-portfolio "Latinxs on the Rise" banner, created by Michelle Sención (2016).

Conclusion

As professors, we arrive to our classrooms understanding that our students possess assets that they have developed because of, not in spite of, their upbringings and the social and cultural factors that have shaped their development. For these students in El Paso and New York City who mostly identified with a variety of Latinx identities, we knew that these beliefs and practices are ones that are not necessarily always honored in hegemonic classrooms. As critical educators, we strongly believe that it is our responsibility to not only honor their identities but also provide students with opportunities and the tools to understand and honor others' identities. While traditionally this has been achieved through the exploration of "diverse" texts but then engaging in classroom discussions with students who, due to the nature of higher education in the United States, oftentimes are similar in race and class, opportunities for more critical discussions and knowledge construction that may be grounded in a greater diversity of lived experiences as well as the texts may be missed. Digital tools enable educators to push the classroom boundaries further to be even more inclusive and to incorporate the voices of knowledge producers, students, who would otherwise be missing in regional classroom discussions about texts that they themselves have lived.

Digital tools also allow us to set the stages for more authentic teaching and learning that is based in trust and care. As we include students who can complement texts with their lived experiences and share across space, we are sure to include pedagogies that have the dual purpose of establishing trust as well as delivering content, developing critical consciousness, and developing essential skills. At a time when the United States is especially polarized with distrust of one another reaching troubling rates, it is important to introduce students to others who live apart from them with whom trust is created. With the increased globalization of information, it is important that students possess national and global networks through which they can obtain trusted information about issues that while far from them in distance, are important in shaping narratives about Latinidad. Just as important is developing critical consciousness about these issues, which again, is best shaped through the dialectical relationships that the students create with each other and the texts. Digital tools facilitate this again, with individual students able to respectfully engage in arguments that are often polemical. With relationships of trust and care established, debates become less defensive and more honest, with students more apt to engage in vulnerable discussions to learn rather to defend their positions across digital platforms. It is this way that students can best develop new knowledges, through these ongoing dialogues that they engage in not only in the classrooms via videoconferences, but also in their homes, as they view phone and computer screens and then communicate and intellectually engage with their colleagues in digital spaces. It is through this active learning occurring across space, based in relationships carefully crafted in trust and care, that our best hopes for rehumanizing Latinx education can occur.

Notes

1. Emma Pérez, "Sexuality and Discourse: Notes from a Chicana Survivor," 1991.

2. Irma Victoria Montelongo and Isabel Martínez, "Decolonizing the Classroom," 2018.

3. National Center of Education Statistics, "John Jay College of Criminal Justice," 2020.

4. Patrik Svensson, "Landscape of Digital Humanities," 2010.

5. Bryan W. Carter, "Communicating with the World," 2013.

6. Patricia McGee, *The Instructional Value of Digital Storytelling*, 2015.

7. Maria del Carmen Salazar, "A Humanizing Pedagogy," 2013; Angela Valenzuela, Subtractive Schooling, 1999.

8. Daniel Solórzano, Octavio Villalpando, and Leticia Oseguera, "Educational Inequities and Latina/o Undergraduate Students in the United States," 2005; Salazar, 2013.

9. Salazar, 2013; Maria E. Fránquiz, and Maria del Carmen Salazar, "The Transformative Potential of Humanizing Pedagogy," 2004; Raul Ybarra, "Latino Students and Anglo-Mainstream Instructors," 2000; W. E. B. DuBois, *The Souls of Black Folks*, 1903.

10. Gina A. García and Nicholas Daniel Natividad, "Decolonizing Leadership Practices, 2018.

11. Aidan Curzon-Hobson, "A Pedagogy of Trust in Higher Learning," 266.

12. Paulo Freire, *Pedagogy of the Oppressed*, 68.; Salazar, 138.

13. The ten principles establish the following: 1) Honoring the lived experience of learners is critical; 2) Critical consciousness is essential for students and educators; 3) Sociocultural resources must be valued; 4) Classroom texts and teaching must be relevant to the students' lives; 5) Students' existing knowledges must be honored in the classroom; 6) Trust and care are essential to engaging in humanization in the classroom; 7) Traditionally honored narratives and rhetoric have a place in these classrooms; 8) Student achievement will occur through their activation of a variety of capacities: social, intellectual, and academic; 9) Students can only be empowered through intentional pedagogical practices; and 10) Educational inequities should be challenged and can lead to change.

14. Aria Razfar, "Repair with Confianza," 2010.

15. Ybarra, 2000.

16. Curzon-Hobson, 2002; Salazar, 2013; Freire, 2006.

17. Jodi Halpern and Harvey M. Weinstein, "Rehumanizing the Other," 2004:568.

18. Halpern and Weinstein, 2004:564.

19. Freire, 2006.

20. Francisco Cantú, *The Line Becomes a River*, 2018.

21. Lorgia García-Peña, "Dismantling Anti-Blackness together," 2020.

22. Rosalyn Negrón, *Ethnic Identification and New York City's Intra-Latina/o Hierarchy*, 2018.

23. Steven Vertovec, "Super-Diversity and Its Implications," 2007; Ybarra, 2000.

24. Daisy Hernández, *A Cup of Water*, 2005; Elizabeth Acevedo, "AfroLatina," 2015.

Bibliography

Acevedo, Elizabeth. "AfroLatina." YouTube. September 21, 2015. https://www.youtube.com/watch?v=tPx8cSGW4k8.

Cantú, Francisco. *The Line Becomes a River: Dispatches from the Border*. New York, NY: Riverhead Books, 2018.

Carter, Bryan W. "Communicating with the World." In *Digital Humanities: Current Perspectives, Practices, and Research*, edited by Bryan W. Carter and Charles Wankel. Bingley, England: Emerald Publishing Limited, 2013.

Curzon-Hobson, Aidan. "A Pedagogy of Trust in Higher Learning." *Teaching in Higher Education*, 7, no. 3 (2002): 265–76. https://doi.org/10.1080/135625 10220144770.

DuBois, W. E. B. *The Souls of Black Folks*. New York, NY: Penguin Classics, 1996/1903.

Fránquiz, Maria E., and Maria del Carmen Salazar. "The Transformative Potential of Humanizing Pedagogy: Addressing the Diverse Needs of Chicano/Mexicano Students." *High School Journal*, 87, no. 4 (2004): 36–53. DOI:10.1353/hsj.2004.0010.

Freire, Paulo. *Pedagogy of the Oppressed*. New York, NY: Continuum Books, 2006.

García-Peña, Lorgia. "Dismantling Anti-Blackness together." NACLA, June 8, 2020. https://nacla.org/news/2020/06/09/dismantling-anti-blackness-together.

Halpern, Jodi, and Harvey M. Weinstein. "Rehumanizing the Other: Empathy and Reconciliation." *Human Rights Quarterly* 26, no. 3 (2004): 561–83. http://www.jstor.org/stable/20069745.

Hernández, Daisy. *A Cup of Water under My Bed*. Boston, MA: Beacon Press, 2014.

McGee, Patricia. *The Instructional Value of Digital Storytelling: Higher Education, Professional, and Adult Learning Settings*. New York, NY: Routledge, 2015.

Montelongo, Irma Victoria, and Isabel Martínez. "Decolonizing the Classroom: Latina/os and Chicana/os Speaking and Learning from the Margins." In *Community Engagement and High Impact Practices in Higher Education*, edited by Gina G. Nuñez and Azuri L. Gonzalez. Dubuque, IA: Kendall-Hunt Publishing, 2018.

National Center for Educational Statistics. "John Jay College of Criminal Justice." US Department of Education, 2020. https://nces.ed.gov/college navigator/?id=190600#.

Negrón, Rosalyn. "Ethnic Identification and New York City's Intra-Latina/o Hierarchy." *Latino Studies*, 16, no. 2 (2018): 185–212. https://doi.org/10.1057/s41276-018-0121-3.

Pérez, Emma. "Sexuality and Discourse: Notes from a Chicana Survivor." In *Chicana Lesbians: The Girls Our Mothers Warned Us About*, edited by Carla Trujillo. Berkeley, CA: Third Woman Press, 1991.

Razfar, Aria. "Repair with Confianza: Rethinking the Context of Corrective Feedback for English Learners (ELs)." *English Teaching: Practice and Critique* 9, no. 2 (2010): 11–31. https://eric.ed.gov/?id=EJ912614.

Salazar, Maria del Carmen. "A Humanizing Pedagogy: Reinventing the Principles and Practice of Education as a Journey towards Liberation." *Review of Research in Education* 37, no. 1 (2013): 121–48. https://doi.org/10.3102/0091732X12464032.

Sólorzano, Daniel G., Octavio Villalpando, and Leticia Oseguera. "Educational Inequities and Latina/o Undergraduate Students in the United States: A Critical Race Analysis of Their Educational Progress," *Journal of Hispanic Higher Education* 4, no. 3 (2005): 272–94. https://doi.org/10.1177/1538192705276550.

Svensson, Patrik. "The Landscape of Digital Humanities." *Digital Humanities Quarterly* 4, no. 1 (2010): https://digitalhumanities.org/dhq/vol/4/1/000080/000080.html.
Valenzuela, Angela. *Subtractive Schooling: The Politics of Caring*. Albany: State University of New York Press, 1999.
Vertovec, Steven. "Super-Diversity and Its Implications." *Ethnic and Racial Studies* 30, no. 6 (2007): 1024–54. https://doi.org/10.1080/01419870701599465.
Ybarra, Raul. "Latino Students and Anglo-Mainstream Instructors: A Study of Classroom Communication." *Journal of College Student Retention* 2, no. 2 (2000): 161–71. https://doi.org/10.2190/GLHT-DT1F-CKCY-1GW8.

Chapter 4

Translanguaging and Multiple Literacies

Podcasting as a Linguistically and Culturally Sustaining Medium in a Multicultural Teacher Education Course

Jen Stacy, Mildred Ramos, and Adriana Correa

Introduction

On September 25, 2017, Jen Stacy, an assistant professor of education at California State University Dominguez Hills (CSUDH), received the following email from Mildred Ramos and Adriana Correa, undergraduate students in her Education in a Multicultural Society class.

> Hi Jen,
>
> Adriana and me are going to work together for the podcast. We know you said we can do it in English or Spanish. Our question is if we can talk in both languages at once? Like, for example, Spanglish?

The students had been assigned to create a podcast exploring class concepts and their relation to education. The podcast assignment had been designed to replace a traditional essay in hopes to better capture and assess students' dynamic ways of thinking, discussing, and concluding about the conceptual foundations of culture and education. Jen found that traditional essays fell short of reflecting students' robust understanding and articulation of concepts that emerged during class discussions. A podcast, she hoped, would offer a more active, social, and constructivist platform for showcasing students' epistemic plurality.[1] Central to the instructions for this assignment was a statement that students could record their podcast in any language.

When Mildred and Adriana tried to record the podcast in only Spanish or only English, they found themselves *translanguaging*, or deploying their "full linguistic repertoire without regard for watchful adherence to the socially and politically defined boundaries of named (usually national and state) languages."[2] Their process and final product pushed Jen to think more critically about what it means to utilize humanizing pedagogies as a way to value and sustain linguistic and cultural capital in teacher education courses at CSUDH, a Hispanic-Serving Institution in Southern California.[3] The students' work exemplifies the power of humanizing pedagogies in teacher education and suggests the ripple effect that incorporating these practices may have in the schooling experiences of Latinx communities.

Hispanic-Serving Institutions (HSIs) play a unique role in preparing future educators. Given that enrollment consists of at least 25 percent of Latinx students, HSI teacher preparation programs contribute to the diversification of the predominantly white teaching profession.[4] At CSUDH, 64 percent of students identify as Latinx, followed by 10.5 percent Black, 8 percent Asian, and 6.6 percent white. A commuter campus, it ranks fourth in the state and eighteenth in the nation in the overall mobility index.[5] There is a national effort to recruit minoritized teachers who share students' social identities so that learning may become more culturally and linguistically relevant.[6] In tandem, research on first-generation college students show that over 40 percent identify as Black or Latinx.[7] Studies have unveiled the unique needs of first-generation college students and have called for institutions to be more systemically responsive to students' realities, a mission that HSIs attempt to uphold.[8] In the CSUDH undergraduate teacher education program, internal data reports that 74 percent of students identify as Latinx and 12 percent as Black. Within this space, teacher educators have a responsibility to model critical pedagogies to promote pedagogical meta-awareness amongst pre-service teachers and to enact counter-hegemonic, humanizing teaching practices that influence the larger sociopolitical context.[9] In this chapter, we explore how podcasting serves as a medium through which to center pre-service teachers' linguistic capital to model, practice, and reflect on humanizing pedagogies.[10] We assert that implementing humanizing pedagogies will have ripple effects throughout Latinx education at large: modeling humanizing practices in teacher preparation programs influences the likelihood that new pre-K-12 teachers will enact such pedagogies in Latinx communities.

Rehumanizing Latinx Education in Teacher Education

Today's educators have been inculcated in the standards movement and teacher preparation programs have not been immune.[11] In efforts to quantify and measure learning in the name of "progress," minoritized students have become victims of "cultural and linguistic eradication" as their complex social identities have been reduced to labels and utilized for categorization and control.[12] It has been common practice for schools to label students' ethnic, linguistic, and ability identities and use these labels to justify deficit approaches to schooling.[13] A clear example is labeling Spanish-speaking youth as English Learners (ELs) as a justification for assimilatory (and ineffective) English-only policies. This process has largely dehumanized students, creating an automated system that generally disposes Latinx youth instead of centering their cultural capital.[14]

Today's pre-service teachers have been socialized in the practices of labeling and teaching from this deficit perspective. Lortie suggests that pre-service teachers first understand teaching through apprenticeship of observation: by the time they arrive at university, future teachers have spent hours observing, analyzing, and reflecting on what constitutes "good" teaching from a personal, intuitive perspective.[15] Given the assimilatory, whitestream ideology that pervades pre-K-12 education, it is not surprising that pre-service teachers may have internalized dehumanizing practices as commonplace.[16] It is also not surprising that our current education system continues to replicate the status quo and achievement gaps/debts between minoritized and white students.[17] If we are to rehumanize education for Latinx students across educational institutions, teacher preparation programs must model humanizing practices so that pre-service teachers embody and enact humanizing practices in their classrooms, breaking the cyclical nature of deficit education.[18]

Humanizing pedagogy is considered one of Paulo Freire's original contributions to education.[19] Freire calls for the oppressed to become fully human and liberated through the pursuit of *conscientização*, critical consciousness, of the systems of oppression in which they are entangled and, often, of which they have internalized.[20] Teachers and students must engage in praxis: reflection and action upon the world in order to transform it.[21] Instruction then ceases to be a manipulative, oppressive tool; instead, students' critical consciousness is centered, making humanization truly ontological.[22]

Humanizing pedagogy is not a sterile set of methods to be transferred into any setting; instead, it is an enveloping practice in which the teacher "recognizes the political nature of education, the reproductive nature of schools, and the schools' continued (yet unspoken) deficit views of subordinated students."[23] Humanizing pedagogy in teacher education, then, is a project of humanization for both professors and students.[24] Both are in process of *becoming* more fully human as they dialogically explore their cultural and political selves situated in broader realms of oppression and participate in critical self-reflection.[25] For effective change, tenets of humanizing pedagogies should be operationalized at the programmatic, curricular, and interpersonal levels of teacher education.[26]

To center the process of becoming and challenge systemic oppression, teacher educators' praxis must sustain students' cultural and linguistic capitals.[27] Culturally sustaining pedagogy seeks to "perpetuate and foster—to sustain—linguistic, literate, and cultural pluralism as a part of schooling for social transformation" while upholding dynamic cultural dexterity as a necessary good.[28] Thus, incorporating culturally sustaining pedagogies is necessary for invoking a humanizing pedagogy at an HSI. When teachers embrace students' cultural practices, such as translanguaging, as a formal part of the curriculum, students' identities are amplified and not erased.[29] By valuing language practices, educators and students become partners in learning and use collective knowledge to pursue social change.[30] Fránquiz and Salazar found that humanizing practices with Latinx students included *respeto* (respect), *confianza* (mutual trust), *consejos* (verbal teachings), and *buen ejemplos* (exemplary models) and fostered youth's healthy educational orientations.[31] Research has documented how humanizing praxis, like ethnic studies courses, has a positive effect on attendance, GPA, and credits toward graduation.[32]

Latinx students enrolled at an HSI may enter the field of education having been socialized into a deficit mode of viewing complex social identities (their own and those of their students) in relation to what counts as valuable in school, what Freire would deem as internalizing the image of the oppressor.[33] Pre-service teachers must unlearn these hegemonic understandings through a humanizing teacher preparation experience. The urgency of humanizing learning is magnified for Latinx pre-service teachers at CSUDH who will eventually teach minoritized students in greater Los

Angeles. Teacher educators have a responsibility to rethink how educational spaces are constructed to sustain minoritized students' cultural and linguistic practices while analyzing systemic, institutionalized oppression. Using new literacies in the digital humanities, such as podcasting, is one way that values show students interact with the world, capture their cultural and linguistic capital, and permit translanguaging.

Linguistic Capital and Translanguaging as Humanizing Pedagogies

To operationalize theoretical assertions, Salazar synthesizes ten principles of humanizing pedagogy, four which emphasize that learning must be generated from students' realities and center their unique identities and abilities:

1. The reality of the learner is crucial.

2. Students' sociocultural resources are valued and extended.

3. Content is meaningful and relevant to students' lives.

4. Students will achieve through their academic, intellectual, and social abilities.[34]

Learning must center Latinx students' myriad forms of cultural capital, or resources and assets, on which they draw to navigate society. It is important to highlight that Latinx students all have linguistic capital: "intellectual and social skills attained through communication experiences in more than one language and/or style."[35] Yosso explains that while linguistic capital includes knowledge of named language systems, such as Spanish and English, it also encompasses students' repertoires of storytelling skills, communication skills, and social tools enacted through language.[36] Given that learning inevitably happens through semiotic exchange, it follows that a humanizing pedagogy must incorporate students' linguistic capital.

In the undergraduate teacher education program at CSUDH, more than 70 percent of students identify as Latinx and have connection to Spanish, whether they speak it as a dominant language or are considered heritage learners (HLs).[37] HLs are "individuals having historical or personal connection to a language such as an endangered indigenous language or immigrant language that is not normally taught in school . . . or may speak or understand the heritage language and are to some degree bilingual in English and the heritage language."[38] While it may seem obvious that one form of linguistic capital that bilingual students have is access to (at least) two named language systems (e.g., Spanish and English), Mildred and Adriana's email point to a common misnomer: the idea that they must operate fully in one named language system or the other and never integrate the two. Otheguy, García, and Reid define a named language system as the language of a nation or social group and argue that the existence of named languages as separate systems exists only from an outsider's perspective.[39] Drawing on data from sociolinguistics and bilingual education about the realities of language use, they propose a theory of translanguaging that captures the point of view of the speaker.[40] Multilingual students' language use is dynamic: their language use is interdependent on context, people, texts, and their relationship with their environment, and is reflective of their entire linguistic repertoire—including features from multiple named language systems.[41] Thus, translanguaging is defined as "the deployment of a speaker's full linguistic repertoire without regard for watchful adherence to the socially and politically defined boundaries of named (and usually national and state) languages."[42] Translanguaging with multilingual students requires understanding language from the "speaker up, and not from the named language down."[43] In other words, an educator must seek first to understand students' linguistic capital in order to center it in learning.[44]

Translanguaging has become a guiding theory for working with multilingual learners and can inform educators' philosophical stance, instructional design, and pedagogical shifts.[45] Studies about teachers who have intentionally centered translanguaging have shown that students feel their social identities recognized and that students' academic engagement and language skills benefit.[46] Not surprisingly, research on translanguaging parallels studies about invoking humanizing and culturally sustaining pedagogies with Latinx students. Reyes III argues that border theory is essential in humanizing education: teachers' praxis must stem from Latinx students' everyday experiences that transcend dichotomous boundaries and encapsulate bicultural practices, like translanguaging, that are identity tools and survival tactics.[47] Fránquiz and Salazar noted that using and discussing fluid language practices while studying literature was critical in supporting students' process toward critical consciousness.[48] Finally, Bucholtz, Casillas, and Lee identified language as the essential element in culturally sustaining pedagogy, as it is the vessel through which culture is produced, experiences understood, and identity developed.[49] Their study of Latinx youth illustrated how valuing translanguaging in multiple facets of learning (topic, process, product, presentation) deepened students' knowledge while sustaining their identities in academic and social endeavors.[50]

Digital Humanities and New Literacies

Teacher education courses can serve as a powerful model as to how critical educators develop philosophical stances, design instruction, and shift pedagogies in connection with students' realities.[51] An interdisciplinary digital humanities approach permits teacher educators to reconsider common assignments and reimagine instructional design. Cro and Kearns document how collaborative engagement with technologies develops students' meaning making while encompassing new literacies. This sweet spot is "the nexus through which community and meaning converge."[52] New Literacy Studies, as it exists within digital humanities, offers a framework for designing culturally and linguistically sustaining assignments that uphold the goals of humanizing pedagogies for Latinx students.[53]

Stemming from ethnographic studies that illuminated how literacy practices were embedded in daily life and how social contexts generated literacies, New Literacy Studies "attempt to understand literacy in terms of concrete social practices and to theorize it in the ideologies in which different literacies are embedded" (The New London Group 1996).[54] Street posits that all forms of literacy must be understood as they are situated within cultures that possess and perpetuate ideologies and power structures.[55] In essence, our understanding of literacy can be expanded beyond traditional notions of printed text to encapsulate the myriad ways in which "people generate, communicate, and negotiate meaningful content through the medium of encoded texts."[56]

A prime example of new literacies are the ubiquitous technologies that permeate our lives.[57] Since the early twenty-first century, a turn in new literacy studies has encompassed digital environments and a range of technologies.[58] Mobile technology can be understood as a new literacy that is already embedded within Latinx students' cultural practices to be leveraged in innovative, humanizing pedagogies that center students' realities and linguistic capital.[59] Wargo illustrated how youth technoliteracies embody individual expressions that capture the individual, place, time, and affect while speaking across audiences and reflecting larger cultural forces.[60] For example, Wargo highlights how nail polish represented one queer youth's identity across real-life and virtual platforms.[61] Painting nails served as an outlet of control and a response to the harassment the student faced about her sexuality and gender presentation; however, online a photo of her nails represented her "girly girl" side. A complicated portrait emerged as "the affective feeling of time and story become impressed upon the body and its relationship to the digital."[62] In their framework on humanizing teacher education, Andrews et al. point to using new literacies as a way for teacher educators to enact epistemological flexibility and to legitimize students' various ways of knowing.[63] Through a humanizing lens, teacher educators incorporate technology as a new literacy that reflects and sustains students' cultural and linguistic capitals. This approach serves two purposes: pre-service teachers' learning becomes more humanizing, and they develop the humanizing pedagogical skills necessary for integrating digital humanities methods in their future classrooms.[64]

The podcast assignment in this study was developed intentionally to create space for students' linguistic capital. A podcast is a digital audio file that centers on a certain theme and may be available in installments, incorporates elements of discussion and/or storytelling, and is available for download or streaming. Scholars have identified podcasting as a genre of digital humanities and critical work has been underway to craft public-facing humanities content through responsive models of podcasting.[65] This genre began as a form of expression largely by the dominant culture but has since been reappropriated as a space for discourse practices of communities of color and, more and more, is being embraced by Latinx populations.[66] Distinct from traditional print literacy, a podcast esteems oral literacy. Shirley Brice Heath's foundational work in this field showcased how oral literacies were intrinsic in the cultural practices of African Americans but were discouraged in and excluded from schools.[67] Oral literacies of Latinx populations have also been documented.[68] Stacy and Aguilar highlighted how multigenerational Latinx students' oracy captured their cultural practices and linguistic knowledge through digital storytelling.[69] Drawing from these perspectives, we view podcasting as a new literacy that engages Latinx students through oral traditional modes of storytelling that are connected to other narrative genres, like hip hop and spoken word, prevalent in their daily lives.

Podcast Assignment Overview

In recent years, podcasts assignments have increased exponentially in elementary to graduate-level humanities classrooms, largely due to their open-ended format for creative forms of narrative storytelling. The podcast assignment for this multicultural education class was designed for similar reasons.[70] Its flexible format permitted the development of students' critical analysis of a key concept through privileging narrative storytelling. Drawing from Adler and Van Doren's framework for critical reading responses, students were guided by three objectives: 1) recover meaning from a text; 2) reconstruct meaning using personal practical knowledge; and 3) link meaning to a broader context, specifically K-12 education.[71] Students chose a relevant course topic/concept, explored its meaning, related it to their lives, and applied it to their future teaching. The assignment instructions and rubric were designed to be open-ended to encourage deep, rich development of ideas but to also permit for individualization.

Podcast development happened during class sessions, spanning approximately three weeks. Students organized their ideas with an outline and collaboratively explored different recording apps. Early on, students used voice recording apps (like Easy Voice Recorder or Voice Memo) on their smartphones. In recent iterations, students use the Anchor podcasting platform.[72] This application permits students to record in segments and add sound effects, resulting in a polished, easily shareable podcast. Students now share their work in an end-of-semester podcast convention.

Research Methods

Mildred and Adriana participated in Jen's course without any interruptions during fall 2017. Their podcast assignment stood out for its quality and for the use of translanguaging. After the semester, Jen asked if they would be interested in analyzing their podcast through a translanguaging lens and reflecting on how this experience might contribute to their future teaching. The students agreed and we met periodically to analyze the podcast and engage in critical reflection. Collaborative analysis was utilized to ensure member-checking and to enact humanizing practices.

We identified several moments in the podcast where the students switched between named languages to explain or explore the complex concept of culture. We felt that these moments were meaningful for several reasons. First, they were essential to developing the students' argument and meeting the assignment's requirements. Second, these moments showcased students' cultural practices. The fact that Mildred and Adriana were using multiple languages at once to explain cultural moments added an additional layer to illustrate how language is a vehicle for culture and vice versa. Finally, these moments captured the multidimensional characteristics of translanguaging.

While Mildred and Adriana were switching between languages, multiple interlocutors could be seen interacting with and influencing their language use. We tracked when and how the different named languages were being used and Adriana and Mildred added commentary to explain their thinking behind each moment. This was our effort to capture their idiolect, or their unique language that includes a "mental grammar that is acquired primarily through, and deployed mostly in, social and personal interaction," to better understand how translanguaging happened.[73]

As Adriana and Mildred guided the analysis, their epistemological plurality was centered, and the professor became the learner.[74] Jen gained deeper insights about the students' lives and linguistic capital. The dialogic process also permitted her to engage in critical self-reflection, raising questions about becoming more intentional in developing opportunities for translanguaging and communicating its value in her teaching. What follows is an analysis of Mildred and Adriana's podcast assignment through a translanguaging lens to better understand how this assignment sustained linguistic and cultural capital while meeting the principles of humanizing pedagogies.

Findings

In addition to being a new literacy that reflected cultural practices, the podcast assignment better aligned with classroom practices. Most class sessions included student-led, small-group Socratic discussions where students studied topics related to culture, justice, and schooling and interrogated their thinking using the Socratic method.[75] Jen noticed that students held rich Socratic discussions that were full of cultural references and translanguaging. However, when asked to write an academic paper, students' essays often lacked the multidimensional luster present in their conversations. A podcast met the general academic learning goals but also captured students' dynamic discussions, cultural connections, and linguistic capital.

In efforts to communicate the value of linguistic capital, Jen included the following clause in the instructions. "Many students in our class are multilingual! You are welcome to use any language you wish when creating your podcast. Jen speaks and understands Spanish. For any other languages, she will reach out to the campus community to assist in grading." Looking at this clause, it is obvious why Adriana and Mildred assumed that they needed to create their podcast in Spanish or English, not both. Based on Jen's learning, the clause has been updated to read "You are welcome to use any language/language variety and/or multiple language/language varieties" to be more encompassing of all linguistic capital.

Participant Identities

Understanding Adriana's and Mildred's identities is necessary to understanding their approach to the podcast. Given that Jen was a key interlocutor throughout the podcast creation (as the professor she was the target audience) and during the analysis, a brief description of her identity is also included.

Adriana

Adriana identifies as Mexican American and was born and raised in Los Angeles, California. Her father is from Zamora, Michoacán, México, and while her mother was born in the US, her maternal grandparents emigrated from Guadalajara, Jalisco, México. Adriana spoke only Spanish until attending public school. In school, Adriana was placed in traditional English Language Learning courses and eventually transferred into mainstream classes. Now, Adriana feels most comfortable speaking in English but maintains a strong connection to Spanish. She continues to speak with her father and maternal grandmother only in Spanish but speaks English or Spanglish with her mother and siblings. Having felt like she "lost her Spanish," Adriana reconnected with Spanish in high school courses where she struggled to feel linguistically comfortable and accepted by her peers. At CSUDH, Adriana studied a concentration in Spanish as a component of her major to further develop her linguistic knowledge and abilities. While she has become more confident in Spanish, she still feels like her academic language skills are stronger in English. Adriana has her elementary teaching credential and integrates her knowledge of bilingualism in mainstream classrooms.

Mildred

Mildred was born in Tiquisate, Escuintla, Guatemala. She spent her childhood in a small village before moving to la Ciudad de Guatemala. Throughout school, Mildred took a few English classes. Once in high school, she studied a degree in *secretaria bilingüe*, bilingual secretary. This program heavily emphasized reading and writing English over speaking it, and to this day Mildred feels more confident in these domains. In 2000, Mildred immigrated to the United States, joined several family members in Los Angeles, and eventually married her husband, also from Guatemala. She spent five years studying English before completing her associate degree and enrolling in the teacher education program at CSUDH. Mildred confidently completed the Spanish concentration courses in her major. She speaks mostly Spanish at home, though sometimes she speaks English with her sons, and feels like her English skills are still developing. Mildred now has her elementary teaching credentials with a bilingual authorization and is currently teaching kindergarten in a dual language program.

Jen

Born and raised in Ohio, Jen learned Spanish as a second language through courses in middle school, high school, and university. As an undergraduate, she traveled to Xalapa, Veracruz, México, and Oaxaca, Oaxaca, México, to study Spanish. She then taught in bilingual schools in Monterrey, Nuevo León, México, for four years and studied a master's degree in education (in Spanish) at La Universidad de Monterrey. She considers herself fluent in Spanish, with a strong foundation in reading and writing; however, Jen always feels like her Spanish skills need work and is eager to practice the language in any domain.

Translanguaging Moments

In this section, we analyze two moments from Mildred and Adriana's podcast that highlight how they draw on their linguistic capital to make sense of a difficult concept: culture. Having read a chapter from the book *Intercultural Communication: A Discourse Approach* by Ron Scollon, Suzanne Wong Scollon, and Rodney H. Jones, the students were exposed to a postmodern understanding of culture as something that people "do" (particularly through language) as opposed to something that people "have."[76] In efforts to understand this concept, Mildred and Adriana first explore what it means and how it applies to their lives. In doing so, they translanguage and, in turn, their translanguaging illuminates another rich element of how they "do" culture. The excerpts are presented in the students' original languages. To ensure understanding, we have presented the exact transcription of the podcast on the left with necessary translation on the right.

Podcast Excerpt #1: Defining Culture

The first podcast excerpt begins after a three-minute introduction during which Adriana and Mildred welcome listeners in multiple languages and discuss their preliminary thoughts about what culture is and its importance. Then, the students attempt to formally define the concept:

Mildred: Entonces, ojalá que nuestro tema sea algo provechoso y puedan entender y agarrar un poquito más de información acerca de este tema que es muy importante, no confundirlo porque a veces creemos que es una cosa y resulta que cuando vamos a leer es algo totalmente diferente de lo que pensábamos. Y yo creo que ahorita Adriana nos va a dar una breve introducción acerca de lo que es realmente cultura. [So, we hope that our topic will be helpful and that you can learn a bit more about this very important topic. We hope that it is not confusing because sometimes we think that something is one thing and when we read about it, it is something totally different from what we thought. And I believe right now Adriana is going to give us a brief introduction about what culture really is.]

Adriana: Okay so, we read an article called *Intercultural Communication: A Discourse Approach*, by Ron Scollon, Suzanne Wong Scollon and Rodney H. Jones. And basically, it talks about how intercultural communication is between two people or two different groups of people from different cultural origins to have a conversation, and when they have this conversation, they . . . find problems in their communication . . . So, the problem is that these people have different definitions as to what culture really is, according to the reading. Some people believe that culture is something you have, like courage or intelligence, and some people might have it more than others . . . Others might see culture as a set of rules, so like in a game, you know, how you have rules, you either break the rules, you conform to the rules . . . Lastly, some people see culture as living inside a country or a building. So like let's say, for example, when people from Latin American come to the United States, they leave their culture behind, they leave their traditions, their language and everything, and assimilate to the American culture because they might be afraid that they're going to be judged by their

110 | Jen Stacy, Mildred Ramos, and Adriana Correa

accent, by their clothing, by their style, by anything, any little thing because, you know, these days it's very hard to try to be yourself with so many people trying to judge you.

Mildred: Sí tienes toda la razón. Cuando andaba investigando y leyendo más acerca de este tema . . . encontré algo muy importante y se me hizo muy interesante, que dice, [*Yes, you are completely right. When I was researching and reading more about this topic, I found something very important and interesting that says:*] "You are not joining this culture, you are not becoming a member of another society, you are not abandoning your own culture. That will be assimilation and that's not what we are after."

In this excerpt, there are four clear players that are adding to the dynamic of Adriana and Mildred's linguistic capital: Adriana and her cultural and linguistic capital, Mildred and her cultural and linguistic capital (including her Mexican friends), the course text, and the internet source. These interlocutors, as they operate within larger sociocultural contexts (e.g., HSI, Los Angeles, immigration history, sociocultural power dynamics), provide insight about the students' dynamic bilingualism. The figure below attempts to capture this reality:

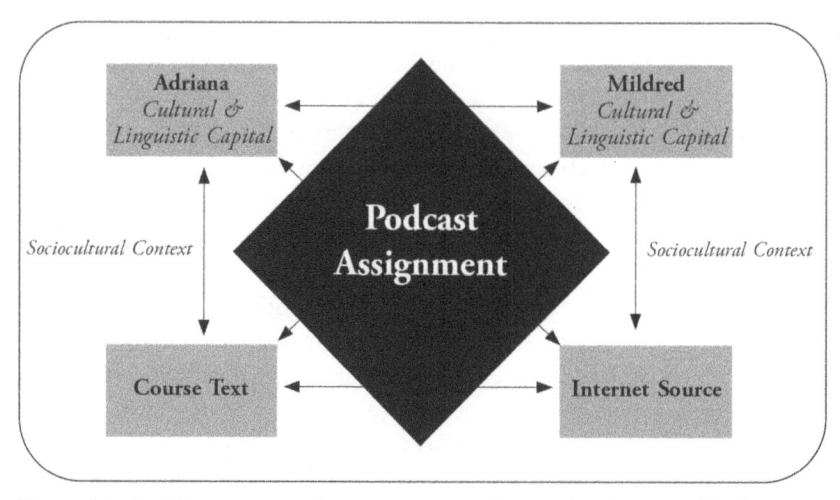

Figure 4.1. Interlocuters in podcast assignment. Source: Jen Stacy, Mildred Ramos, and Adriana Correa.

At the beginning of the podcast, Adriana follows what Mildred is saying in Spanish and, in sections not featured, she joins the conversation in Spanish. However, in the moment where they begin defining culture, Adriana draws upon her comfort with academic English. She deepens the conversation with quotes and summaries from the text. (It is worth noting that incorporating course readings was a requirement for the assignment and all course readings were in English.) Without missing a beat, Mildred contributes to these ideas in Spanish ("Sí, tienes toda la razón . . .") and then draws on an Internet source in English to compliment the book's definition of culture. Mildred's personal response is in Spanish yet her academic response, with a citation, is in English. Particularly interesting is when Mildred points out that operating within a different culture does not require complete assimilation; however, her use of an academic source in English is telling. What "counts" as an official source for a university assignment? And what norms should one follow (or assimilate to) when presenting an idea for school as opposed to outside of school? The academic source is in English and how she makes sense of the source is in English. On one hand, this highlights how Mildred translanguages as a college student at CSUDH: she completes most of her formal academic work in English, yet her processing in Spanish is always present. She operates through one linguistic system that shows itself in the form of named languages dynamically and depending on the context.[77] On the other hand, it illuminates an oversight in Jen's attempt to humanize learning.

Andrews et al. call on teacher educators to enact ontological and epistemological plurality: while Jen made space for students' linguistic capital, the message of privileging written, academic English in course texts was clear.[78] This moment permitted her to reflect critically on what texts she privileges, how she inadvertently communicates this to her students, and what changes could be made to value different epistemologies. Integrating new literacies and multiple modes of production by students is one indicator of an epistemological shift but professors must also consider which literacies are being deemed worthy of study and if they sustain students' cultural practices.[79]

After citing the internet source, Mildred's linguistic turn captures the dynamics of her background and cultural experiences—including her relationship with Adriana.

> **Mildred:** Entonces, este, a veces, nosotros confundimos que asimilar una cultura es dejar nuestras culturas atrás, como renunciar

a la cultura de mi país. Le decía a Adriana, nos estábamos riendo un poquito, ¿verdad?, porque le digo que nosotros, a los guatemaltecos nos dicen "chapines." Y le digo que para nosotros es bien fácil, este, [ríe] cambiar de cultura— [So sometimes we confuse that assimilating to a culture is leaving our culture behind, like giving up the culture from my country. I was telling Adriana, and we were laughing a little, right, because I was telling her that they call us Guatemalans "chapines" (a name used specifically for Guatemalans). And I told her that for us it is easy to (laughs) change cultures—]

Adriana: Sí. [*Yes.*]

Mildred: Porque yo lo he experimentado. Yo tengo muchas amistades que son de México . . . y es algo muy chistoso porque cuando a veces me reúno con un grupo muy grande donde hay personas mexicanas, yo hablo como ellos. Por ejemplo, los mexicanos tienen un dicho que ellos dicen, cuando te despides de alguien dicen, "Okay, pues, ándale, nos vemos." [Because I have experimented. I have many Mexican friends . . . and this is something very funny because sometimes when I get together with a big group where there are Mexican people, I speak like them. For example, Mexicans have a saying, when you say goodbye to someone they say, "Okay, well, alright then, we'll see each other soon."]

Adriana: Ah sí, ajá. (laughs) [*Ah, yes, haha.*]

Mildred uses the phrase *chapines* to analyze her identity as Guatemalan using her developing postmodern understanding of culture. Mildred explains how *chapines* captures her shifts in cultural practices while highlighting language as the vehicle through which she practices this plurality. Mildred has amplified her linguistic repertoire, or idiolect, with the Mexican variety of Spanish, including the phrase *ándale pues*. Otheguy et al. point out that monolingual people constantly deploy their entire idiolect: they translanguage between lexical and structural repertoires of the same named language depending on context.[80] Through this lens, we can understand Mildred's use of the phrase *ándale pues* as a type of translanguaging: she moves between Guatemalan Spanish and Mexican Spanish.

In her reflection, Mildred explained communicating in Spanish was easiest for her, but she looked for opportunities to connect with Adriana, knowing her comfort in English. In analyzing the way that she spoke about culture, she said, "Los dos [cultura y lenguaje] van de la mano porque sin lenguaje no podemos comunicarnos con la sociedad, la cual representa la cultura en la que vivimos." [Culture and language go hand in hand because without language we cannot communicate with society, which represents the culture in which we live.] Mildred's developing philosophy about the interconnectedness between language and culture explains her approach to translanguaging and her example of shifting between Spanish varieties. While it has been documented that Central Americans often feel pressure to "silence" their identities by using the Mexican dialect of Spanish—and one must consider the power dynamics at play here—Mildred is making sense of her experience as one of intercultural discourse, capturing her flexible linguistic knowledge.[81] Adriana's laughter and agreement evidences how Mildred's cultural practices have served her in forming relationships in the United States and shows commonalities amongst the students' idiolects. Together, these suggest the power of translanguaging in not only sustaining cultural and linguistic practices amongst Latinx college students, but in serving as a tool for cultural flexibility.

Podcast Excerpt #2: Exploring Culture as Practice

As the podcast continues, Mildred and Adriana discuss how culture can be understood as practice. Their examples and explanations of culture begin to go beyond markers of identities into daily practices. Additionally, they explore the changing nature of culture.

> **Mildred:** Algo muy interesante que leí en el libro es esta cita [que] dice, "Cultural tools evolve in social groups and change over time as they are passed down from generation to generation . . . They also might be taken off by other social groups and adapted to fit their need." Y aquí nos está dando un ejemplo del idioma inglés, ¿verdad?, que dice que . . . el idioma inglés no nació realmente aquí en este país . . . [Something very interesting that I read was this quote that says, "Cultural tools evolve in social groups and change over time as they are passed down from generation to generation . . . They also might be taken off by other social

groups and adapted to feed their need." And there they give us the example of English, right? They say that the English language did not originate in this country . . .]

Mildred: . . . Otro ejemplo que yo le daba yo [a Adriana] el ejemplo de cuando las mamás le están dando pecho o están alimentando a sus niños con leche materna. En mi país es muy normal ver a una señora dándole pecho a su bebe y así, destapada, te sacas un pecho, el baby está mamando y es algo muy normal allá . . . Pero al venir a este país . . . ya no voy a hacer lo mismo que hacían en allá en mi comunidad . . . Aquí ya la sociedad requiere que te pongas una manta encima para taparte el pecho, ¿verdad? [. . . Another example that I gave to Adriana was the example of when mothers breastfeed their babies. In my country it is very normal for a woman to breastfeed her baby, just like that, uncovered, you take out your breast and the baby nurses and it is something very normal there . . . But to come to this country . . . I am not going to do the same thing that they do back in my community . . . Here society requires that you put a blanket on to cover your breast, correct?]

Adriana: Sí. No, y luego es interesante porque también en el—In the readings, it was talking about lo que hacer—Las cosas que hacemos cada . . . [*Yes. No and then it's interesting because in the—in the readings, it was talking about what to do, the things that we do every . . .*] Most of the time we don't know why we do it. We just do it because we learned from our parents, from our friends, from our teachers, from our community, y estas cosas van cambiando, estas [*these things continue to change*], you know, that your beliefs keep changing, you know. My-my mom and my dad are Catholic, and I didn't grow up religious, I didn't grow up going to church every Sunday . . . So, you know, sometimes I tell my mom like, "I don't know if I'm Catholic. I don't know what I believe in. I don't know—," and you know, sometimes she's like, "Are you serious?" you know like—Como que se molesta un poquito. Y le digo, "Pos, ¿cómo crees que yo voy a crecer creyendo esas cosas si nunca me enseñastes o nunca me—[*Like it bothers her a little. And I tell her, "Well, how can you think that I am going to grow up believing these things if* *you never taught me or you never . . ."*] You didn't expose me to anything." Exactly. So, it's crazy how things change. And I think from generation to generation, it's just—Everything's changed in culture . . . And it's a constant change . . .]

Here, Adriana and Mildred utilize their linguistic skills to explore culture as a contrastive space. After citing a formal academic reference in English, Mildred uses Spanish to compare the practices of breastfeeding in Guatemala versus in the United States. Mildred captures how power dynamics regulate cultural practices when she notes that US society "requires" a mother to cover up. Adriana supports Mildred's ideas by following up in Spanish before switching to English: "Sí. No, y luego es interesante porque también en el—in the readings, it was talking about lo que hacer—Las cosas que hacemos cada . . . Most of the time we don't know why we do it." Again, we see how the academic readings interject as an interlocutor, indicating a switch to English. In this moment, Adriana's full linguistic system is at work. In her first linguistic turn, she acknowledges that Mildred has used Spanish. Next, she makes a connection back to the course reading in English. Then, perhaps to enter back into the relational space with Mildred, she switches back to Spanish before continuing in English.

Adriana's linguistic capital permits her to explore her changing cultural practice (and identity) regarding Catholicism. She mostly uses English as she challenges how she could be considered Catholic if she didn't grow up attending church. Given that Adriana attributes English as the primary language of her upbringing, it is not surprising that she uses this named language to express these thoughts. However, when she reflects on the conversation she had with her mother about the topic, she begins using Spanish. In her analysis, Adriana stated that she began explaining in English because she remembers the conversation happening with her mom mostly in English. However, because she and her mother often speak Spanglish and because it feels natural to speak with Mildred in Spanish, she switched to Spanish. She switched back to English towards the end when she could not come up with how to say *expose* in Spanish. Her use of multiple named languages to explain this cultural practice embodies the sociocultural reality she has navigated to enact the evolving practice. Adriana reiterates that "everything's changed in culture . . . And it's a constant change." As much as this phrase applied to the students' cultural anecdotes, it also provides ontological insight of how shifting cultural practices happen through, and are represented by, linguistic shifts.

If to uphold humanizing practices teacher educators must embrace ontological plurality, then it is necessary to accept the integral role of translanguaging in capturing Mildred's and Adriana's understanding of changing cultural practices.[82] First, their linguistic interactions with each other represent a reality that Latinx communities live every day: first-generation immigrants who speak mostly Spanish (or Indigenous languages) interacting with Latinx folks who have lived in the United States for several generations. Their existence in "contact zones" continuously connects them with language and cultural practices from their or their family's sending country along with new languages and cultural practices.[83] Adriana and Mildred's discussion illuminates a) the contrastive cultural experiences that each have had either between generations (e.g., Adriana and her mother) or between countries (e.g., Mildred and the breastfeeding example) and b) the plurality of the Latinx experience in Southern California.

Second, it must be understood that the students' translanguaging was essential to conveying their knowledge about the concept of culture: it captured their ontological position in society as a first-generation Guatemalan immigrant and a 2.5-generation Latinx woman. Mildred's and Adriana's knowledge was intertwined with their translanguaging: had they not drawn on their entire linguistic capital, they would not have accurately represented their lived cultural reality and would not have authentically defined the concept of culture. Without translanguaging, their podcast would lack depth, texture, and knowledge. The students' use of translanguaging was culturally sustaining; it nurtured their social identities and cultural ways of being while they achieved academically.[84] The podcast, a literacy, authentically captured this, fully humanizing Mildred and Adriana within the learning process.

Conclusion

Hispanic-Serving Institutions are charged with expanding educational opportunities for Latinx communities while "enhance[ing] the academic offerings, program quality, and institutional stability" of universities that serve Latinx students.[85] Teacher preparation programs at HSIs are in a unique position to uphold both goals. Latinx teachers will continue to play a critical role in contributing to the quality of educational access in Latinx communities. HSIs must ensure that new generations of teachers have foundational experiences in humanizing practices that both enhance their learning and influence their teaching ideologies.[86]

Tomorrow's teachers will be essential in carrying out the critical call to rehumanize Latinx education. HSI teacher education programs must adapt humanizing pedagogies and work arduously to operationalize them. The case of Adriana and Mildred's podcast assignment is an example of how teacher educators can draw on theories that support humanizing pedagogies, like translanguaging, by using multiple literacies that center students' linguistic capital.[87] Central to our study was the practice of critical reflection amongst students and professors.[88] Jen engaged in critical reflection before, during, and after the podcast assignment while the students participated in critical reflection twice, once as they completed the assignment and a second time while writing this chapter. Collaborating with Adriana and Mildred elevated the process of critical reflection and proved to be a type of humanizing pedagogy in and of itself.

Future Possibilities

Our argument at the beginning of this chapter suggests that integrating humanizing pedagogies in teacher education will have a ripple effect throughout the education of Latinx populations at large. Aspiring teachers who have experienced humanizing education know its value and bring conviction to enact real change in their classrooms and, subsequently, in their communities. If humanizing practices are at the center of pre-service teachers' training, the new generation of Latinx educators will be well-equipped to draw on new literacies, like podcasts, whilst centering linguistic and cultural capital. In this case, Adriana and Mildred experienced firsthand the power of responsive technoliteracies and are positioned to enact humanizing practices with their students while pushing the envelope on integrating new literacies and sustaining linguistic practices. The COVID-19 pandemic has only intensified the role that the digital humanities play as both vessels for and products of culturally and linguistically meaning making. Now is the time for teachers of color to enact new literacy futurisms with their students of color at the nexus of "intersectionality, translanguaging, decoloniality, ancestral, play, and collectivity" (p.428) and to recognize podcasting as one literacy medium through which this becomes possible.[89]

As a way to imagine future possibilities for humanizing education for pre-K-20 Latinx learners, we end with the voices of future teachers. Below, Adriana and Mildred synthesize their teaching philosophies after completing their undergraduate teacher preparation program at CSUDH. Their words illuminate the impact that a humanizing approach to teacher education has had in their preparation and offer insight to the humanizing practices that they will enact as teachers with future Latinx students.

Adriana: Teaching is a way to help students to understand that they are not limited to the messages that they receive from society or even the norms in their communities. All students can pursue higher education. I want to teach students to want to learn, to want to better their situations. I will use current data and articles about the realities of society across the curriculum so that students can be exposed to topics, challenge norms, and think critically about expectations. Students should have the liberty to use all their languages. It will benefit them because they can express themselves, participate, and feel comfortable inside and outside of the classroom. Allowing students to use all their native language will prevent them from losing it, which is an important component in their future and culture.

Mildred: Enseñar es tomar a mis estudiantes de la mano para guiarlos y ayudarlos a descubrir y desarrollar sus habilidades. Es poner en sus corazones una semillita que lentamente se está cuidando y alimentando en todas las etapas de su crecimiento hasta llegar a dar su fruto. Mi meta como maestra es apoyar y ayudar a mis alumnos con paciencia, devoción, amor y dedicación, para que ellos tengan las **herramientas** necesarias para enfrentar y vencer todos los obstáculos que vengan en su camino educacional y llegar a la meta con éxito. Para lograr mi objetivo estaré mezclando el hogar, la escuela y la comunidad. Creo que estos tres lugares deben de formar siempre parte en el aprendizaje de los estudiantes porque esto les ayudará a sentirse aceptados, seguros y apoyados por sus maestros y familiares y comunidad alrededor. Hablarles en su idioma—o mezclando los dos—manda un mensaje que, "yo me pertenezco aquí." [Teaching is taking my students' hand to guide them and help them discover and develop their skills. It is planting a seed to be slowly cultivated until it bears fruit. My goal as a teacher is to support and help my students with patience, devotion, love, and dedication so that they have the tools to face and overcome obstacles and successfully reach their goals. As a teacher, I will mix home, school, and community. I believe that these three places should always be part of student learning because this will help them feel accepted, safe, and supported by their teachers and family and community. Speaking to students in their language—or mixing two languages—sends the message that "I belong here."]

Notes

1. Stephanie M. Palenque, "The Power of Podcasting," 2016.
2. Ricardo Otheguy, Ofelia García, and Wallis Reid, "Clarifying Translanguaging and Deconstructing Named Languages," 283.
3. Lilia Bartolomé, "Beyond the Methods Fetish," 1994; Tara Yosso, "Whose Culture Has Capital?" 2005.
4. US Department of Education, "Hispanic-Serving Institutions (HSIs)," 2019.
5. CSUDH, "California State University, Dominguez Hills: Our Students," 2020.
6. Albert Shanker Institute, "A Look at Teacher Diversity," 2016; Sonia Nieto, *The Light in Their Eyes*, 2010.
7. US Department of Education, Office of Planning, Evaluation and Policy Development, Policy.
8. Milagros Castillo-Montoya, "Deepening Understanding of Prior Knowledge," 2017; Rob Longwell-Grice et al., "The First Ones," 2016.
9. Saili Kulkarni, Jen Stacy, and Heather Kertyzia, "Collaborative Self-Study," 2019; Paul Gorski, "What We're Teaching Teachers," 2009.
10. James Paul Gee, *Social Linguistics and Literacies*, 2012; Yosso, 2005.
11. Marta Baltodano, *Appropriating the Discourse of Social Justice in Teacher Education*, 2015. The standardization movement across pre-K-20 education is largely attributed to the 1983 report *A Nation at Risk*, which utilized test scores to assert the need for increased standardization with regard to high school coursework and college acceptance. Federal legislation has further codified these expectations through the No Child Left Behind Act of 2002 and the Every Student Succeeds Act of 2015. States extend these standardized expectations to teacher preparation programs. See for example, the *California Teacher Performance Expectations*.
12. Bartolomé, 176; Reynaldo Reyes III, "In a World of Disposable Students," 339.
13. María del Carmen Salazar, "A Humanizing Pedagogy," 2013.
14. Reyes III, 2016; Yosso, 2005.
15. Dan Lortie, *Schoolteacher*, 1975.
16. Sandy Marie Anglas Grande, "American Indian Geographies of Identity and Power," 2000; Salazar, 2013.

17. National Center for Education Statistics, "Achievement Gaps," 2011.
18. Dorinda Carter Andrews et al., "Beyond Damage-Centered Teacher Education," 2019.
19. Salazar, 2013.
20. Paulo Freire, *Pedagogy of the Oppressed*, 1972.
21. Freire, 1972.
22. Freire, 1972.
23. Bartolomé, 175.
24. Dorinda Carter Andrews and Bernadette M. Castillo, "Humanizing Pedagogy for Examinations of Race and Culture in Teacher Education," 2016.
25. Andrews et al., 2019.
26. Andrews et al., 2019.
27. Samy H. Alim and Django Paris, "What Is Culturally Sustaining Pedagogy and Why Does It Matter?" 2017.
28. Alim and Paris, 12.
29. Mary Bucholtz, Dolores Inés Casillas, and Jin Sook Lee, "Language and Culture as Sustenance," 2017.
30. Bucholtz, Casillas, and Lee, 2017.
31. Maria E. Fránquiz and Maria del Carmen Salazar, "The Transformative Potential of Humanizing Pedagogy," 2004.
32. Thomas Dee and Emily Penner, "The Causal Effects of Cultural Relevance," 2017.
33. Freire, 1972.
34. Salazar, 138.
35. Yosso, 78.
36. Yosso, 2005.
37. 2021 undergraduate student demographics in the College of Education were gathered through an internal report generated by CSUDH.
38. Valdés, 37–38.
39. Otheguy, García, and Reid, 2015.
40. Otheguy, García, and Reid, 2015.
41. CUNY-NYSIEB, "What Is Translanguaging?" 2018.
42. Otheguy, García, and Reid, 283.
43. Ofelia García and Tatyana Kleyn, *Translanguaging with Multilingual Students*, 23.
44. Yosso, 2005.
45. García and Kleyn, 2016.
46. García and Kleyn, 2016; Ofelia García, Susana Ibarra Johnson, and Kate Seltzer, *The Translanguaging Classroom*, 2017.
47. Reyes III, 2016; Cynthia Bejarano, *Que Ónda?*, 2005; Antonia Darder, *Culture and Power in the Classroom*, 1991.
48. Fránquiz and Carmen Salazar, 2004.

49. Bucholtz, Casillas, and Lee, 2017.
50. Bucholtz, Casillas, and Lee, 2017.
51. García and Kleyn, 2016.
52. Cro and Kearns, 2020, paragraph 1.
53. Andrews et al., 2019.
54. Shirley Brice Heath, *Ways with Words*, 1983; Moll et al., "Funds of Knowledge for Teaching," 1992; Victoria Purcell-Gates, *Other People's Words*, 1995; Denny Taylor, *Family Literacy*, 1983; Gee, 76.
55. Brian Street, *Social Literacies*, 1995.
56. Colin Lankshear and Michele Knobel, "Sampling 'the New' in New Literacies," 64.
57. Lankshear and Knobel, 2007.
58. Mills, 2010.
59. Jen Stacy and Jodi Aguilar, "Connection, Culture, and Creativity," 2018.
60. Jon Wargo, "Literacy Sponsorscapes and Mobile Media," 2016.
61. Wargo, 2016.
62. Wargo, 2016.
63. Andrews et al., 2019.
64. Kennedy, 2017.
65. SDSU, "Podcasting the Humanities: Creating Digital Stories for the Public," 2022.
66. Exposito, 2022.
67. Heath, 1983.
68. Guadalupe Valdés, *Con Respeto*, 1996.
69. Stacy and Aguilar, 2018.
70. For complete assignment, rubric, and resources visit: https://bit.ly/3axWECR.
71. Mortimor J. Adler and Charles Van Doren, *How to Read a Book*, 1972.
72. You can access by going to https://anchor.fm/.
73. Otheguy, García, and Reid, 289.
74. Freire, 1972; Andrews et al., 2019.
75. Richard Paul and Linda Elder, "Critical Thinking," 2007.
76. Ron Scollon, Suzanne Wong Scollon, and Rodney H. Jones, *Intercultural Communication*, 2012.
77. Otheguy, García, and Reid, 2015.
78. Andrews et al., 2019.
79. Andrews et al., 2019.
80. Otheguy, García, and Reid, 2015.
81. Magaly Lavadenz, "Como Hablar en Silencio (Like Speaking in Silence)," 2014; Scollon, Scollon, and Jones, 2012.
82. Andrews et al., 2019.
83. Mary Louise Pratt, "Arts of the Contact Zone," 1991.

84. Bucholtz, Casillas, and Lee, 2017.
85. US Department of Education, 2019.
86. Andrews et al., 2019.
87. Otheguy, García, and Reid, 2015; Gee, 2012; Yosso, 2005.
88. Andrews et al., 2019.
89. The Literacy Futurisms Collective-in-the-Making, 2021.

Digital Materials

A public folder containing resources for podcasting and translanguaging can be found by following the link below or by the QR code.

Translanguaging and Multiple Literacies: Podcasting in Teacher Ed: Digital Materials https://bit.ly/3axWECR.

Bibliography

Adler, Mortimor J., and Charles Van Doren. *How to Read a Book: The Classic Guide to Intelligent Reading*. New York, NY: Touchstone, 1972.

Albert Shanker Institute. "A Look at Teacher Diversity." *American Educator* 40, no. 3 (2016): 18–19.

Alim, Samy H., and Django Paris. "What Is Culturally Sustaining Pedagogy and Why Does It Matter?" In *Culturally Sustaining Pedagogies: Teaching and Learning for Justice in a Changing World*, edited by Paris Django, Samy H. Alim, and Celia Genishi, 12–32. New York, NY: Teachers College Press, 2017.

Andrews, Dorinda Carter, Tashal Brown, Bernadette M. Castillo, Davena Jackson, and Vivek Villanki. "Beyond Damage-Centered Teacher Education: Humanizing Education for Teacher Educators and Pre-Service Teachers." *Teachers College Record: The Voice of Scholarship in Education* 121, no. 6 (2019): 1–28.

Andrews, Dorinda Carter, and Bernadette M. Castillo. "Humanizing Pedagogy for Examinations of Race and Culture in Teacher Education." In *Race, Equity, and the Learning Environment: The Global Relevance of Critical and Inclusive Pedagogies in Higher Education*, edited by Frank Tuitt, Chayla Haynes, and Saran Stewart, 112–28. Sterling, VA: Stylus, 2016.

Baltodano, Marta. *Appropriating the Discourse of Social Justice in Teacher Education*. Lanham, MD: Rowman & Littlefield, 2015.

Bartolomé, Lilia. "Beyond the Methods Fetish: Toward a Humanizing Pedagogy." *Harvard Educational Review* 64, no. 2 (1994): 173–94.

Bejarano, Cynthia. *Que Ónda?: Urban Youth Culture and Border Identity*. Tucson: University of Arizona Press, 2005.

Bucholtz, Mary, Dolores Inés Casillas, and Jin Sook Lee. "Language and Culture as Sustenance." In *Culturally Sustaining Pedagogies: Teaching and Learning for Justice in a Changing World*, edited by Paris Django, Samy H. Alim, and Celia Genishi, 53–70. New York, NY: Teachers College Press, 2017.

Castillo-Montoya, Milagros. "Deepening Understanding of Prior Knowledge: What Diverse First-Generation College Students in the U.S. Can Teach Us." *Teaching In Higher Education* 22, no. 5 (2017): 587–603. https://doi.org/10.1080/13562517.2016.1273208.

Cro, Melinda A., and Sara K. Kearns. "Developing a Process-Oriented, Inclusive Pedagogy: At the Intersection of Digital Humanities, Second Language Acquisition, and New Literacies." *Digital Humanities Quarterly* 14, no. 1 (2020). http://www.digitalhumanities.org/dhq/vol/14/1/000443/000443.html.

CSUDH. "California State University, Dominguez Hills: Our Students." California State University, Dominguez Hills. 2020. https://www.csudh.edu/Assets/csudh-sites/career-center/docs/2020-csudh-demographics.pdf.

CUNY-NYSIEB. "What Is Translanguaging?" CUNY-NYS Initiative on Emergent Bilinguals. 2018. https://www.cuny-nysieb.org/translanguaging-resources/.

Darder, Antonia. *Culture and Power in the Classroom: A Critical Foundation for Bicultural Education*. Westport, CT: Bergin & Garvey, 1991.

Dee, Thomas, and Emily Penner. "The Causal Effects of Cultural Relevance: Evidence from an Ethnic Studies Curriculum." *American Educational Research Journal* 54, no. 1 (2017): 127–66. https://cepa.stanford.edu/sites/default/files/wp16-01-v201601.pdf.

Exposito, Suzy. "Podcasts Made by and or Latinos Finally Make Mainstream Inroads." *Los Angeles Times* (Los Angeles, California), February 15, 2022. https://www.latimes.com/entertainment-arts/music/story/2022-02-15/latino-podcast-chalino-sanchez-sonoro-futuro-spotify.

Fránquiz, Maria E., and Maria del Carmen Salazar. "The Transformative Potential of Humanizing Pedagogy: Addressing the Diverse Needs of Chicano/Mexicano Students." *High School Journal* 87, no. 4 (2004): 36–54. https://doi.org/10.1353/hsj.2004.0010.

Freire, Paulo. *Pedagogy of the Oppressed*. New York, NY: Herder and Herder, 1972.

Garciá, Ofelia, Susana Ibarra Johnson, and Kate Seltzer. *The Translanguaging Classroom: Leveraging Student Bilingualism for Learning*. Philadelphia, PA: Caslon Publishing, 2017.

García, Ofelia, and Tatyana Kleyn. *Translanguaging with Multilingual Students: Learning from Classroom Moments*. New York, NY: Routledge, 2016.

Gee, James Paul. *Social Linguistics and Literacies: Ideology in Discourses*. 4th ed. New York, NY: Routledge, 2012.

Gorski, Paul. "What We're Teaching Teachers: An Analysis of Multicultural Teacher Education Coursework Syllabi." *Teaching and Teacher Education* 25, no. 2 (2009): 309–18. https://doi.org/10.1016/j.tate.2008.07.008.

Grande, Sandy Marie Anglas. "American Indian Geographies of Identity and Power: At the Crossroads of Indigena and Mestizaje." *Harvard Education Review* 70, no. 4 (2000): 476–98. https://doi.org/10.17763/haer.70.4.47717110136rvt53.

Heath, Shirley Brice. *Ways with Words: Language, Life and Work in Communities and Classrooms*. Cambridge, MA: Cambridge University Press, 1983.

Kennedy, Kara, "A Long-Belated Welcome: Accepting Digital Humanities Methods into Non-DH Classrooms." *Digital Humanities Quarterly* 11, no. 3 (2017): http://www.digitalhumanities.org/dhq/vol/11/3/000315/000315.html.

Kulkarni, Saili, Jen Stacy, and Heather Kertyzia. "Collaborative Self-Study: Advocating for Democratic Principles and Culturally Responsive Pedagogy in Teacher Education." *The Educational Forum* 84, no. 1 (2019): 4–17. https://doi.org/10.1080/00131725.2020.1679932.

Lankshear, Colin, and Michele Knobel. "Sampling 'the New' in New Literacies." In *A New Literacies Sampler*, edited by Michele Knobel and Colin Lankshear. New York, NY: Peter Lang Publishing, 2007.

Lavadenz, Magaly. "Como Hablar en Silencio (Like Speaking in Silence): Issues of Language, Culture, and Identity of Central Americans in Los Angeles." In *Latinos and Education: A Critical Reader*, 2nd ed., edited by Antonia Darder and Rodolfo D. Torres. New York, NY: Routledge, 2014.

Longwell-Grice, Rob, Nicole Zervas Adsitt, Kathleen Mullins, and William Serrata. "The First Ones: Three Studies on First-Generation College Students." *NACADA Journal* 36, no. 2 (2016): 34–46. https://doi.org/10.12930/NACADA-13-028.

Lortie, Dan. *Schoolteacher: A Sociological Study, Second Edition*. Chicago, IL: University of Chicago Press, 1975.

Mills, Kathy Ann. "A Review of the 'Digital Turn' in the New Literacy Studies." *Review of Educational Research* 80, no. 2 (2010): 246–71. https://doi.org/10.3102/0034654310364401.

Moll, Luis C., Cathy Amanti, Deborah Neff, and Norma Gonzalez. "Funds of Knowledge for Teaching: Using a Qualitative Approach to Connect Homes and Classrooms." *Theory into Practice* 31, no. 2 (1992): 132–41. https://doi.org/10.1080/00405849209543534.

National Center for Education Statistics. "Achievement Gaps." Institute for Education Sciences: National Center for Education Statistics. 2011. https://nces.ed.gov/nationsreportcard/studies/gaps/.
Nieto, Sonia. *The Light in Their Eyes: Creating Multicultural Learning Communities*. New York, NY: Teachers College Press, 2010.
Otheguy, Ricardo, Ofelia García, and Wallis Reid. "Clarifying Translanguaging and Deconstructing Named Languages: A Perspective from Linguistics." *Applied Linguistics Review* 6, no. 3 (2015): 281–307. https://doi.org/10.1515/applirev-2015-0014.
Palenque, Stephanie M. "The Power of Podcasting: Perspectives on Pedagogy." *Journal of Instructional Research* 5 (2016): 4–7.
Paul, Richard, and Linda Elder. "Critical Thinking: The Art of Socratic Questioning." *Journal of Developmental Education* 31, no. 1 (2007).
Pew Hispanic. "Hispanic Population and Origin in Select U.S. Metropolitan Areas, 2014." Pew Research Center. 2016. https://www.pewhispanic.org/interactives/hispanic-population-in-select-u-s-metropolitan-areas/.
Pratt, Mary Louise. "Arts of the Contact Zone." *Profession* 91 (1991): 33–40. https://www.jstor.org/stable/25595469.
Purcell-Gates, Victoria. *Other People's Words: The Cycle of Low Literacy*. Cambridge, MA: Harvard University Press, 1995.
Reyes III, Reynaldo. "In a World of Disposable Students: The Humanizing Elements of Border Pedagogy in Teacher Education." *The High School Journal* 99, no. 4 (2016): 337–50. https://doi.org/10.1353/hsj.2016.0013.
Salazar, María del Carmen. "A Humanizing Pedagogy: Reinventing the Principles and Practice of Education as a Journey toward Liberation." *Review of Research in Education* 37, no. 1 (2013): 121–48. https://doi.org/10.3102/0091732X12464032.
Scollon, Ron, Suzanne Wong Scollon, and Rodney H. Jones. *Intercultural Communication: A Discourse Approach*. 3rd ed. Hoboken, NJ: Wiley-Blackwell, 2012.
SDSU. "Podcasting the Humanities: Creating Digital Stories for the Public." NHC Graduate Student Public Humanities Podcasting Institute. 2022. https://sites.google.com/sdsu.edu/nhc2022winterinstitute/home.
Stacy, Jen, and Jodi Aguilar. "Connection, Culture, and Creativity: Using Mobile Technology as a Medium for Storytelling in an Intergenerational Classroom." *Multicultural Education* 25, no. 2 (2018): 28–35.
Street, Brian. *Social Literacies: Critical Approaches to Literacy in Development, Ethnography, and Education*. New York, NY: Pearson Education, 1995.
Taylor, Denny. *Family Literacy: Young Children Learning to Read and Write*. Exeter, NH: Heinemann Educational Books, 1983.
The Literacy Futurisms Collective-in-the-Making. "'We Believe in Collective Magic': Honoring the Past to Reclaim the Future(s) of Literacy Research." *Literacy Research: Theory, Method, and Practice* 70 (2021): 428–47. https://doi.org/10.1177/23813377211036475.

US Department of Education, Office of Planning, Evaluation and Policy Development, Policy and Program Studies Service. *The State of Racial Diversity in the Educator Workforce*. US Department of Education. July 2016. Report. https://www2.ed.gov/rschstat/eval/highered/racial-diversity/state-racial-diversity-workforce.pdf.

US Department of Education. "Hispanic-Serving Institutions (HSIs)." White House Initiative on Advancing Educational Equity, Excellence, and Economic Opportunity for Hispanics. 2019. https://sites.ed.gov/hispanic-initiative/hispanic-serving-institutions-hsis/.

Valdés, Guadalupe. *Con Respeto: Bridging the Distances between Culturally Diverse Families and Schools: An Ethnographic Portrait*. New York, NY: Teachers College Press, 1996.

Valdés, Guadalupe. "Heritage Language Students: Profiles and Possibilities." In *Heritage Languages in America: Preserving a National Resource*, edited by Joy Kreet Peyton, Donald A. Ranard, and Scott McGinnis, 37–77. Washington DC: Center for Applied Linguistics, 2001.

Wargo, Jon. "Literacy Sponsorscapes and Mobile Media: Lessons from Youth on Digital Rhetorics." *Enculturation* 23 (2016). http://enculturation.net/literacy-sponsorscapes.

Yosso, Tara. "Whose Culture Has Capital? A Critical Race Theory Discussion of Community Cultural Wealth." *Race, Ethnicity and Education* 8, no. 1 (2005): 69–91. https://doi.org/10.1080/1361332052000341006.

Chapter 5

US Latinx Digital Humanities
Rehumanizing the Past through Archival Digital Pedagogy

Gabriela Baeza Ventura, Lorena Gauthereau,
and Carolina Villarroel

Introduction

In 1991, under the direction of Nicolás Kanellos, a group of US Latinx[1] Studies scholars[2] began discussions to strategize a plan dedicated to combatting the underrepresentation of the Latinx presence and contributions to the United States. With initial funding from the Rockefeller Foundation, these scholars founded Recovering the US Hispanic Literary Heritage (Recovery Program or Recovery), a nonprofit archival organization housed at the University of Houston (UH), one of three Hispanic-Serving Research Institutions (HSIs), and one of the most ethnically diverse research university campuses in the nation.[3] The Recovery Program's founding scholars defined the organization's mission as one dedicated to recovering, documenting, preserving, and making available the written legacy of Latinx populations in the United States. These scholars recognized the urgent need to recover the Latinx documentary history as they acknowledged how institutional archives failed to represent the extensive written legacy of Latinx communities. Indeed, evidence of Latinx literary culture prior to the 1960s was virtually nonexistent in the archives, due to strict appraisal guidelines developed in the 1950s.[4] This was in direct contrast to their own research, as well as that of their colleagues, through which they had already uncovered significant archival evidence of the written culture of Latinx communities in the United States.

From its inception, the Recovery Program began microfilming, digitizing, and archiving community histories to fight against institutional and environmental erasure of Latinx voices. The first cohort of graduate students and scholars began working against time to identify and locate newspapers and other publications that documented the existence of a Latinx community in the United States. Together, they documented the presence of hundreds of authors, publishers, and locations significant to the Latinx knowledge production. They set to work on implementing archival protocols to capture and describe these materials. This resulted in the creation of databases, microfilm images, digital surrogates, and physical collections that established Recovery's digital and analog archive.

In order to make this rich archive available to the public, Recovery publishes scholarly editions of recovered works through Arte Público Press[5] and through the US Latinx Digital Humanities Center (USLDH) digital images of archival documents (newspapers, manuscripts, correspondence, historical documents, etc.) in databases (EBSCO and Newsbank, Inc.),[6] and scholarly editions on APPDigital.[7] The materials are in analog and digital format and are accessible through UH's Special Collections and the Recovery Program.

The location of the Recovery Program at a Hispanic-Serving Institution in the ethnically and linguistically diverse city of Houston speaks to the importance of curating collections and creating content through the lens of the Latinx community, rather than replicating the Eurocentrism of institutional archives. Rodrigo Lazo (2009) maintains that archives and projects such as the Recovery Program offer a new way of understanding American Studies and contesting canonical US history.[8] Personal or community archives can contain narratives of lived experiences from the perspective of historically marginalized communities, in this case, the Latinx community. Michelle Caswell, Marika Cifor, and Mario H. Ramírez support this claim when they explain that: "community archives are responses not only to the omissions of history as the official story written by a guild of professional historians, but the omissions of memory institutions writ large, and they can thus be read as directly challenging the failure of mainstream repositories to collect a more diverse representation of society."[9] The Recovery Program creates a community archive that documents narratives left out of the canonical archive, but also curates a community archive that is specifically developed

by Latinx scholars whose goal it is to preserve and share Latinx historical accounts of their lives and contributions in the United States.

From the program's creation, a community of Recovery scholars developed dedicated to the preservation and study of these materials that dismantle the colonial perspective of history in the United States. In 2022, almost thirty-five years later, Recovery's collections include a range of transnational, multilingual, and multicultural materials from the colonial period to 1980.[10] Due to the immense efforts of the founding scholars and the growing community of Recovery scholars and graduate students at universities around the United States and abroad, the program's archives contribute directly to the field of US Latinx Studies itself, as well as to American Studies, by filling in the gaps of documentary history.[11] Using these archives in the classroom rehumanizes the Latinx community as students bear witness to firsthand accounts that challenge the hegemonic narrative of national history. We understand rehumanizing the past as an action that amplifies voices in Latinx collections, allowing them to take space and to speak for themselves, by providing alternate historical accounts to those that depict them negatively.[12]

In 2019, the Mellon Foundation awarded UH a grant to establish a first-of-its-kind US Latinx Digital Humanities Center (USLDH) in the College of Liberal Arts and Social Sciences. USLDH grew out of the Recovery Program's mission to preserve, document, and make available alternative histories. It draws on the program's vast collection of written materials and provides opportunities for scholars to use computational tools such as data curation, visualization, spatial analysis, and metadata creation to share knowledge from these archival materials.[13] As a natural extension, the center's approach to digital humanities is based on theories of social and linguistic justice, decolonialism and praxis, women of color (WOC) feminism, and historically marginalized community archiving.[14]

Developing a Latinx Feminist Pedagogical Practice

Through the process of elaborating different digital projects, we have developed pedagogical practices that go beyond the mission of preserving history by involving students (high school, undergraduate, and graduate) and community members directly in knowledge production. We ground this pedagogical practice in Latinx intersectional feminist thought. Particularly, we rely on the framework defined by Recovery board member and scholar María E. Cotera who points out that digital archives do not have to be sites of hierarchical knowledge delivery; instead, they have the radical potential to serve as "an active space of exchange and 'encuentro' between the present and the past."[15] We understand *encuentro* to mean a communal encounter or interactive conversation that does not replicate traditional archival tendencies to own collections and speak on behalf of others. Thus, an *encuentro* recognizes the ways that community records can or would have spoken for themselves. Cotera's article specifically references the Chicana por mi Raza Digital Collective (CPMR),[16] a digital repository of oral histories and personal archives that documents the contributions of Chicana feminists during the long civil rights movement. CPMR enacts a Chicana feminist praxis that puts civil rights activism into practice to combat the erasure of the lived experiences of Chicanas through "a networked transgenerational community of scholars, activists, archivists, and students working collaboratively to produce knowledge by and about Chicanas."[17] Like Cotera, we recognize the transgenerational work that forms the foundation of current feminist thought and activism, yet our work with archives, which is representative of diverse Latinx origins prior to the 1960s, requires us to widen the lens.

Extending from Cotera's "Chicana digital praxis," thus, we theorize a Latinx intersectional feminist praxis founded on the work of Latinx feminist thought prior to the 1960s, such as Luisa Capetillo (1879–1922), Sarah Estela Ramírez (1881–1910), Loreley (María Luisa Garza) (1887–1980), and María Amparo Ruiz de Burton (1832–1895).[18] By necessity, Latinx feminists prior to the 1960s worked across national boundaries and identities to advocate for their communities. Take for example, the work done by Elena Arizmendi, publisher and editor of *Feminismo Internacional*, a magazine published in New York between 1922 and 1923. Arizmendi sought to create a feminist network throughout the United States, Latin America, and Europe by compiling news about women's rights in the different countries and publishing Latina feminist thought that countered Anglo feminism. As seen in this example, we recognize the intersectional work of Latinx feminists through their attention to intersecting concerns of gender, ethnicity, nationality, language, labor, bodily autonomy, education, religion, sexuality, and much more. By theorizing a Latinx feminist praxis, we consider how these historical Latinxs advocated on behalf of their communities. As *Feminismo Internacional* demonstrates in its various issues, cultural norms often barred Latinas from speaking out on their own behalf, but their advocacy for their community produced change that addressed the needs of women and themselves. We contend that this methodological framework provides the tools to interrogate how knowledge is produced and how power is embedded in the process itself. It requires an awareness of the provenance of archival items. That is, we must keep in mind that these items are often records, photographs, documents, newspapers, and journals kept by members of the Latinx community that narrate alternative perspectives of US history. Yet, such records are kept out of official institutional archives because they do not belong to famous people and do not echo the narrative of Anglo-American progress that makes up the majority of the standard high school, college, and university history curriculum.

A digital pedagogy elaborated from the starting point of Latinx intersectional feminist praxis requires collaboration that extends beyond that of archivists and scholars. Digital humanities grounded in this praxis lends itself to collaboration, as it draws from community knowledge (archives, oral histories, community historians, scholars, activists) and fosters a space to connect people inside and outside of the institution to work together. When students work with archival material and curate a collection, they have the opportunity to actively participate in the production of knowledge and, in the case of a Hispanic-Serving Institution, such as UH, become advocates for their community's histories. As a result of UH's student demographics, Houston's large immigrant and Latinx population, and the location of the UH main campus in a Latinx neighborhood, UH students are exposed to Latinx culture quite regularly. Hands-on work with historically marginalized archives, such as the Recovery Program's collections, allows undergraduate students the opportunity to see the role the Latinx community has played in US history and begin to recognize the ways that the history curriculum edits or erases minority contributions.[19]

Using Omeka in the Undergraduate Classroom

Omeka is an open-source web publishing platform that is specifically geared toward hosting digital archival collections and exhibits: "Omeka provides an open-source infrastructure for organizing collections of objects and displaying them as an online exhibition. It brings together the convenient aspects of a content management system for building websites with the organization of item-level metadata employed by libraries, museums, and archives."[20] Some examples of Omeka sites include the Bracero History Archive, the Colored Conventions Project, Recovering the US Hispanic Literary Heritage

Digital Collections, and Take Back the Archive. Our team has found that using Omeka in the undergraduate classroom in combination with underrepresented community archives allows students to interact with history in a more personalized way.[21] Omeka provides a venue for sharing archival collections with a larger audience but can also function as a pedagogical tool for encouraging students to learn and contribute to knowledge production. As students work through the various tasks to complete the project, they critically engage with the archive, learn how to curate a digital collection, make decisions about metadata, and become familiar with the history embedded in the archival collection itself. Such close interaction with the archive puts students in contact with untold stories contextualized by critical Latinx theory.[22] Moreover, this platform allows them to share content that is scholarly, creating opportunities to question where these stories lie and to ponder why they are not part of the historical and literary discourse of the United States.

Omeka allows curators to link related material to each item in its Dublin Core metadata.[23] Linked data creates connections between items with the same subject headings and other metadata. Students can also use the Omeka metadata field "Relation" to link directly to digital content, such as an Omeka exhibit, a digital timeline, a network analysis, or a digital map. In this way, students could potentially link their own work with existing projects related to their subject and create a network of materials and stories that present various perspectives on a particular subject.

Scaffolded Assignment

In this Omeka exercise, undergraduate students were given instructions to curate an exhibit that featured items from a historically marginalized archive housed at the Recovery Program or at the Special Collections at the University of Houston.[24] Many, if not most, of these students had never visited or worked with archives. The assignment was scaffolded into various activities: 1) introduction to Omeka with training from a USLDH team member and digital humanities librarian where students created logins for Omeka and learned how to use the platform; 2) students created journals in Google Drive that were shared with the instructor to log in all activities conducted toward the completion of the project; 3) the class and instructor visited the archival collections (online or in person); 4) each student identified two or three archives that they wanted to work with; 5) each student scheduled an appointment with the archivist(s) to discuss copyright and access to the collection of their interest; this meeting determined the availability of the collections for an online exhibit; 6) each student made a decision on which archive to use for their assignment; 7) students scheduled time(s) to review the collection to identify topic(s) for the digital exhibit and to begin assessing which items to select; 8) students selected forty items for their Omeka collection; 9) students communicated with archivist(s) to digitize the selected items (if they had not already been digitized) and proceeded to scan if there was no digital surrogate; 10) students drafted the organization of the forty items in a thematic manner; 11) students created Excel sheets with metadata for each item following Dublin Core: title, author, description, year, etc.; 12) students created a collection on the Omeka site; 13) students uploaded digitized files to Omeka; 14) students created Library of Congress Subject Headings (LCSH–controlled vocabulary used to describe an specific subject matter[25]) for each item (English and Spanish, depending on the class); 15) students selected twenty items for their exhibit; 16) students conducted research on the archival materials selected in order to write an introduction (approximately five hundred words) to provide context for the exhibit; 17) using the journal that they kept, students drafted a document that explained the protocols they followed to complete the project. The document was published in the exhibit and included the student's name, affiliation, course name, archives visited, archivist(s) who helped them and rationale in selecting images organization, etc.;[26] 18) students shared the Introduction and Protocols document with instructor to receive feedback before uploading those files to Omeka; 19) students prepared bibliography; 20) students organized exhibit on Omeka; 21) students presented the exhibit to instructor and classmates for feedback; 22) students addressed feedback and published the exhibit; and 23) students wrote a short reflective essay on the exercise and turned in all materials for a grade. Throughout the process, the instructor scheduled one-on-one appointments with students to discuss archive selections, thematic organization, metadata, and other issues encountered.

Part of the preparation in working with archives from underserved communities included reading and discussing ethics of care. Virginia Held in *The Ethics of Care: Personal, Political, Global* (2006) explains that when you practice ethics of care you ensure that students think about subjects not as mere objects of study that serve academic purposes, but rather someone to whom we have a responsibility, whose emotions are acknowledged, valued, and appreciated. This helped students to connect rather than remove themselves, and to value the differences between the private and public spheres. In the end, ethics of care allowed students to create a connection and to produce more meaningful and respectful scholarship.[27]

In addition to ethics of care, students read scholarship on archives, archivists, historically marginalized communities, and Latinx literature and history so that they could have a general understanding of the field.[28] Through class discussions, students were invited to think about the role that archivists, scholars, academia, and governing bodies play in advocating for and curating archives from underserved communities. The discussion also included thinking about the physical spaces that underrepresented archives occupy in our cities to further consider the role they play in our own lives.

Journal

Students wrote weekly entries in a journal to document the progress on their project, which they submitted for a grade. This journal included the failures and successes of the decisions they made as they organized their collection and exhibit. For instance, students were encouraged to explain how they chose to organize the items so that they could think about the pros and cons of that decision. They had to determine if they had enough items to support the organization and if the metadata and subject headings created conformed to their decision. They then decided if they had to modify the initial organization.

Final Projects

Some examples of the archives selected by students in these courses include *Feminismo Internacional*, the Leonor Villegas de Magnón Collection, the Candy Torres Collection, and the Planned Parenthood Collection.[29] In these examples, students chose to speak on themes of Latin American women leaders, Latin American female celebrities, the Mexican Revolution and women, activism and women, and women in STEM. As they prepared metadata and subject headings for the items, students were able to identify links between items in the collection that they did not know existed previously. Their historical and theoretical research helped to contextualize the primary resources and allowed students to notice the silences in national narratives that excluded their chosen archives. When students published their final exhibits, the exhibit clearly identified their roles as knowledge producers who curated the collection, created metadata, and contextualized the historical information. During these classes, students expressed their commitment to honoring the legacy and histories contained in the archives demonstrating that they understood the ethics of care and the stakes of grounding the project in a Latinx versus a hegemonic perspective.

Lessons Learned

In processing materials using metadata with Dublin Core standards, students learned how their exhibits could then be integrated into algorithms where Latinx identities would not have appeared otherwise. Standardized metadata makes the collections discoverable and connects them to other documents related to canonical history. By using this platform, students were able to see the ways that archival items filled in gaps of history and the power behind naming things with controlled vocabulary. Their practice in managing Library of Congress Subject Headings and other metadata specifically taught them how to wield these academic tools for the benefit of underserved communities. For the Spanish language class, students created metadata in both English and Spanish to increase searchability. Using Spanish ensured that we honored the language in which the collections were produced and increased accessibility to the collections tied to the history of Spanish-speaking countries. In the end, students became aware of the critical thinking required in knowledge production and contributed to the rehumanization of the Latinx archive.

Furthermore, Omeka projects such as these are an interdisciplinary opportunity to learn firsthand from experts in the fields of humanities, library studies, and technology. This pedagogical model enacts Paulo Freire's "pedagogy of the oppressed" as both students and educators coincide in their efforts to "engage in critical thinking and the quest for mutual humanization"[30] not only in the humanization of the archival subject, but also for students as they gain the trust to become active producers and preservers of their community's histories.

Encouraging work on archives provides students with access to primary source materials, encouraging new knowledge production. Project-based learning (PBL) using digital tools engages them and allows them to present the result of their research in innovative ways. This experience of working with Latinx and historically marginalized archives enhances the classroom dynamic to a collaborative environment, enacting a Latinx feminist praxis. This teaching and learning environment becomes a collaboration not only between professor and student-researcher, but perhaps more importantly, between archival subject and researcher. Given that these archives would have remained hidden or lost, this engagement with technology allows contributors to bring the archival subjects to digital platforms in the twenty-first century to reclaim their humanity and space in the historical and literary record. Working closely with archives gives students the opportunity to feel connected to the material, to learn history from a primary source that is oftentimes personal.

Future Possibilities: Community Outreach

Using a Latinx feminist praxis to structure this type of Omeka project can also extend into the community itself. As previously mentioned, a Latinx feminist praxis prioritizes a relationship with the community and urges the creators of digital content to work not only with community archives (such as local Latinx historical documents), but also to get feedback, allow interaction between, and share content with the community represented in said archives. Extending projects from the classroom to the community helps to humanize Latinx education precisely through the embodiment of that history.

Despite the perceived democratization of digital content-production, Internet content is largely produced by and about the Global North in English. In terms of numbers, this amounts to approximately 20 percent of the world (or less) being responsible for shaping "our understanding of 80% of the world."[31] Digital humanities projects also reflect this skewed knowledge production online and reproduce the colonial record by highlighting hegemonic voices, archives, and epistemologies. Considering the high stakes of creating content about, by, and for underrepresented communities, student digital collections and exhibits can make an impact beyond the classroom walls by offering alternative sources for research projects in English and Spanish. Digital humanities training does not have to be limited to undergraduate and graduate students. Instead, it can be offered to middle and high school students, as well as teachers themselves. For example, education majors can create more pedagogical content in the form of exhibits, which can then encourage students of different academic levels (K-12 and higher education) to interact with digital archives.

Furthermore, extending digital projects into the community can allow for cooperative work with the owners of collections, valuing their input on the acquisition, processing, and dissemination of the historical materials. In fact, students expressed their desire to extend their work into the public sphere by conducting oral history interviews with community members and developing collaborations to fill in the gaps of missing information. Their written reflections demonstrated that they viewed the historical accounts as human experience rather than a static object.

In our own work in the Recovery Program, particularly in USLDH, we ground ourselves in the archive to rehumanize the communities that have been erased from the official US record. We see the archive as a pivotal point from which Latinx digital humanities can extend to a multitude of projects, beyond the archival exhibit, such as geospatial visualizations, text mining, interactive timelines, 3D printing, etc. USLDH's Latinx feminist praxis prioritizes ethics of care, bilingual metadata, community involvement, community training, and education to humanize Latinx archive as a daily practice. As scholars we are constantly thinking about strategies to incorporate historically marginalized voices in the classroom in innovative and responsible ways that have long-lasting impacts on the student, often transforming them into allies and advocates for their own communities. These recovered archives contextualize and locate Latinx lived experience, not only through memories of discrimination and oppression, but also through survival, thriving, and joy. These archival memories help to fill in the gaps, provide a more complete history and understanding of the United States, and offer a lesson in learning how to reckon with the stakes and responsibilities attached to working with historically marginalized archives.

Notes

1. We use the term Latinx and Latina throughout this chapter. We recognize that the term Latinx is anachronistic in reference to the historical work and people described here, as it is a contemporary term. People of Latin American descent prior to the 1960s tended to use national terms of origin (Puerto Rican, Dominican, etc.) to identify themselves, rather than the terms Latina or Latino. We have decided to

use Latinx here not to force twenty-first-century values onto the past, but rather, to account for all the voices whose identities may have been erased through gendered language. This includes transgendered and non-binary people who may have been forced to hide their identity because of strict legal, religious, and cultural regulations of the time period. We also use the term Latina when specifically grappling with women's rights and representation.

2. These scholars included Edna Acosta-Belén, Antonia Castañeda, Rodolfo Cortina, José Fernández, Juan Flores, Erlinda González Berry, Román Gutiérrez, Laura Gutiérrez-Witt, Virginia Sánchez Korrol, Luis Leal, Clara Lomas, Genaro Padilla, Raymond Paredes, Nélida Pérez, Gerald Poyo, María Herrera Sobek, and Roberto Trujillo.

3. "The University of Houston Now an Hispanic-Serving Institution." *University of Houston,* 2012.

4. In the 1950s, US archivist and archival theorist Theodore R. Shellenberg instituted guidelines that categorized items as historically significant only if they pertained to widely-known persons or events, thereby marginalizing materials related to communities of color. Considering that Latinx and other ethnic minorities figures were relatively unknown outside of their communities, they did not meet the criteria for archivization. Studies conducted by Carey McWilliams and Cecil Robinson on Mexican-American documentary history during the 1950s reveal that archivists dismissed Latinx records because of linguistic barriers and racism. See Theodore R. Shellenber, "Informational Values," 1956; Carey McWilliams, *North from Mexico,* 1949; Cecil Robinson, *With the Ears of Strangers,* 1963; and Gabriela Baeza Ventura, Lorena Gauthereau, and Carolina Villarroel, "Recovering the US Hispanic Literary Heritage," 17–27.

5. The Recovery Program is the historical arm of Arte Público Press, the largest publisher of contemporary and recovered literature by U.S. Latinx authors. https://artepublicopress.com/.

6. The EBSCO database, available through library subscription services, includes the *Arte Público Hispanic Historical Collection,* an archive of publications focused exclusively on US Hispanic history, literature and, culture from colonial times until 1960. It is available in two series. *Series 1* focuses on the creative life of US Latinos and Hispanics. Context is written, indexed and searchable in Spanish and English. *Series 2, The Latino-Hispanic American Experience: Leaders, Writers and Thinkers,* offers a three-themes collection of almost 300,000 pages chronicling Latino-Hispanic civil rights leaders, religious thinkers, and Latina writers in the United States from the late nineteenth to mid-twentieth century. The *Hispanic American Newspapers (1808–1980)* collection on the Newsbank, Inc. database contains the single largest compilation of Spanish-language newspapers printed in the United States during the nineteenth and twentieth centuries. This distinctive collection features hundreds of titles, including many published bilingually in Spanish and English.

7. APPDigital is built on the Manifold Scholarship platform and contains interactive scholarly editions that can be highlighted and annotated by readers. https://artepublicopress.manifoldapp.org/.

8. Rodrigo Lazo, "Migrant Archives," 36–38.

9. Michelle Caswell, Marika Cifor, and Mario H. Ramirez. "'To Suddenly Discover Yourself Existing,'" 56–81.

10. This includes a microfilm collection of approximately 1,400 newspapers; feminist publications, such as the the League of Iberian and Hispano-American Women's official 1922–23 publication, *Feminismo Internacional* (International Feminism); a variety of religious newspapers; photographs; manuscripts; books; and personal papers belonging to Latinx community members of different national origins. Aside from the Recovery Program's archives, other Latinx collections can be found in libraries such as the University of California-Berkeley's Bancroft Library, The University of Texas at Austin's Lilia Benson Latin American Collection, University of Miami Special Collections, and CUNY-Hunter College's Center for Puerto Rican Studies.

11. José F. Aranda, Jr., "Recovering the US Hispanic Literary Heritage," 476–84.

12. See for example John Morán González's discussion of the vilification of Mexicans at the Battle of the Alamo in *Border Renaissance: The Texas Centennial and the Emergence of Mexican Literature*. Austin: University of Texas, 2009 and more recently, Donald Trump's negative characterization of Latinx immigrants in Lizzy Gurdus, "Trump: 'We have some bad hombres and we're going to get them out.'" CNBC. 19 Oct. 2016.

13. An example of a project that stemmed from this grant is "Visual Bibliography of Hispanic Periodicals in the US" which reveals the written legacy of US Latinxs in serial publication form and creates awareness of the historical extent to which the Latinx community has made their presence in the United States. The information is based on the book *Hispanic Periodicals in the United States: Origins to 1960 a Brief History and Comprehensive Bibliography* by Nicolás Kanellos and Helvetia Martell. For a list of current and ongoing USLDH projects, please visit https://artepublicopress.com/projects.

14. This includes the work of digital practitioners, archivists and non-DH scholars and community members and organizations, such as Antena Aire, María E. Cotera, Lorgia García Peña, Marisa Duarte, Mario H. Ramírez, Ruja Benjamin, Moya Z. Bailey, Sonia Saldívar-Hull, Roopika Risam, Dorothy Kim, Emma Pérez, Andrea Roberts, Linda García Merchant, Nicole Hannah Jones, Carolina Criado Pérez, David Contreras, Mikaela Selley, the Colored Conventions, and the African American History, Culture, and Digital Humanities (AADHum) Initiative, among others.

15. María Cotera, "Nuestra Autohistoria," 489.

16. See http://chicanapormiraza.org/. Cotera is a Recovery board member, director of CPRM, and associate professor at the University of Michigan. She

supervised the creation of CPMR together with co-director, Linda García Merchant, and in collaboration with the Institute for Computing in the Humanities, Arts and Sciences at the University of Illinois Urbana Champaign.

17. María Cotera, "Nuestra Autohistoria," 489.

18. Sample works by and about these writers include Luisa Capetillo, *A Nation of Women*, 2004 and *Absolute Equality*, 2008; Diane Telgen, *Notable Hispanic American Women*, 1993; Vicki L. Ruiz and Virginia Sánchez Korrol, *Latinas in the United States, set*, 2016; Inés Hernández, "Sara Estela Ramírez: Sembradora," 1989; Loreley, *La novia de Nervo*, 1922 and *Los amores de Gaona*, 1922; María Amparo Ruiz de Burton, *Who Would Have Thought It?*, 1995 and *The Squatter and the Don*, 1997.

19. Recent examples of this include Arizona's ban on Mexican-American Studies courses, as well as the struggle in Texas to revise the state curriculum to include Mexican-American Studies. See Kelly McEvers (host), "Arizona's Ethnic Studies Ban in Public Schools Goes to Trial," 2017; Mary Tuma, "SBOE Passes Mexican-American Studies, but Whitewashes the Name," 2018; Andrea Zelinski, "Professors: Mexican-American History Textbook Is 'Offensive.'" 2016.

20. Gretta Tritch Roman, "Review: Scalar and Omeka," 122–23.

21. The assignment described herein may also be adapted for high school and graduate students, as well as community outreach programs. The assignment can also be adapted to use other platforms instead of Omeka, such as Wix, Wordpress, Jekyll, or even Instagram.

22. See sample syllabus, Gabriela Baeza Ventura, "SPAN 3394: From the Archive to the Digital: Intro to US Latino.

23. "The Dublin Core schema is a small set of vocabulary terms that can be used to describe digital resources (video, images, web pages, etc.), as well as physical resources such as books or CDs, and objects like artworks," see https://www.dublincore.org/specifications/dublin-core/.

24. This exercise was originally adapted from assignments created by Leandra Zarnow at the University of Houston and examples from Claire Battershill and Shawna Ross, *Using Digital Humanities in the Classroom*, 2017. USLDH staff guided Clara Lomas's students from the Colorado College in a week-long workshop based on this exercise. Additionally, the assignment was further modified for use in an upper-level Spanish language course and a Women, Gender & Sexualities Studies taught by Latinx Studies experts Gabriela Baeza Ventura and Carolina Villarroel at the University of Houston.

25. Library of Congress Subject Headings (LCSH) http://id.loc.gov/authorities/subjects.html.

26. For the structure of the protocols the program follows Collections as Data Facets, and the specific example used for La Gaceta de la Habana digitizations project: https://collectionsasdata.github.io/facet7/.

27. Virginia Held, *The Ethics of Care*, 2006. An example on the use of this theory is the work done by Purdom Lindblad and Jeremy Boggs, "Advocacy by Design," 2017.

28. See syllabus and USLDH Bibliography, bit.ly/USLDHbib.

29. See sample student projects on *Recovering the US Hispanic Literary Heritage Digital Collections*: Cory Castillo, "La lucha por los derechos de las mujeres latinas" https://usldhrecovery.uh.edu/exhibits/show/luchaporderechos; Mary Jaquez, "Escritoras famosas del siglo XX" https://usldhrecovery.uh.edu/exhibits/show/escritoras; Areli Navarro Magallón, "Respecting Beauty: Angela de Hoyos' Visual Art" https://usldhrecovery.uh.edu/exhibits/show/visualartadh; Elaina Roher "Una colección de artistas latinos de la década veinte" https://usldhrecovery.uh.edu/exhibits/show/artistasfemenismointernacional/latinoartists1920shome; Walker Shores, "Candy Torres: A Technorican" https://usldhrecovery.uh.edu/exhibits/show/candytorrestechnorican.

30. Paulo Freire, *Pedagogy of the Oppressed*, 1970.

31. Mark Graham and Anasuya Sengupta, "We're All Connected Now," 2017.

Digital Materials

Baeza Ventura, Gabriela. "SPAN 3394: From the Archive to the Digital: Intro to US Latino Digital Humanities." Department of Hispanic Studies. Houston, TX: University of Houston, 2019. https://drive.google.com/drive/search?q=3394%20syllabus.

Battershill, Claire, and Shawna Ross. *Using Digital Humanities in the Classroom: A Practical Introduction for Teachers, Lecturers, and Students*. Web Companion. 2017. https://scalar.usc.edu/works/digital-humanities-in-the-classroom-a-practical-introduction/index.

Castillo, Cory. "La lucha por los derechos de las mujeres latinas." Recovering the US Hispanic Literary Heritage Digital Collections. Arte Público Press. 2019. https://usldhrecovery.uh.edu/exhibits/show/luchaporderechos.

Jaquez, Mary. "Escritoras famosas del siglo XX." Recovering the US Hispanic Literary Heritage Digital Collections. Arte Público Press. 2019. https://usldhrecovery.uh.edu/exhibits/show/escritoras.

Navarro Magallón, Areli. "Respecting Beauty: Angela de Hoyos' Visual Art." Recovering the US Hispanic Literary Heritage Digital Collections. Arte Público Press. 2019. https://usldhrecovery.uh.edu/exhibits/show/visualartadh.

Recovering the US Hispanic Literary Heritage Digital Collections. Arte Público Press. University of Houston, Houston, TX. http://usldhrecovery.uh.edu/.

Roher, Elaina. Una colección de artistas latinos de la década veinte. Recovering the US Hispanic Literary Heritage Digital Collections. Arte Público Press. 2019. https://usldhrecovery.uh.edu/exhibits/show/artistasfemenismointernacional/latinoartists1920shome.

Shores, Walker. Candy Torres: A Technorican. Recovering the US Hispanic Literary Heritage Digital Collections. Arte Público Press. 2020. https://usldhrecovery.uh.edu/exhibits/show/candytorrestechnorican.

Bibliography

Aranda Jr., José F. "Recovering the US Hispanic Literary Heritage." In *The Routledge Companion to Latino/a Literature*, 476–84. New York, NY: Routledge Press, 2015.

Baeza Ventura, Gabriela, Lorena Gauthereau, and Carolina Villarroel. "Recovering the US Hispanic Literary Heritage: A Case Study on US Latina/o Archives and Digital Humanities." *Preservation, Digital Technology & Culture* 48, no. 1 (2019): 17–27. https://doi.org/10.1515/pdtc-2018-0031.

Battershill, Claire, and Shawna Ross. *Using Digital Humanities in the Classroom: A Practical Introduction for Teachers, Lecturers, and Students.* London & New York: Bloomsbury Academic, 2017.

Capetillo, Luisa. *A Nation of Women: An Early Feminist Speaks Out/Mi Opinión sobre las libertades, derechos y deberes de la mujer.* Houston, TX: Arte Público Press, 2004.

Capetillo, Luisa. *Absolute Equality: An Early Feminist's Perspective/Influencias de las ideas modernas.* Houston, TX: Arte Público Press, 2008.

Caswell, Michelle, Marika Cifor, and Mario H. Ramirez. "'To Suddenly Discover Yourself Existing': Uncovering the Impact of Community Archives." *The American Archivist*, vol. 79, no. 1 (June 2016): 56–81. DOI:10.17723/0360-9081.79.1.56.

Cotera, María. "Nuestra Autohistoria: Toward a Chicana Digital Praxis." *American Quarterly* 70, no. 3 (2018): 489. https://doi.org/10.1353/aq.2018.0032.

de Burton, María Amparo Ruiz. *The Squatter and the Don.* Houston, TX: Arte Público Press, 1997.

de Burton, María Amparo Ruiz. *Who Would Have Thought It?* Houston, TX: Arte Público Press, 1995.

Freire, Paulo. *Pedagogy of the Oppressed.* Translated by Myra Bergman Ramos. New York, NY: Continuum International Publishing Group, Inc., 1970.

Graham, Mark, and Anasuya Sengupta. "We're All Connected Now, so Why Is the Internet so White and Western?" *The Guardian.* 5 October 2017. https://www.theguardian.com/commentisfree/2017/oct/05/internet-white-western-google-wikipedia-skewed.

Held, Virginia. *The Ethics of Care: Personal, Political, Global.* Oxford; New York: Oxford University Press, 2006.

Hernández, Inés. "Sara Estela Ramírez: Sembradora." *Western Women Writers* 6, no. 1 (1989): 13–26.

Lazo, Rodrigo. "Migrant Archives: New Routes in and out of American Studies." In *States of Emergency: The Object of American Studies*, edited by Russ Castronovo and Susan Kay Gillman, Chapel Hill: University of North Carolina Press, 2009, 36–38.

Lindblad, Purdom, and Jeremy Boggs. "Advocacy by Design, a Design Framework for Critical Engagement Centered in Advocacy." Maryland Institute for Tech-

nology in the Humanities. University of Maryland, 2017. https://mith.umd.edu/news/advocacy-design-moving-theory-practice-part-1/.
Loreley. *La novia de Nervo.* Liberería de Quiroga, 1922.
Loreley. *Los amores de Gaona.* San Antonio, CA: Art Advertising Co.,1922.
McEvers, Kelly. "Arizona's Ethnic Studies Ban in Public Schools Goes to Trial." *NPR.* July 14, 2017. https://npr.org/2017/07/14/537291234/arizonas-ethnic-studies-ban-in-public-schools-goes-to-trial.
McWilliams, Carey. *North from Mexico: The Spanish-Speaking People of the United States.* Philadelphia, PA: JB Lippincott, 1949.
Robinson, Cecil. *With the Ears of Strangers: The Mexican in American Literature.* Tucson: University of Arizona Press, 1963.
Roman, Gretta Tritch. "Review: Scalar and Omeka," *Journal of the Society of Architectural Historians* 77, no. 1 (2018): 122–23. https://doi.org/10.1525/jsah.2018.77.1.122.
Ruiz, Vicki L., and Virginia Sánchez Korrol. *Latinas in the United States, Set: A Historical Encyclopedia.* Bloomington: Indiana University Press, 2016.
Shellenber, Theodore R. "Informational Values." *Bulletins of the National Archives* 8 (October 1956), *Archives and Records Management Resources*, US National Archives. archives.gov/research/alic/reference/archives-resources/appraisal-informational-values.html.
Telgen, Diane. *Notable Hispanic American Women.* Germany: VNR AG, 1993.
"The University of Houston Now an Hispanic-Serving Institution." *University of Houston,* March 29, 2012. Press Release. https://uh.edu/news-events/stories/2012/march/3292012HSIDesignation.php.
Tuma, Mary. "SBOE Passes Mexican-American Studies, but Whitewashes the Name." The Austin Chronicle. May 13, 2018. https://austinchronicle.com/daily/news/2018-04-13/sboe-passes-mexican-american-studies-but-whitewashes-the-name/.
Zelinski, Andrea. "Professors: Mexican-American History Textbook Is 'Offensive.'" *Houston Chronicle.* 18 July 2016. https://houstonchronicle.com/news/politics/texas/article/Professors-Mexican-American-history-textbook-is-8385586.php?utm_campaign=chron&utm_source=article&utm_medium=https%3A%2F%2Fwww.chron.com%2Fnews%2Fhouston-texas%2Fhouston%2Farticle%2FState-Board-of-Education-to-weigh-standards-for-12824376.php.

Chapter 6

The Delis Negrón Digital Archive
A Pedagogical Approach to Latinx Familial and Community Archives

Sylvia Fernández Quintanilla and Annette M. Zapata

Introduction

The archive of the Puerto Rican Delis Negrón was almost lost to the ages as it sat in the attic of his daughter Delia Negrón García's home. According to Delia Negrón García, her father "was always reading, writing, and sharing his make-believe fables with us. Negrón also taught English classes, wrote and directed live theater—he acted and performed in his own shows. He established his own newspapers in Laredo and Del Rio, [Texas], and was a reporter and editor-in-chief at *La Prensa* in San Antonio."[1] Prior to finding his archive, his family was unaware of his literary and journalistic trajectory in the United States and Mexico, a legacy that brought his Puerto Rican heritage to the México-Texas borderlands.

The personal collection contains family photographs, poems, newspaper clippings, manuscripts, correspondence, and handwritten notes. The poet's physical collection was donated to Recovering the US Hispanic Literary Heritage (Recovery) at the University of Houston (UH) by his family during the twenty-fifth anniversary Recovery conference with the intention of having a digital archive created.[2] The inclusion of Delis Negrón in the archive and the creation of its digital version brings to the forefront the pedagogical importance of telling stories by recuperating and assembling, composing, constructing, building and facilitating digital archives by and for the Latinx community within and outside of academia.[3]

While an estimated fifty-four million Latinxs live in the US, with forty-three million Spanish speakers, most versions of United States history often do not acknowledge Latinx stories as part of the official history.[4] This can be attributed to a lack of consideration when it comes to Latinx archives, or even to what is considered an archive or as pertinent historical material or resources. This chapter proposes the use of community and familial archival sources through digital storytelling practices to transform and rehumanize Latinx education, provide an opportunity to understand emotions and experiences documented in archival material, and structure and present these stories digitally through accessible and interactive technologies. Through this process we present a counter narrative to the often-used tropes of invasion that have accompanied influxes of immigration from undesired groups registering alternative histories and experiences of Latinx people in the United States with their own archives and stories.

The recovery, preservation, and transformation of Delis Negrón's archive to its digital version provides a way to tell his story and address issues of silences and gaps found in familial archives, (im)migrant and diasporic history, Latinx literary legacy, United States history, and transnational contributions.[5] Through postcolonial digital humanities, this project models a familial and community digital archive that makes use of digital spaces and tools to record and expand access to their story and history, similar to Roopika Risam's emphasis on tackling the colonial and neocolonial echoes in the digital cultural record in *New Digital Worlds*.[6] In effect, the creation of this familial digital archive provides an example for the preservation of community and familial archives, in their various physical and/or digital conditions, and the creation of digital storytelling projects that intervene in the history of the Americas from personal, local, national, and transnational perspectives.

Finally, we discuss the contributions of Hispanic-Serving Institutions and the relevance of involving Latinx students in the creation of familial and community digital archives as digital storytelling projects. Through collaborations that engage students, academics and community members, digital storytelling practices can formulate new methods of creating digital resources with community and familial archives in conditions not always suitable for digital technologies. Overall, this article addresses the necessity of working with familial and community archives to address Latinx histories and experiences in the analog and digital cultural record.

These resources allow us to learn about historical and or cultural experiences that may not have been included in official histories, such as the participation of Puerto Rican Delis Negrón in the south Texas border region. His digital archive provides a window into Mexican-American culture and politics, LULAC activities, US Latinx literature, and the legacy of a Puerto Rican in the diaspora. As interpreted by Alfredo Lucero-Montano, Walter Benjamin indicates historical materialism does not reconstruct history by repeating the past, it constructs interferences in the present. In this way, Negrón's archive forms part of the discontinuities that Benjamin points out, which constructs an alternative history.[7] Joining the political, social, and cultural activities of the United States breaks with the system of racial and cultural hierarchy that excludes Latinxs. The writings and the participation of Negrón in the community through political and social activities gives testimony to a historical aspect of the culture displaced by the political and hegemonic discourses of the United States and within Latin America.

Practices in Latinx Familial and Community Digital Archives

The Delis Negrón Digital Archive serves as a pedagogical tool to guide in the creation of familial digital archives using documents and materials available to individuals in their familial and/or community histories incorporating digital storytelling practices.[8] Familial and community digital archives are a way we can decolonize the archive by utilizing accessible resources available to communities outside of academia. This is vital for the decentralization of institutional archives that usually prioritize large scale, organized, focused archives that support certain ideologies or aspects of national history.

Markus Friedrich argues that archives are often seen as an integral component and indicator of a well-organized administration and, therefore, count as important elements in the development of the nineteenth-century European nation. National archives are created through these nations and support the ideological construction of national histories . . . placing archives as part of infrastructures of colonial oppression.[9] In this way, familial and community digital archives create a postcolonial digital cultural record for stories and histories that are often overlooked or excluded by institutions.

The postcolonial digital cultural record, as Risam states, allows us "to tell new stories, shed light on counter-histories, and create spaces for communities to produce and share their own knowledge should they wish."[10] This is what the Delis Negrón Digital Archive does by creating a resource for the family and the Latinx community through digital storytelling.

Latinx familial and community (digital) archives are often multilingual, dispersed, incomplete, in some cases uncontextualized, and have the potential to provide a space for individuals "to challenge the authority of the national building" by opposing and adding to the official history of the United States that has excluded local Latinx stories from historical memory.[11] The preservation of non-typical community and familial archives that do not represent the ideal Western family is not usually a focus for institutional, traditional archives. According to María Cotera in " 'Invisibility Is an Unnatural Disaster': Feminist Archival Praxis after the Digital Turn," "traditional archival methods often nourish an invisibilizing feedback loop in which one's access to power determines one's presence in the archive, and one's presence in the archive shapes knowledge, which, in turn, informs the system of values that shapes the collecting priorities of institutions. So those farther away from the mechanisms of power . . . are rarely represented in institutional archives. Consequently, their lives and interventions are rarely the subject of historical meaning-making."[12] This control of the traditional archive not only causes a lack of knowledge in the importance and value of familial documents, but also generates a disjunction between the traditional archive and the Latinx community. This reality is reflected in Negrón's collection since this digital archive only reflects a part of his writings. Many documents were not preserved and others are scattered in other national repositories such as the *Newspaper Archive*, where his voice is not highlighted.

The historian Vicki Ruiz in "Nuestra América: Latino History as United States History" expands on the situation of Latinxs in the United States, stating, "[y]et, the narratives of these people remain within the American experience, overshadowed by the national implications of conquest referred to in one text as 'the fruits of victory.' "[13] However, there is an extensive tradition of "cross-cultural archival comparison" that is not limited to European examples.[14] Friedrich explains that "[s]cholarly attention has begun to shift away from the history of archives as institutions to the history of archiving as social practice" that makes it possible to decentralize archival history towards previously unconsidered archives.[15] By preserving and making digitally available archives such as Negrón's, the archive, history, and literature are decolonized through the representation of these excluded communities within Western knowledge spaces as homi bhabha and other scholars such as Gloria Anzaldúa, Cherrie Moraga, and Gayatri Spivak refer to in their reference of postcolonialism.

While the history and archives of the Americas do not generally reflect this notion, it is imperative to resist these structures of institutional power by finding and creating other methods of representation. One such method can be found in postcolonial digital humanities, where historical and cultural materials from underrepresented communities look for ways to preserve and shed light to their own stories. As Risam describes: "Digital archives perform and resist colonial violence, examining how scholarly organizations influence digital humanities practices on a global scale, teaching students that they can intervene in the digital cultural record and understanding the forms of the human that are sanctioned through digital humanities scholarship. At the intersections of postcolonial thought and digital humanities lie the possibilities for transforming the practices of digital knowledge production."[16] This intersection opens digital spaces to tell these histories and stories in ways that facilitate collaboration between the communities themselves and scholars versed in preservation and digital creation. This is where digital storytelling enters the conversation. By digital storytelling, we are referring to the use of archival materials to tell a story on a digital platform with multimodal templates, which can include oral or written accounts, but is focused on the curated documents and/or visual aids the community and/or family is trying to preserve and share. According to Sonia Chaidez, instructional technologist, in her blog post "Digital Storytelling in Digital Humanities?," "Digital storytelling shares the ethos of the digital humanities: the willingness to collaborate, to experiment, to share, to fail, to be transparent, to iterate, and to make public. Digital storytelling like DH is modular in its ability to remix and alter the format to fit different disciplines. Digital storytelling is less about expertise and making expert knowledge public or leveraging open data for research and more about centering teaching and learning experiences."[17] As we emphasized before, familial and community archives can oftentimes be found in precarious conditions. Considering this, it is important to use digital storytelling practices in the creation of community and familial digital humanities projects that take into account various ways to exhibit the material in relation to its condition of preservation, organize and divide the material in a way that allows for interaction, and, most importantly, take into consideration the personal stories and connections the family or community shares when preserving their materials.

The act of preserving the Delis Negrón archive and seeing its potential as a Latinx pedagogical digital project is an act of decentralization and social practice that brings into consideration not only this archive, but also others like it that have been excluded by the concept of the European archive. Engaging students and community members in hands-on interventions with their familial and community digital archives permits them to "directly [intervene] in the representation, visibility, and legibility of postcolonial literary and cultural production online," making them active participants in the preservation of their stories.[18]

The Creation of a Familial Digital Archive

As mentioned above, student engagement is a priority in the creation of familial and community digital archives. The Delis Negrón Digital Archive demonstrates this as it was curated, archived, digitized, and transferred to a digital version by a team of four Latina graduate students working as research assistants at Recovery. After the donation of the physical archive, the team performed the following procedures for the physical documents to be preserved, digitized, and saved in Recovery's digital repository.[19] Firstly, the documents were curated and digitized by Sylvia Fernández, project lead, according to the preservation guidelines of the Library of Congress.[20] Photos and documents were scanned at a 300 dpi in their original form and condition, excluding no document or fragment. An Excel sheet was created to catalog the archive as it was scanned and maintain the "original order" of the documents as provided by the family, including the sections they classified the materials under. The metadata in the Excel sheet was organized into six sections: family, poetry, press, manuscripts, correspondence, and notes. Fernández also included identification numbers, subject headings, and name tags for all materials scanned.

After the completion of the metadata, the team that worked on the transition of the physical archive to the digital project was formed. Initially this project was assigned to Fernández, but after a lecture by Tom Scheinfeldt of Greenhouse Studios at the University of Connecticut, Fernández together with Isis Campos, Victoria Moreno, and Annette Zapata, fellow RAs with Recovery, made the decision to implement within the project a "new culture of collaboration" that focuses on new attitudes between colleagues of distinct disciplines in order to produce digital scholarship.[21] In the case of the Negrón project, the colleagues involved took what was an individual task and decided to form a partnership among the RAs following an organic methodology to create this project. The team was already responsible for the preservation of this material and others like it that Recovery has worked with since its foundation in 1992. The transformation of this archive into a digital project allowed the team to put into practice what is emphasized in postcolonial digital humanities: collaboration. As Gabriel Griffin and Matt Steven state, "Collaboration is a complex, intersectional activity in which multiple forms of co-working often occur simultaneously, even as they are differentially privileged, acknowledged or, as in some instances, not acknowledged at all."[22] With the now formed team, the process of transforming the familial archive of Delis Negrón into a digital storytelling project began.

The first discussion the team had was to select a platform while considering the archive's precarious state and several missing pieces. We chose Wix since it allowed us to select various templates to present the archival material available through storytelling practices. As Chaidez states, digital storytelling tells stories using computer-based tools like graphics, audio, video, and web publishing, some of which can be low-tech and accessible to anyone.[23] While the use of a commercial platform like Wix might lead some to question the academic value of this project and this archive, this platform was selected because it is user friendly and approachable to creators and facilitates interaction with communities outside of academic spaces. As Arjun Sabharwal in *Digital Curation in the Digital Humanities: Preserving and Promoting Archival and Special Collections* notes:

> Recent advances in technology and various debates in the digital humanities have, however, placed increasing emphasis on computing, digital technologies, and social media, bringing into question the scholarly and theoretical scope of digital humanities practices as well as the relationship between archives and the humanities. Digital Humanities projects, such as thematic research collections, continue to demonstrate the value of archives through this continuing relationship because archivists have expanded their expertise to cover digital curation in order to preserve, promote, and provide long-term access to digital—that is, digitized and born-digital—collections as well as quantitative data for non-narrative humanities projects.[24]

While Sabharwal is discussing institutional or academic digital archival collections, we take the idea further to include familial and community digital storytelling projects as "thematic research collections." This continues Friedrich's notion of decentralizing archives, making the Negrón digital platform an interactive archive of social practice.[25]

The decision to use Wix was agreed upon and a template was chosen based on its functionalities, like the use of slides and videos. The documents were uploaded to the platform, which functions as a digital repository, and categorized in a similar manner as established in the Excel data, while combining the subjects in those categories.[26] Several aspects, in addition to the original archive, were included on the site: family quotes, poetry recitations, photographs documenting the donation of the collection, and reflections by family members and the RAs that created the digital project. The images uploaded to the site were documented using Dublin Core Metadata Initiative with the information available from the documents.[27]

Each section was designed by an RA, keeping the original web page template, but organizing the page in a format that allowed for the best presentation and interaction with the whole collection. For example, the manuscripts are displayed individually, with all of their pages in a slideshow that can be enlarged page by page, while the postcards are in gallery format that can also be enlarged. Additionally, various digital components created by the Negrón's family were integrated into the sections on the website, such as the *Palabras*-poetry collection that was made digitally available by the family, and videos of students reciting Negrón's poetry from his Facebook page. The category "Collection" and subsection "Reflections" were added to include moments from the donation of the archive to Recovery and reflections from the family and the scholars that worked on the project. This added to the storytelling aspect that the team wanted to document, from the donation of the material to the physical (and now digital) materials available and the memories that the family had from Delis Negrón.

Engagement with Latinx Communities as an HSI

The familial digital archive of Negrón emerged because of the desire of his family to preserve his memory and work in a way that could be shared with the academic and Latinx community. The partnership between the Negrón family and Recovery made that possible. The Recovering the US Hispanic Literary Heritage program is housed within Arte Público Press (APP) at the University of Houston. In 2012, UH received the designation of Hispanic-Serving Institution (HSI), for "consistently rank[ing] among the top colleges and universities in the nation for conferring bachelor's degrees and doctorates on Hispanic students."[28] The support and efforts taking place at UH as an HSI allowed the RAs, Latinas in the Hispanic Studies PhD program at this institution, to work with Recovery and their archival and digital initiative. They gained experience working collaboratively on this project, not only with each other, but also with the Negrón family. Therefore, one of the main objectives of this project was to encourage the application of "documentation strategies and engage communities to actively participate in archival practice [to] help remedy some of the historical lacunae that affect[s] many underrepresented groups and will empower them to take an active part in the process of documenting their stories and history, rather than remaining the passive object of 'preservation.'"[29] This is seen in the Delis Negrón Digital Archive through the collaboration of Latinx scholars and community members in the preservation of this material, making them active participants in the practice and knowledge production of this familial digital archive.

In Sabharwal's words, "The recent decades have brought even greater visibility and public role to archivists [and humanities scholars] whose work can shape community memory and identity through more creative outreach practices."[30] This project and the work of the team members attempts to preserve the community memory through these practices in the hope of bringing figures like Negrón out of the archival shadows. These types of initiatives are working towards filling and/or making visible the silences and absences that traditional archives, digital humanities practices, and official histories reflect.

Recovery has emphasized creating digital and public projects with the archives available to them, leading to their US Latino/a Digital Humanities Initiative. As Gabriela Baeza Ventura, Lorena Gauthereau, and Carolina Villarroel mention, their "DH center (#usLdh), Recovery, and Arte Público Press continue[s] making use of all the tools available to help US Latinas/os occupy spaces from which they can speak and act with the certainty that their heritage, history, language, and ethnic identity take center stage within all hegemonic discourses."[31] Thus, the creation of the Delis Negrón Digital Archive emerged as a necessity to document and to continue the dialogue regarding the Latinx community, their transnational and diasporic ties, their multiple and complex identities, and their belonging to the history of the Americas.

Through this process, the team learned that collaboration and engagement between Latinx scholars and communities outside of academia was a major aspect in the development of this digital archive. Firstly, the Negrón family helped guide the structure of the project, specifically in certain gaps that Negrón's trajectory presents through its documents. Because of their active part in the archival process, LULAC documents that mark Negrón as editor were donated. Additionally, through his literary works, his ties to his Puerto Rican identity, something not commonly seen in his newspaper publications, and his appreciation of Mexican history and culture is showcased, like in the poems "Palabras," "Bandera," and "Las soldaderas" or in his manuscripts with the various titles of "Cantinflas."[32]

The diverse intersections of his literary and cultural production are a crucial aspect to highlight since it is an example of a Puerto Rican's life working outside of the traditional East Coast trajectory. The conversations with the family members were essential, because, with their stories, the team was able to understand their reasons for donating the material. For further community engagement, the public is also invited to interact with certain sections, such as the transcription of Delis Negrón's personal notes that will be done using crowdsourcing methods.[33] Additionally, as it is a continuous process of recovering and locating documents relating to Delis Negrón from different archives, they are encouraged to contribute to the project if they know about any documents that can be incorporated into his digital archive.[34]

These collaborative community efforts are becoming more popular and necessary as postcolonial digital humanities projects take on more ethical ways to represent community stories. Similarly, as an HSI, it is important to reflect the diverse, personal histories and stories of Latinx communities in history, the archives, and the digital cultural record. This inclusion leads toward a broader knowledge of the cultural and literary production of Puerto Ricans in the United States. Frances Aparicio indicates that,

> the production of literature by Puerto Ricans in the United States has also been historically silenced. Despite the fact that Puerto Rican migration is not as recent as many believe, literary and cultural scholars have neglected to document and to rescue contributions of this important Latinx sector throughout the early part of the century (with the exception of research done at the Center for Puerto Rican Studies at Hunter College). Most scholarship on Puerto Rican literature has principally focused on the contemporary period, that is, from the beginning of the Nuyorican movement (late 1960s and early 1970s) until now.[35]

This archive brings to light that Puerto Rican migration has been present long before the Nuyorican movement. Puerto Ricans have not only established their own communities along the East Coast but have also integrated themselves into other Latinx communities and have presented their contributions in newspapers, collections, and other literary and cultural productions and events. While Latinx archives have traditionally been excluded and oppressed, subjecting the identities of entire communities and nations to marginalization, familial and community (digital) archives and collaboration practices, as seen with the Negrón project, can serve as an example of ways to reconstitute the memory.

Working with programs and institutions, like Recovery and HSIs, that prioritize working with and supporting voices and stories that are often overlooked, helped facilitate the interactions between the Negrón family and the graduate student RAs to create this organic digital storytelling project. This opens the door for Latinx students to intervene in spaces that have been dominated by Western knowledge and applied methodologies, thus offering new ways to approach familial and community (digital) archives from communities that have been disregarded by institutional archives.

The Future of Latinx Familial and Community Digital Archives

It is important to note that even in the digital era Latinx familial and community archival material continue to be overshadowed at the institutional and digital level by initiatives that prioritize canonical figures or the maintenance of centralized Western or Latin American knowledge and culture. In regards to Latinx archives, Rodrigo Lazo describes these collections as "the texts of the past that have not been written into the official spaces of archivization."[36] The efforts made here to preserve a small familial and community collection, the initiative to make it digital and public, as well as establishing a model to work directly with the family, breaks with traditional forms and highlights alternative practices for archival spaces. This facilitates access to the material in order to incorporate new interpretations, histories, and representations in the digital cultural record. In this way, moving the physical archive of Negrón to a digital version allows not only access to a particular history of a Puerto Rican in the diaspora, but, in a broader context, also recomposes the intellectual and literary history of the Latinx community in the United States and its contribution to the political, cultural, and social contingency of the country.

The Delis Negrón Digital Archive does not intend to make a record of his life, but rather to give access to his personal records, professional career, and his participation in the community through the available documents. This is with the intention of emphasizing an organic exploration and interaction with the documents accessible in order to interpret it in different ways, as well as to connect other documents that are dispersed in various archives in the United States or elsewhere. Familial and community digital archives serve as a pedagogical example for other families, communities, and students to build or help consolidate this kind of collaborative work. The methodologies applied when working with this digital archive create awareness within the Latinx community of the importance of maintaining and preserving their familial stories with the materials available to them.

In this way, the procedures and practices followed in the Delis Negrón Digital Archive disclose the need for familial and community archives created by or engaging with members of their own communities in order to preserve the personal memories within the national and transnational histories. As Ruiz mentions, "It is crucial to understand their [Latinx] histories within and beyond the borders of the United States and to contextualize present and projected demographic realities by exploring the pasts that preceded them."[37] Latinx familial and community archives expand the knowledge of what Latinx history, culture, literature, and migration represents in the Americas. In this we hope that other Latinx students and community members take up the mantle and continue to add to the cultural record with their stories and history. Ruiz describes, "Contrary to popular media depictions of Latinxs as people who arrived the day before yesterday, there exists a rich layering of nationalities, generations, and experiences" that have shaped and continue to develop the American experience in the United States.[38] With this in mind, the curation and creation of this digital archive, and future archives like it, leads to the continued development of an inclusive history of the Americas.

Conclusion

The gaps and absences within Delis Negrón's physical archive led the team to create a digital archive through storytelling approaches in order to work in filling the lacunae of this collection. As Sabharwal indicates, "Archives have been, still are, and will be collecting materials from the past when historical records were produced in print, but at the same time, they can also participate in the transition to digitally oriented and reconfigured landscape."[39] Therefore, the creation of the Delis Negrón Digital Archive reconfigures the landscape in its transition to using the benefits of technologies to connect with other communities beyond geographical and institutional borders. It is also an example of collaborative work towards the digitization of familial and community archives, in this case among Latinx community members, scholars, and HSIs.

The Delis Negrón Digital Archive represents one small effort to shed light on a personal, familial, and community collection that involved recuperating, preserving, and making visible the history of a Puerto Rican in the Mexico-Texas border region. The fact that the archive is incomplete does not mean it cannot become a digital project. On the contrary, through pedagogical digital storytelling practices, postcolonial digital humanities, and collaboration between scholars and the community, Latinx archives can be expanded. As described by Sabharwal, "Interdisciplinary research, postmodernist and postcolonial, Marxist, and feminist methods of representation, and the growing corpora of born-digital materials have informed historical analysis and writing, which in turn inform academic and public discourse on history, including local history and cultural heritage."[40] The Delis Negrón archive provides another aspect of the local and transnational history and heritage that he and his family participated in.

For this reason, the digital version was designed in an organic manner to encourage individual, unique, and multidisciplinary interpretations by those that make use of the documents provided in this Latinx familial digital archive. With the material exhibited in the digital repository, other work can be initiated contributing to transform and rehumanize Latinx education. Literary and historical analysis can be expanded through his poetry or his newspaper publications. His publications reflect the documentation of events in the south Texas border region that have potential for a future project that emphasizes the continued recovery of documents and periodicals that expand knowledge on the Mexico-United States border region and its communities.

While some of Negrón's records may be beyond recovery, this does not take away from the impact that the documents available provide for the Latinx, Puerto Rican, and Mexican communities, as well as their impact on the academic and historical research community. Through this project there is an argument for a postcolonial, intersectional gaze of the archives in the creation of digital humanities community projects. In other words, it is proposed that this digital archive be used as an example for the formation of Latinx familial and community projects considering the digital tools, methodologies, and procedures discussed in this chapter. This will help break away from the idea that a valued archive or historical material or resources is found nicely stored in a library, digital repository, or elsewhere. This proposition intends to expand the view of the Latinx experiences beyond borders and skewed historical representations in the digital cultural record that have been established by changing the way communities document their legacies and stories.

Notes

1. Facebook Page, "Delis Negrón, Poet."
2. The initial curation of the physical archive of Delis Negrón was made possible through the efforts of the Recovery archival team and their community interactions, which focus on Latinx outreach as part of their mission and the mission of the University of Houston, as a Hispanic-Serving Institution. Recovery "is an international program to locate, preserve and disseminate Hispanic culture of the United States in its written form since colonial times until 1960." For more information, visit https://artepublicopress.com/recovery-program/.
3. We use the term *Latinx* to refer to people in the US with a familial connection to a Latin American or Caribbean country. We maintain the use of Latinx throughout the chapter outside of direct quotes and book/article/organization/program titles.
4. Erin Blackmore, "The Brutal History of Anti-Latino Discrimination in America."
5. We refer to *(im)migrant* in the sense that Puerto Ricans are technically migrants in the US, but many times are treated or perceived as immigrants.
6. Roopika Risam, *New Digital Worlds*, 13.
7. Alfredo Lucero-Montano, "On Walter Benjamin's Historical Materialism," 130.
8. Delis Negrón Digital Archive, 2017.
9. Markus Friedrich, "Epilogue," 421.
10. Friedrich, 5.
11. Rodrigo Lazo, "Migrant Archives," 37.
12. María Cotera, " 'Invisibility Is an Unnatural Disaster,' " 785.
13. Vicki Ruiz, "Nuestra América," 660.
14. Ruiz, 424.
15. Ruiz, 422–23.
16. Ruiz, 19.

17. Sonia Chaidez, "Digital Storytelling in Digital Humanities?"
18. Roopika Risam, *New Digital Worlds*, 93.
19. Recovery makes every effort to preserve all archival collections in their digital repository, whether it is a permanent collection they house or is a digital humanities project.
20. Archive preservation guidelines by the Library of Congress: https://www.loc.gov/preservation/.
21. "Design Process," Greenhouse Studios.
22. Gabriel Griffin and Matt Steven, "Collaboration in Digital Humanities Research."
23. Sonia Chaidez, "Digital Storytelling in Digital Humanities?"
24. Arjun Sabharwal, *Digital Curation in the Digital Humanities*, 27.
25. Sabharwal, 422–23.
26. Wix functions as a digital repository to store the material that is visualized and presented, but it is not a permanent one. Being aware of this, the Delis Negrón Digital Archive website is archived on Archive-It, a web archiving service, in addition to the physical and digital archive preservation held by Recovery at Arte Público Press.
27. The Dublin Core Schema is a small set of vocabulary terms that can be used to describe digital resources (video, images, web pages, etc.), as well as physical resources such as books or CDs, and objects like artworks. For more information, see *Bioinformatics Challenges at the Interface of Biology and Computer Science: Mind the Gap*, 2016, Teresa K. Attwood, Stephen R. Pettifer, and David Thorne.
28. Marisa Ramírez," The University of Houston Now an Hispanic-Serving Institution," 2012.
29. Valerie Love and Marisol Ramos, "Identity and Inclusion in the Archives," 15.
30. Love and Ramos, 50.
31. Gabriela Baeza Ventura, Lorena Gauthereau, and Carolina Villarroel, "Recovering the US Hispanic Literary Heritage," 25.
32. Mario Moreno (Cantinflas) was a Mexican comic film actor, producer, and screenwriter and an iconic figure in Mexico and Latin America.
33. The transcription feature through crowdsourcing methods would be a collaboration through the Recovery Program.
34. "Protocols," Delis Negrón Digital Archive, 2017.
35. Frances R. Aparicio, "From Ethnicity to Multiculturalism," 20.
36. Aparicio, 37–38.
37. Aparicio, 671.
38. Aparicio, 672.
39. Aparicio, 33.
40. Aparicio, 49.

Digital Materials

Bracero History Archive. Center for History and New Media. University of Texas, El Paso, TX. 2021. http://braceroarchive.org/.

Chaidez, Sonia. "Digital Storytelling Guidebook for Educators." Sonia Chaidez. 2019. https://soniachaidez.com/digital-storytelling/.

Chicana por mi Raza Digital Memory Project and Archive. The Institute for Computing in Humanities Arts and Sciences, University of Illinois Urbana Champaign, IL. 2015–2019. https://chicanapormiraza.org/.

Delis Negrón Digital Archive. Recovering the U.S. Hispanic Literary Heritage Digital Collections. Arte Público Press. 2017. https://recoveryprojectapp.wixsite.com/negrondigitalarchive.

Medina, Cruz. "Digital Latinx Storytelling: Testimonio as Multimodal Resistance." In *Racial Shorthand: Coded Discrimination Contested in Social Media*. Edited by Cruz Medina and Octavio Pimentel. Computers and Composition Digital Press, 2018. https://ccdigitalpress.org/book/shorthand/chapter_medina.html.

(@PALABRASporDelisNegron). "Delis Negrón, Poet." Facebook, December 19, 2016. https://www.facebook.com/PALABRASporDelisNegron/.

"Palabras Poesías." Poetry by Delis Negrón. 2022. http://delisnegron.com/.

"StoryCenter: Listen Deeply . . . Tell Stories." StoryCenter. 2022. https://www.storycenter.org.

Bibliography

Aparicio, Frances R. "From Ethnicity to Multiculturalism: An Historical Overview of Puerto Rican Literature in the United States." In *Handbook of Hispanic Cultures in the United States: Literature and Art*, edited by Francisco Lomelí, Nicolás Kanellos, and Claudio Esteva-Fabregat, 19–39. Houston/Madrid: Arte Público Press and Instituto de Cooperación Iberoamericana, 1993.

Baeza Ventura, Gabriela, Lorena Gauthereau, and Carolina Villarroel. "Recovering the US Hispanic Literary Heritage: A Case Study on US Latina/o Archives and Digital Humanities." *Preservation, Digital Technology & Culture* 48, no. 1 (2019): 17–27.

Blackmore, Erin. "The Brutal History of Anti-Latino Discrimination in America." September 27, 2017. Accessed July 26, 2022. https://www.history.com/news/the-brutal-history-of-anti-latino-discrimination-in-america.

Chaidez, Sonia. "Digital Storytelling in Digital Humanities?" August 30, 2018, Accessed July 26, 2022. https://soniachaidez.com/digital-storytelling/digital-storytelling-in-digital-humanities/.

Cotera, María. "'Invisibility Is an Unnatural Disaster': Feminist Archival Praxis after the Digital Turn." *South Atlantic Quarterly* 114, no. 4 (2015): 781–801.

Delis Negrón Digital Archive. Recovering the US Hispanic Literary Heritage. Accessed July 26, 2021. https://recoveryprojectapp.wixsite.com/negrondigitalarchive.

"Delis Negrón, Poet." Facebook Page. Accessed July 20, 2018. https://www.facebook.com/PALABRASporDelisNegron/.

"Design Process." Greenhouse Studios. University of Connecticut. Accessed July 2018. https://greenhousestudios.uconn.edu/design-process/.

Friedrich, Markus. "Epilogue: Archives and Archiving across Cultures—Towards a Matrix of Analysis." *Manuscripts and Archives: Comparative Views on Record-Keeping*, Edited by A. Bausi, C. Brockmann, M. Friedrich, and S. Kienitz, 421–45. Berlin/Boston: Walter de Gruyter GmbH, 2018.

Griffin, Gabrielle, and Matt Steven. "Collaboration in Digital Humanities Research—Persisting Silences." *Digital Humanities Quarterly* 12, no. 1 (2018). Accessed July 20, 2018. http://www.digitalhumanities.org/dhq/vol/12/1/000351/000351.html.

Lazo, Rodrigo. "Migrant Archives: New Routes in and out of American Studies." In *States of Emergency: The Object of American Studies*, edited by Ross Costronovo and Susan Gillman, 36–54. Chapel Hill: University of North Carolina Press, 2009.

Love, Valerie, and Marisol Ramos. "Identity and Inclusion in the Archives: Challenges of Documenting One's Own Community." In *Through the Archival Looking Glass: A Reader on Diversity and Inclusion*, edited by Mary A. Caldera and Kathryn M. Neal, 1–22. Chicago, IL: Society of American Archivists, 2014.

Lucero-Montano, Alfredo. "On Walter Benjamin's Historical Materialism." *Astrolabio. Revista internacional de filosofía*, no. 10 (2010): 126–31.

Ramírez, Marisa. "The University of Houston Now an Hispanic-Serving Institution Federal Designation Underscores Goal to Prepare Diverse Populations for Global Competitiveness," UH News and Events, March 29, 2012, Accessed July 26, 2022. https://www.uh.edu/news-events/stories/2012/march/3292012HSIDesignation.php.

Risam, Roopika. *New Digital Worlds: Postcolonial Digital Humanities in Theory, Praxis, and Pedagogy*. Evanston, IL: Northwestern University Press, 2019.

Ruiz, Vicki L. "Nuestra América: Latino History as United States History." *Journal of American History* 93, no. 3 (2006): 655–72.

Sabharwal, Arjun. *Digital Curation in the Digital Humanities: Preserving and Promoting Archival and Special Collections*. Boston, MA: Chandos Publishing, 2015.

Chapter 7

Crossing Pedagogical Front|eras through Collaborative World-Making and Digital Storytelling

Jeanelle D. Horcasitas and Olivia Quintanilla

Introduction

The impact that the 2020 pandemic had across the US was unimaginable, and it certainly disrupted the educational experiences for many students. Community colleges (CC) in particular were forced to pivot their curriculum and schedule to accommodate a virtual learning environment. At the same time, economic downturn, social unrest, political turmoil, and more brought forth many injustices and inequities on various institutional levels. Interestingly, however, in 2019 we created a choose-your-own adventure game called Front|eras. This game imagined what the consequences of virtual reality and increased racial injustices would be in the year 2049. But it was the year 2020 that many of these dystopian realities we imagined had manifested in ways we never thought possible.

The COVID-19 pandemic presented us with the opportunity to reflect on what we have done in the past and how it has influenced our present, and be intentional as we work toward shaping a better future. More specifically, Front|eras was the catalyst for changing our pedagogical methods to center the experiences of our students and what we call their "everyday ways of knowing"[1] to rehumanize Latinx education. We also began implementing more digital tools that could be used alongside assignments and projects, focusing on science fiction and speculative fiction. We call this approach *speculative tools of knowledge*, a methodology we created that draws from speculative fiction and science fiction as a source of inspiration, collaboration, thought experiments, creativity, and world making to produce new forms of knowledge, critique, and insight. As community college educators and first-generation women of color in the academy, we recognize the urgency to rehumanize Latinx education and will outline our pedagogical methods and case studies in the following chapter.

Rehumanizing Latinx Education at CCCs

At the California community college (CCC) level, Latinx students are the largest ethnic group represented in this system.[2] In fact, many CCCs operate under the definition of a Hispanic-Serving Institution (HSI), which the US Department of Education defines as an institution with at least 25 percent of Hispanic full-time enrolled students. As community college professors and former students ourselves, we recognize that attending a community college is sometimes the only way to access higher education, especially to transfer to California State University (CSU) and University of California (UC) higher education institutions. Unfortunately, despite the high enrollment of Latinx students in the CCC system, many are unsuccessful transferring, obtaining a certificate, or completing a degree.[3] Growing up in low-income households, we understand the struggle to navigate college and to feel seen in these spaces for our unique backgrounds and knowledge. As a result, we believe in rehumanizing our educational institutions to cater to our Latinx communities so that they can have bright and successful futures. We argue that using speculative tools of knowledge and everyday ways of knowing practices in community college classrooms through various assignments or projects like Front|eras, can help reimagine a future Latinx voice (especially transborder identities) that are visible and powerful because they are grounding stories from Latinx people as knowledge-producing agents of innovation in a socio-historically situated and extrapolated future San Diego.

Historically, Latinx students have been forced to navigate a negative racial climate on campus, including microaggressions, stereotype threat, and assimilation. In Tara J. Yosso's *Critical Race Counterstories along the Chicana/Chicano Educational Pipeline*, she highlights why Latinx students struggle among their peers, and the barriers they face when trying to navigate the academic pipeline.[4] According to data in 2005 about 70 percent of Chicana/o students enroll in community college in pursuit of a four-year university degree, and only 17 percent of those students will successfully transfer.[5] Not only do Chicanas/os complete the fewest number of bachelor's degrees (only seven out of one hundred Chicana/o elementary school students will graduate with their bachelor's), they also only make up about 1 percent of the professoriate.[6]

Almost a decade later, the UCLA Chicano Studies Research Center produced a report that revisited the pipeline for Latinx students and found they were still far behind many other racial and ethnic groups in the US.[7] This study reports that Latinx students comprise up to 54 percent of all K-12 students in California alone, yet they are severely underrepresented the further they get in the educational pipeline.[8] For example, Latinx only make up about 8 percent of master's degrees, would need to increase their attainment of doctorates by fourfold to catch up with other ethnic/racial groups, and represent only 4 percent of the nation's faculty.[9] The data conveys that "In California in 2013, Latina/o academic faculty comprised 14 percent of faculty in the CCC system, 9 percent in the CSU system, and 6 percent in the UC system."[10]

However, there is a larger issue at hand when it comes to providing Latinx students with the support they need to be successful in their education. Students of color have long fought for their educational curriculum to reflect their realities and communities such as the push for African-American Studies, Chicano Studies, Asian-American Studies, and Ethnic Studies in the 1960s. Back then, the fight was primarily about inclusion in existing spaces. Even at that time, Latinx students and scholars were still placed in a space of exclusion and alienation since the academic institution is embedded with historical processes that were not designed for their success. Access to culturally competent courses is half the battle. Students need more from us to be successful. Rehumanizing Latinx education can change that, and we argue this is possible by ensuring we check in with our students on the varying aspects of their lives. We situate our pedagogy within this historical context and employ rehumanization as a core function of our educational philosophy and practice.

We understand that students are tired of being treated like overpaying customers and are exhausted from being overworked from readings that do not speak to their realities. They are deterred from expressing themselves and often feel like they have no rights as learners. This is primarily caused by the "deficit-based thinking" that many institutions have toward students of color, rather than recognizing them for the "cultural wealth Latinos employ to overcome and survive adversity."[11] Latinx students are also exhausted because of the academic culture that pushes toxic habits like studying late and glorifying high grades before everything else. In reality, we want our students to enjoy their educational journey. We do not want them to wait to enjoy life until after they graduate. We honor their need for rest, family, and leisure.

We also need to be speaking to our students one-on-one and building solidarity and community by discussing these challenges as a class to reinforce these ideas of well-being and self-care. We put validation theory into practice for our students of color because its "asset-based approach to working with students as knowledgeable and capable of college-level work, and build supportive relationships between validating agents and students" is a valuable aspect of empowering our students to be active in shaping their own futures.[12] People of color often feel pressured to make up for lost social status by engaging in overproductivity leading to burnout. We want to keep those ambitions sustainable and achievable by grounding them in the resources found within community care.

We pose the question: What keeps us going in the pursuit of our studies when life throws us seemingly unmanageable hardships? One of the precious capacities we enjoy as humans is the ability to be creative and to explore ourselves and our world through our imagination. We have witnessed our Latinx students repressing their own ideas and expressing shame and embarrassment for proposing their interpretations and presenting their questions. We see these self-defeating habits repeat themselves every semester with different cohorts of students. The role of education in developing one's ethnic identity is key. If students feel positively about their ethnic identity and cultural connections, they are more likely to engage and participate in spaces beyond the classroom that encourage collaboration and community building.

Pedagogical Approaches and Methods

Everyday Ways of Knowing

As an interdisciplinary field, ethnic studies has historically spanned the humanities and social sciences by using research methods from a wide range of disciplines such as history, geography, sociology, anthropology, and Indigenous studies. We approach ethnic studies from an Indigenous and Latinx framework, specifically one that centers everyday ways of knowing and begins with the understanding that categories of identity are always already intersected, in flux, and transforming together across time and space. Our interpretation of everyday ways of knowing builds on the concepts brought forth by validation theory, as well as a "culturally validating Latino student successful framework [that] dismantles the deficit-based grand narrative and poses the consideration that students have cultural wealth they employ to success in their own way."[13] Moreover, our teaching practices are influenced by a liberatory pedagogy that is rooted in an inclusive curriculum, various ways of knowing, and especially Rendón's *Sentipensante* [Sensing/Thinking] *Pedagogy* that "views individuals as whole human beings, connects inner and outer learning, deeply engages the learner through the use of contemplative practices, promotes the acquisition of both knowledge and wisdom, and emphasizes activism, liberation, healing and social change."[14]

Our methodology of collecting the everyday experiences and knowledge from our Latinx students is distinct from the traditional bottom-up approach. The bottom-up approach is derived from the language of business and project management. For our project, we sought to reclaim and reinvent this concept of the bottom-up by allowing our Latinx students to collectively share resources with one another and generate the knowledge about how they want to make and envision their future worlds, especially when it comes to their educational and career paths. Our everyday ways of knowing approach employs knowledge sharing as a methodology and relies on the alternative resources and knowledge from our communities that may not be recognized by large institutions. We want our Latinx students to reclaim this power over their future by acting as agents of change, the ones driving the tools and resources to get them where they want to be. Front|eras is just a starting point. If more projects such as this one can be created by students, it can provide opportunities to Latinx students because it gives them a foundation and space to tell their unique stories, to share their own resources, and think critically about how they want to shape their futures.

Speculative Tools of Knowledge

We argue that speculative tools of knowledge are necessary for empowering students in shaping their futures. Science fiction and speculative fiction are not simply bodies of text about unrealistic futures. Rather, these narratives are powerful speculative tools of knowledge for people of color to practice their own world making and shape the futures they want. As a result, this encourages students to generate alternative stories about the past, present, and future, and actively change their own narratives by reimagining and envisioning multiple possibilities for their futures.

While Latinx science fiction and speculative fiction is not particularly well-represented in the literary canon or film industry, those that do engage with it have made significant extrapolations from the past and present to capture the ways Latinx people have been alienated in professional and academic spaces. Literary scholar Lysa Rivera emphasizes the importance of writing US/Mexico borderlands science fiction because it is a way to "articulate experiences not only of alienation, displacement, and marginalization but also those of survival, resistance, and resilience."[15] We recognize that Latinx students need to feel empowered and hopeful about their future, despite the challenges and barriers they will inevitably face from institutionalized racism.

Applying These Methodologies to Our Pedagogy

We implement both everyday ways of knowing and speculative tools of knowledge in the classroom because we believe it is our responsibility to nurture a student's (ethnic) identity development and build up their confidence as leaders, innovators, and creative thinkers. We also build on these methodologies by approaching them through a lens of transferable skills. We tell students our goal as the instructor is to build their confidence in transferable skills they will use once they leave us. These skills include creative thinking, writing, analytical skills, using project management tools, leadership development, and recently speculative design. It matters how we treat our students. Kindness and authenticity go a long way. Instead of only posing prompts that ask what they critique, we ask what they would change. By making a safe space for discussions and activities of our curriculum's readings and content, this pivots our students onto equal footing in the classroom so that they can ask questions and more importantly, actively propose their own solutions. This is what using speculative tools of knowledge does for our students. It allows them to take control of their futures and gives them the power over their own narratives.

We acknowledge the harsh realities of many of our Latinx students, but we do not overemphasize them because that work is already being done for us through the media, political actors, and other classes. A (re)focus on the everyday means recognizing the joy, the love, and the growth experienced, especially during times of struggle. Our students are likely to continue experiencing disproportionate amounts of hardships and we want to be clear that those struggles do not define them. We equip our students with effective tools to recognize and celebrate goodness and growth when they see it and to use periods of crisis as opportunities to use speculative tools of knowledge that regroup, reframe, and keep pushing them toward creating the changes they want to see. Our approach to teach students literature and history through speculative design and policy making, and through the lens of the everyday, starts with an understanding of them as trustworthy innovators, leaders, and full human beings.

In our particular CC classrooms, recognizing the value in the everyday knowledge production of our Latinx students addresses a larger goal to strengthen and empower our communities in this collaborative and interdisciplinary approach. This is a primary reason our Front|eras project focused on the San Diego border region. We wanted the struggles of our Latinx students to be represented in these future narratives, especially those crossing the border each day for work or education, and ultimately, demonstrate that they can take part in shaping them as well.

Case Studies Overview

In the following sections, we discuss three case studies that move between Hispanic-Serving Institutions (HSIs), including the University of California San Diego and the San Diego Community College District, and that transcend institutional parameters through community-based Digital Ethnic Studies to showcase how we are approaching the interface of digital humanities, speculative fiction, community building, and skill building for minoritized students. On the surface, the Front|eras game, an exercise on world building in the classroom, and the digital storytelling deployed by the Critical Refugee Studies Collective (CRSC), and the DRSOJ project appear as unrelated projects. We put these projects in conversation to illustrate critical and creative interdisciplinary methods of digital ethnic studies that work to rehumanize education.

CASE STUDY 1: FRONT|ERAS

Setting the Scene

Imagine the world thirty years from now. A world where virtual reality technology allows for elite classes to escape the dystopian present. But this is at the cost of exploiting people of color for cheap labor, especially Latinx immigrants. A deteriorating future society where enclaves of resistance like a group called ContraVR has emerged to destroy and rebuild the systems in place. This was the premise of our choose-your-own-adventure game, Front|eras, which ultimately begs the question: Could this fictional world be our nightmarish reality in the future? While we can spend a lot of time speculating on the future's possibilities, we can also make use of that time by enacting change now and preparing the next generation to reimagine and create more equitable and sustainable futures. This type of thought experimentation and world making practice is vital to our students, especially our Latinx students, whose voices and narratives are often left out of history books, and more important, the way we think about our futures.

The idea for Front|eras emerged from a year-long program titled San Diego 2049 run by the UC San Diego Arthur C. Clarke Center for Human Imagination and School of Global Policy and Strategy. While a total of three groups were formed, our group was the most interdisciplinary, representative of the humanities, arts, and social sciences, and had more than one woman and more than one person of color on the team. We recognized early on that our group was unique because our diverse perspectives and experiences united to envision a future from a socio-political perspective that got people to think about the future, but also be encouraged to make their own stories about the future, too. When we created this game, we did so with the purpose of making a long-lasting impact. One of those goals was to share this game with the broader community and our students.

We named this project Front|eras to represent both the new frontiers that the future will bring, but also the existing *fronteras*, or borders, that pose both a physical and abstract barrier to Latinx communities. This game addresses US-based institutional policies regarding surveillance, immigration, tourism, virtual reality technology, and future laborers, and creatively examines how existing frameworks affect Latinx populations currently and imagines how such systems will evolve in the future.

Front|eras imagines San Diego thirty years from now as a technological playground with virtual reality technology that provides an escape to those wealthy enough to pay for it. People become so immersed in this virtual world that they stay for extended periods of time, completely neglecting their physical bodies in the real world. As a result, many *transfronterizeros* cross the border each day to perform the hospice type of labor to make a living and survive in a world that is on the cusp of collapse. Additionally, we wanted to provide stories from different perspectives to give our users a choice and so they could feel part of the story itself and recognize that they are the ones who shape their own future. We also wanted to convey moments of hope with groups such as ContraVR that resist and fight for better futures and send a call to action that we need to be critical of the current political, sociological, and environmental conditions to prevent this type of future from happening. By sharing this project with our Latinx students, we hope they will recognize what is at stake and that they have a critical role to play in world making and being changemakers. We need to teach our Latinx students how to actively envision and write themselves into these futures, because their narratives do matter.

This project transformed the way we think about our future and the concept of world making. Hours of conversations and thought experiments about our concerns and how we could tackle these issues in our future made us recognize we can enact change now, and the best place for this to begin is in our classrooms. Front|eras is certainly not the solution, but rather the beginning of using speculative tools of knowledge that can be created by anyone. We believe that projects such as this one will rehumanize Latinx education because students will not only feel represented in these narratives, but they will also be the ones engaging with and creating them. Our students are the knowledge-producing agents of the future and as educators for a majority Latinx community college student population, we believe they need to be the focus of our pedagogical discussion and the leaders and creators of our future worlds.

Projects like Front|eras are not meant to be fixed and static; rather, this game encourages our Latinx students and community to take part in shifting the narrative, in taking charge of representing themselves, and embracing the fluidity and evolving nature of their identities. For this reason, we have shared our game in highly visible and public spaces, such as Comic-Con. During the Comic-Con convention in 2019 held in San Diego, California, we were invited to speak about Front|eras on a panel titled "San Diego 2049: World Building and the Future at UC San Diego." We engaged in thought-provoking conversations with SF (science fiction) scholars and writers about what is at stake in our future.[16] We explained how Front|eras achieved its goal to provide accessibility (a game anyone can play or create for that matter) and represent marginalized communities. Our project is a living digital artifact that we want people to expand and develop even further, specifically our Latinx students in the classroom. This project aims to influence and rehumanize Latinx education by providing our students the opportunity to imagine problem-solving scenarios they may face amidst some of the dystopian realities that our technological world is creating. Science fiction is one of the most effective tools to use in the classroom because it extrapolates our present issues and urges our students to think critically about how they could change them.

Using Front|eras to Re-Imagine Education through an SF Lens

Our methods for Front|eras move beyond just thinking creatively or critically about our present and future, but also offer technical skills to our students, such as learning to do simple code on a digital storytelling platform. The digital humanities (DH) played a major role in the creation of our project because we used it to represent a marginalized voice in a field that Tara McPherson infamously wrote about in her chapter titled "Why Are the Digital Humanities So White? Or Thinking the Histories of Race and Computation?"[17] We developed our own collaborative and interdisciplinary methodology using a digital humanities framework that brought together the expertise of a computer scientist, a visual arts designer, literary writers, and social scientists. We established this methodology for this project because we did not want to limit the possibilities of what stories we wanted to tell, nor limit the creative digital tools we could use to tell them and make them more interactive for our users. Therefore, we decided to use the digital storytelling platform Twine. Twine can be described as an "open-source tool for telling interactive, nonlinear stories" and this aligned with our goal to share this project with as many people as possible. We also advocate for open access and open-source tools that allow for anyone and everyone to take advantage of them and share resources. This type of digital commons disrupts the stereotype that scholars must protect their work and block others from seeing it with paywalls, ultimately restricting the engagement of their work with selective elite circles. Again, we value the everyday knowledge production that is out there and want people to eliminate the barriers to allow more connection and collaboration.

We also want to emphasize the interdisciplinary and collaborative aspect of our methodology that teaches our Latinx students to work together, form collectives, and be knowledge-producing agents of change. Twine itself is meant to be collaborative with story maps that show the interconnected stories or "choices" people can be led to as they navigate the game. Students can create the content and represent themselves the way they want. They also can have control of the design and the narrative structure, whether it follows a fixed or non-linear path. Twine is multi-modal and can integrate sounds and images. The creation of a Twine story is simple as well and does not require high-level coding skills beyond HTML to change fonts, colors, backgrounds, etc. Our story mapping method, however, also stems from other projects that use the digital humanities as an alternative storytelling tool for refugees. We will discuss this more in our next case study.

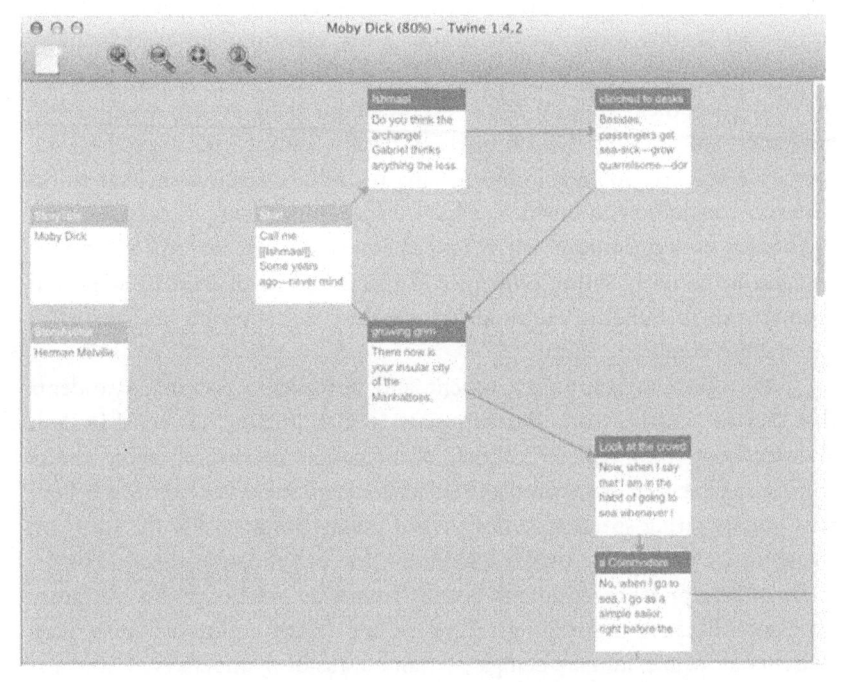

Figure 7.1. Bird's-eye view of a story map, courtesy of Twinery.com.

174 | Jeanelle D. Horcasitas and Olivia Quintanilla

Case Study 2: Classroom Assignments and Projects

Re-imagining and Creating San Diego's Future Waterfront

One example of teaching through the lens of the everyday ways of knowing is a popular week-long world-making exercise run for our US history course from a Chicano perspective for students at the community college, who are primarily Latinx, Chicanx, and Mexican nationals. Students work in small groups to read and discuss various methods, histories, and strategies for world making and speculative design, and then we apply them to San Diego's downtown waterfront. Students are tasked with designing a mock-up of the San Diego downtown area in 2050 with a story to explain their scenario. They also present, display, and put their future worlds into conversation with other reimaginings of the future at the end of the exercise.

We press them for details about this future world they are imagining, and they must build it out their vision from our current realities. If they envision robotic care workers rolling down San Diego's sidewalks, which they have, we follow up with questions such as: How did we get from today to the care worker robots of the future? These questions are overwhelming and at times, frustrating to students. They go back to their groups puzzled, but this gives them time to think deeply about their present realities and how they are shaping their futures. Typically, during the next check-in, they have mocked up an environmentally friendly sewage system that works with our natural environment and have engaged in intense discussions with their peers over the future San Diego they want to see, not just what they perceive to be likely future outcomes. These are some of the first steps and groundwork to building our students' capacity to contribute to alternative storytelling about the future.

We use each planning moment and obstacle to encourage students that they can do this work. By enthusiastically reinforcing our belief in their abilities, soon they believe in their participation in shaping these future worlds, maybe even as urban planners who design these systems. We believe that incorporating speculative design and policy brings to life the focus on social justice and equity that is inherently part of validation theory. Historically underrepresented students benefit from this practice and a liberatory classroom because it means as teachers, we "work compassionately with students as whole human beings . . . and transform underserved students into powerful learners who overcome past invalidation and oppression" and therefore, are motivated to engage in world making and reimagining what the future for them could be.[18]

For this assignment, we make time in our class agenda to build out our ideas and nurture their creativity. We challenge them because we know they can do it and know they need time and practice to feel confident in completing the task to be successful. This is a pedagogical and arguably political decision, to take up class time to do this work, but it is necessary because it matters to our students. We recognize it takes time to relearn pivotal areas of education and critical thinking that our society has favorably structured according to the realities of non-Latinx students. Rehumanizing education in the every day means taking the time to do the work it takes to get to know our students, nurture their identities and ideas, and encourage them to build community with one another to envision the futures they want.

Story Maps with the Critical Refugee Studies Collective

The Critical Refugee Studies Collective (CRSC) founding faculty are among the leading scholars in the field who have extensive expertise in community-engaged research. In 2017, Olivia joined the collective as the graduate student researcher and launched the Story Map project on criticalrefugeestudies.com. Artist Tiffany Chung argues, "Because for me, maps represent life. If there is no life, no society, no culture, there would be no maps . . . maps not only define borders, they are also about people."[19] On these pages, we take the cue from Chung that "maps represent life." We endeavor to reconstruct maps about refugees to tell a different story by refugees; that is, how they came from a history of militarism; how they have rebuilt their communities; and how they continue to survive and thrive, telling stories, rewriting history, and making art, literature, poetry, and films along the way.

This alternative story mapping is inspired by the concepts of counter storytelling in critical race theory. The counter story itself is described as "a tool for exposing, analyzing, and challenging the majoritarian stories of racial privilege. Counter stories can shatter complacency, challenge the dominant discourse on race, and further the struggle for racial reform."[20] These story maps are one component of the website to provide counter stories that include refugee archives, an "open archive," and virtual forum for the archiving of refugee stories. Users can upload poetry, art, film, and music of all genres on these pages. There is also a collective bibliography, list of critical vocabularies built from public submissions, a repository for

CRSC inspired curriculum and teaching activities, and a community blog where anyone is invited to submit a written proposal.

In Olivia's role with the CRSC, she taught herself how to create these story maps through the digital mapping tool ArcGIS. GIS is the acronym for geographic information system and is used as a tool to gather and manage data. In turn, ArcGIS provides a new way to analyze space by enabling users to combine text, interactive maps, and other multimedia to create inspiring immersive stories. One example that shows the significance of counter storytelling and story mapping is when Olivia tried to upload a story submission based in Palestine. Although she tried repeatedly to upload the story, she learned from the tech consultant that the Palestine coordinates would not go through because Google maps did not recognize this territory—it was as if it were invisible. Olivia and the CRSC team, however, were able to approximate the coordinates, but it was not the original location of the story. This was a reminder for us to be critical about what we can do when our creative mapping solutions still edit our (counter)archives.

Story mapping is another amazing example of a speculative tool of knowledge that teaches us about storytelling, digital technologies, and the digital humanities. Story mapping activities are consistently brought up by former students as their favorite assignment, and new students say it is what attracted them to taking the class. Projects like Front|eras and CRSC's story mapping can motivate our students to learn the skills required to do this kind of work.

World Making with Multimodal Tools like Scalar

Our vision for the Latinx students in the classroom is to implement this type of world making and speculative tools of knowledge on our syllabi and curriculum. We want to invite our students to develop their own Twine projects based on their perspectives of what the future might look like. We will provide guidance by facilitating conversations, or thought-experiments, to generate creative discussions about what is happening now, what has happened before, and what will be in the future. Moreover, we will emphasize our interdisciplinary and collaborative methods by requiring students to form teams. We hope that this will help to foster relationships among students from diverse backgrounds and generate authentic knowledge production from their projects.

The students in Jeanelle's transfer-level English 101 course which was taught through a Science Fiction perspective had the option to create their own Scalar project as part of the honor's component of the syllabus. Scalar can be defined as a similar multimodal online platform that can be used by multiple users and uses various types of media to present information. Scalar, however, is not as easy to navigate between various tabs; and Twine's story mapping will give students the ability to mind map their ideas and collaborate more effectively. Students who choose to do a Scalar project also do so individually, and therefore, Twine will help eliminate isolated projects and encourage students to work collaboratively toward a goal. As you can see, we have piloted this type of project with programs like Scalar and feel that our own success using Twine will have a transformative impact on our future Latinx students.

The future of our Front|eras project is to cross the pedagogical borders that exist in the academic pipeline for many Latinx students and make space for them to forge their own valuable forms of knowledge. We are committed to giving students the opportunity to experiment with Twine and develop new possible pedagogical frameworks that empower them to use digital tools, collaborate, and form interdisciplinary connections. We also want to move beyond the borders that exist in our communities, whether that be a result of institutional racism, oppression, exploitation, etc. We realize that Front|eras is also a public humanities project that is meant to be shared with the wider community and prompt conversations from people outside of academia. Returning to the value of everyday knowledge production, we believe our Latinx students, people of color, and other historically underrepresented communities, should be represented in our futures and we hope that projects such as Front|eras will give them the tools, access, and encouragement to do so.

Our experiences as educators, researchers, and first-generation women of color from low-income and immigrant families has shaped our own visions of the future and the long-lasting impact we hope to make. The work we have done in our classrooms with our students, and the community with Front|eras and CRSC, have also inspired a larger initiative we call #DRSOJ.

Case Study 3: DRSOJ Initiative to Cultivate Community and Collaboration

Our DRSOJ initiative reimagines and reinvents professional and personal growth experiences for communities of color seeking educational opportunities. DRSOJ represents the authors, Drs. Olivia and Jeanelle, two PhDs in Ethnic Studies and Literature/Cultural Studies, respectively, who coined this professional partnership in 2015 to empower one another during the first years of our doctoral programs to overcome imposter syndrome by visualizing our success, together. DRSOJ played a key role in maintaining our positivity and momentum in graduate school while we pursued limitless visions of ourselves and our goals that seemed beyond the scope of our doctoral programs. We like to share our journey with others by posting photos of us at work, having fun at conferences and learning new skills, and writing and doing the research we are so passionate about. We tag our photos with the DRSOJ hashtag to remind ourselves that our everyday work and process is part of our bigger plan. Together we created a public facing collective and collaborative identity based in valuing our labor and grounded in friendship that was shareable and taggable, a form of cultural production that gains its meaning and significance through its (re)sharing and dissemination to others, to inspire other students to keep going. We enhanced the visibility of our community-centered partnership through social media which garnered the attention of faculty and staff from local universities and community colleges. As a result, we began receiving invitations to design and facilitate in-person and online workshops and curriculum for programs that serve first-generation students and students of color at UC San Diego and the University of San Diego. We covered topics such as applying to graduate school, sustainable leadership, time management, financial literacy, project management, digital humanities tools, pedagogy, and career paths. These experiences taught us the importance of designing tailored DH curriculum for specific audiences such as community college students and highlighted the need for DH from Ethnic Studies perspectives. In response, DRSOJ began designing Digital Ethnic Studies curriculum.

During summer 2020 in the height of the pandemic we piloted our Digital Ethnic Studies curriculum through a five-week virtual workshop series we titled "World Making for Stories and Life." This workshop series was hosted through the Arthur Clarke Center for Human Imagination in partnership with the San Diego Futures Foundation. Also during the summer of 2020, we designed a two-part virtual digital humanities workshop series for the Preparing Accomplished Transfers to the Humanities (PATH) program, a collaborative transfer support program between the San Diego Community College District and the University of California, San Diego Division of Arts and Humanities. PATH guides transfer students from City, Mesa, and Miramar colleges into arts and humanities majors. Our positionalities and experiences informed our approach to designing DH curriculum and virtual workshop space for PATH students and community college adjuncts. As a method to rehumanize the (virtual) education space, we intentionally embedded confidence-building and professional-growth activities, and insight on navigating higher education as a first-generation and student of color, alongside DH skill building.

New initiatives addressing the nexus of Ethnic Studies and Digital Humanities fields are making headway across the US such as the Digital Ethnic Futures Consortium, or DEFCon. DEFCon is a digital humanities research and teaching community of digital ethnic studies practitioners that create professional development opportunities for research and teaching for ethnic studies fields, funded by a $3-millon-dollar grant from the Andrew W. Mellon Foundation. Like DEFCon, DRSOJ also aims to "increase national capacity for digital humanities curriculum engaged with minoritized communities," and "emphasize the importance of reciprocal and redistributive relationships with communities through digital humanities praxis." DEFCon supports critical work but leaves out those not affiliated with a four-year public university, community college adjuncts, and those without full-time faculty positions from existing funding opportunities. DRSOJ addresses this gap by focusing on community college students and adjuncts.[21]

Our Digital Ethnic Studies curriculum focuses on best practices for teaching DH across transitional stages 1) entering the college system, 2) the transition from community college to university, and 3) the four-year degree to graduate school. The future is bright with Ethnic Studies curriculum implementation in K-12, California State Universities, Community Colleges across California, and more ethnic studies faculty hires. As of this writing, Olivia is the first tenure-track faculty hire in the brand new Ethnic Studies department at MiraCosta Community College in Oceanside, California.

Our blueprint for Digital Ethnic Studies, especially in the community college context, furnishes student support services through speculative tools of knowledge and everyday ways of knowing from historically underrepresented perspectives. We build on and pivot from much of the existing DH curriculum to chart Digital Ethnic Studies approaches to teaching and learning that center our audience as knowledge producers, innovators, and leaders from the start. Our case studies, classroom and community examples, and DRSOJ initiative exemplify our commitments to uplifting and empowering our communities through critical and creative pedagogies that reimagine intersections among DH, Ethnic Studies, and education in this new era of change and possibility. We hope this knowledge sharing of the various ways we self-advocated for resources and opportunities to reimagine DH through a lens of Ethnic Studies and community college can support others in their pursuit of new visions and collaborations.

Notes

1. We will discuss how we define "everyday ways of knowing" as a methodology in our pedagogical practices in a later section.
2. Lindsay Pérez Huber et al., "Still Falling through the Cracks," 8.
3. Pérez Huber et al., 9.
4. Tara J. Yosso, *Critical Race Counterstories*, 2013.
5. Yosso, 80.
6. Yosso, 80–81.
7. Lindsay Pérez Huber et al., "Still Falling through the Cracks," 1.
8. Pérez Huber et al., 6.
9. Pérez Huber et al., 15.
10. Pérez Huber et al., 15.
11. Laura I. Rendón, Vijay Kanagala, and Ripsimé K. Bledsoe, "Shattering the Deficit Grand Narrative," 223.
12. Rendón, Kanagala, and Bledsoe, 228.
13. Rendón, Kanagala, and Bledsoe, 232.
14. Rendón, Kanagala, and Bledsoe, 229.
15. Lysa Rivera, "Future Histories and Cyborg Labor," 415.
16. This discussion included Dr. Shelley Streeby, a scholar doing cutting-edge research on speculative fiction and science fiction and who wrote *Imagining the Future of Climate Change: World-Making through Science Fiction and Activism* (2017), as well as the eminent science fiction writer Annalee Newitz who wrote the novels *Autonomous* (2017) and recently *The Future of Another Timeline* (2019).
17. Tara McPherson in *Debates in Digital Humanities*, ed. by Matthew K. Gold and Lauren F. Klein, 2012.
18. Laura I. Rendón and Susana M. Muñoz, "Revisiting Validation Theory," 28.
19. Tiffany Chung, "Story Maps," 2017.
20. Tara Yosso et al., "Critical Race Theory in Chicana/o Education," 95.
21. Recent programs that address Digital Ethnic Studies include the University of Nebraska's the "New Storytellers: The Research Institute in Digital Ethnic Studies," and at UCB's Center for Race & Gender through its Working Group in Digital Ethnic Studies.

Digital Materials

"The Alliance for Networking Visual Culture." Andrew W. Mellon Foundation. https://scalar.me/anvc/.
"The Critical Refugee Studies Collective: Critical Research, Teaching, and Public Initiatives on Refugees." Critical Refugee Studies Collective. www.criticalrefugeestudies.com.

"Front|eras." UCSD-Fronteras. https://ucsd-fronteras.itch.io/fronteras.
"Twine." Interactive Fiction Technology Foundation. https://twinery.org/.

Bibliography

Chung, Tiffany. "Story Maps." *The Critical Refugee Studies Collective.* https://criticalrefugeestudies.com/story-maps.

McPherson, Tara. "Why Are the Digital Humanities So White? Or Thinking the Histories of Race and Computation?" In *Debates in Digital Humanities*, edited by Matthew K. Gold and Lauren F. Klein. Minneapolis: University of Minnesota Press, 2012.

Pérez Huber, Lindsay, Maria C. Malagón, Brianna R. Ramirez, Lorena Camargo Gonzalez, Alberto Jimenez, and Verónica N. Vélez." Still Falling through the Cracks: Revisiting the Latina/o Education Pipeline." *UCLA Chicano Studies Research Center (CSRC) Research Report*, no. 19 (2015): 1–22.

Rendón, Laura I., and Susana M. Muñoz. "Revisiting Validation Theory: Theoretical Foundations, Applications, and Extensions." *Enrollment Management Journal* 5, no. 2 (2011): 12–33.

Rendón, Laura I., Vijay Kanagala, and Ripsimé K. Bledsoe. "Shattering the Deficit Grand Narrative: Toward a Culturally Validating Latino Student Success Framework." In *New Directions: Assessment and Preparation of Hispanic College Students*, edited by Alfredo G. de los Santos Jr., Laura I. Rendón, Gary Francisco Keller, Alberto Acereda, Estela Mara Bensimón, and Richard J. Tannenbaum, 223–39. Arizona: Bilingual Review Press, 2018.

Rivera, Lysa. "Future Histories and Cyborg Labor: Reading Borderlands Science Fiction after NAFTA." *Science-Fiction Studies* 39, no. 3 (2012): 415–36.

Yosso, Tara J. *Critical Race Counterstories along the Chicana/Chicano Educational Pipeline.* New York, NY: Routledge, 2013.

Yosso, Tara, Octavio Villalpando, Dolores Delgado Bernal, and Daniel G. Solórzano. "Critical Race Theory in Chicana/O Education." *National Association for Chicana and Chicano Studies Annual Conference Proceedings* 9 (2001): 89–104. http://scholarworks.sjsu.edu/naccs/2001/Proceedings/9.

Chapter 8

Developing Action Research Projects for Latinx Students in a Predominantly White Institution

GERARDO MANCILLA AND DONNA VUKELICH-SELVA

Introduction

The Latinx[1] population is the fastest growing group in the United States today. According to *Excelencia in Education*, in 2016, Latinx individuals made up 18 percent of the total population in the United States and 25 percent of the K-12 population.[2] Higher education institutions with "an enrollment of undergraduate full-time equivalent students that is at least 25 percent Hispanic students" can apply to the US Department of Education to be federally designated as Hispanic-Serving Institutions (HSIs).[3] Schools with the HSI designation are eligible to apply for federal grants and additional funding to serve Latinx students. *Excelencia in Education* also noted that the national college graduation rate for all students is 52 percent while the graduation rate for Latinx students is 41 percent.

In Wisconsin, *Excelencia in Education* reported that Latinx students are 7 percent of the total population and 12 percent of the K-12 population.[4] College graduation rates are similar to the national average with 43 percent for Latinx students and 55 percent for white students. Most of the Latinx population is located in Milwaukee County. At Alverno College in Milwaukee, over 10 percent of the student body was Latinx for many years, and in 2017, Alverno College became the first higher education institution to be designated as a HSI in Wisconsin and was one of fourteen such institutions in the Midwest.[5] According to data from the Hispanic Association of Colleges & University (HACU), in the year 2020–21, Wisconsin has three HSIs and six emerging HSIs.[6] The second-largest concentration of Latinxs in Wisconsin is in Dane County, where the capital city, Madison, is located. According to a report entitled *Cuéntame Más*, in 2014 Dane County's Latinx population was 6.1 percent of the total population.[7] The report further notes that in Madison, the largest school district in Dane County, Latinx students represent 20.5 percent of the population. According to the United States Census Bureau, Dane County's Hispanic or Latino population was at 6.9 percent in July 2021.[8]

Edgewood College is a small Catholic liberal arts school located in Madison, WI. It is a predominantly white institution (PWI) serving students from Dane County and other areas in Wisconsin, with a small number coming from out of state. Edgewood College's Latinx population has increased from 6.1 percent in the 2017–18 academic year to 7.3 percent in 2018–19, and 8.7 percent in 2019–20. The Latinx population had grown to 11 percent by the fall 2021 semester.[9] The total undergraduate enrollment for that academic year was 1,233 students. The four-year graduation rate for that school year was 42 percent with a six-year graduation rate of 62 percent. The six-year graduation rate is 65 percent for white students and 36 percent for Latinx students. As the Latinx population continues to increase, it is important for the institution to explore various ways to best serve its Latinx students.

Garcia and Okhidoi conducted a case study with one HSI institution, examining what it means to *serve* Latinx students.[10] Their research explored how a Chicana/o Studies Program and the Educational Opportunity Program (EOP) were important services to provide culturally relevant curricula and programs, and to institutionalize cultural programs across campus to benefit all students. Edgewood College has taken many steps along these lines to develop curricula and programs that serve Latinx students. The college has an Ethnic Studies program that gives students the opportunity to enroll in courses focusing specifically on race and ethnicity in the United States. The college also has two courses focusing on immigration for freshman and sophomore students that explore various aspects of immigration. Both courses are part of the college's COR Program, which prompts students to consider their role in building a more just, compassionate, and sustainable world. The college also has an Office of Student Inclusion and Involvement that supports student organizations and events. In 2011, the Association of Latina/o Students (AL@S) was established with the help of a Latina faculty member. The organization has now changed its name to the Latinx Student Union (LSU) and continues to work on events and programming for the college. In 2021, the college created a new position, hiring a vice president for mission, values, and inclusion (MVI). The new VP is an immigrant from Ecuador and a Latino theologian who is leading an office that will be instrumental in developing further recruitment and retention efforts for Latinx students. Garcia further questioned what it means to truly *serve* Latinx students. She stated that "in order for any institution to serve racialized students, they must transform their organizational structures, practices, culture, climate, and decision-making policies."[11] Edgewood College can qualify to be identified as an emerging HSI and we are working to reach that benchmark. We need to rethink structures and practices to make our institution more welcoming for Latinx students and to better serve our students.

This chapter explores how faculty members in the School of Education created the Leadership Institute for Borderland Research and Education (LIBRE) as an action research project to help serve Latinx students. The project included a weeklong trip to the Arizona borderlands to learn more about immigration, including immigration policies and activist responses to these policies. During the trip, the students engaged in many ways of processing the information they were acquiring, including using digital technology to support their learning. As various digital artifacts were collected, they were posted on our website educatorsandimmigration.com/libre, which was designed to disseminate LIBRE's research.

Rehumanizing Latinx Education and Theoretical Framework

Rehumanizing Latinx education is about seeing, validating, and engaging Latinx students as they learn about themselves and the issues that impact them. Qualitative research methods allow for this to be done in a respectful way, recognizing and validating the lived experience of the participants.[12] Latina/o critical theory (LatCrit) and critical race theory (CRT) emerged from critical legal studies and challenge the notion of hegemony by drawing attention to how the dominant culture perpetuates ideas and uses language to maintain power and control over other marginalized communities.[13] CRT acknowledges the historical and contemporary realities of race, racism, and white privilege.[14] CRT also challenges race-neutral, color-blind, meritocratic, and apolitical policies structures.[15] LatCrit provides a lens to explore the intersectionality of language, immigration, ethnicity, culture, identity, phenotype, and sexuality.[16] LatCrit calls for both social and legal transformation on topics impacting the Latinx population. Solórzano and Delgado Bernal explain how LatCrit and CRT can build on school resistance literature and provide a "framework that examines and explains Chicana and Chicano student resistance in an urban context."[17] The authors focus on the students' human agency, resistance, and actions in their response to the anti-Latino and anti-affirmative-action climate.

A particularly powerful aspect of LatCrit is the call for counter-stories.[18] Counter-stories recount the experiences of racism and resistance from the perspective of marginalized communities.[19] The LIBRE research project was a way for students to engage with immigration that are of particular relevance to their lives. This program design, according to Solórzano and Yosso, follows a critical race methodology, which "offers space to conduct and present research grounded in the experiences and knowledge of people of color."[20]

The project focused on action research as a way to explore the various research pathways that could be explored in the examination of different issues dealing with immigration, and also allowed the Latinx students to see themselves in the curriculum. The project gives students the chance to explore a topic that is personal and impacts their daily lives.

In addition to LatCrit, we used the theoretical concept of *testimonio* in working with the students to understand the richness and authenticity of the stories they were hearing not *only* as stories, but also as authentic and legitimate sources of a much broader knowledge. *Testimonio* emerged out of the resistance and liberation struggles in Latin and Central America and was initially a way to process traumatic events of war, violence, and dictatorship. *Testimonio* helped change the standard narrative around immigration with the nonimmigrant students (and faculty/staff) at our college. Its importance is in placing "the protagonists very explicitly at the center of the stories being told—both in terms of the specifics of the narratives but also . . . in terms of whose voice is constructed as 'expert' and worth listening to."[21] LIBRE makes the intentional connection from the *testimonios* of earlier, more explicitly violent moments to the ongoing psychic violence caused by current immigration policies and the anti-immigrant narrative promoted at the very highest levels of government.

The LIBRE project focused on closing the student participation gap at Edgewood College. The trip was important for raising awareness about what is happening at the US-Mexico border but also focused on the impact the program had on the cultural climate of the institution. The focus of the project was on immigration as something that is extremely relevant to our Latinx students. Many of our Latinx students come from families with very recent immigrant experiences and many of those families are mixed status—a number of DACA recipients have parents who are undocumented, along with younger siblings who were born in the US. The project had three goals: to support Latinx students, to impact other students at the institution, and to promote a more welcoming classroom environment by engaging other faculty and staff.

Rehumanizing Education and Immigration

The political climate leading up to the 2016 presidential elections sparked a significant surge in anti-immigrant sentiment and uncertainty for immigrant communities. During the presidential campaign, then candidate Trump pledged to rescind the Deferred Action for Childhood Arrivals (DACA) program that took effect in June 2012 and offered recipients some respite from deportation, along with access to work permits. College students who had previously received protection from deportation experienced increasing anxiety and fear. Faculty found themselves in a difficult situation trying to support DACAmented[22] and undocumented students. The Trump administration was pursuing increasingly punitive immigration policies and hope for passage of the DREAM Act or comprehensive immigration reform died with the increasingly contentious congressional politics ruling the day. There was a very real fear of deportation that caused families deep concern.[23] This fear is constant and leads to ongoing hypervigilance and mounting stress, all of which was intensified by the Trump administration's rhetoric.[24]

One aspect of rehumanizing education was to be responsive to student needs around immigration. As Ladson-Billings states, culturally relevant teachers need to "help students accept and affirm their cultural identity while developing critical perspectives that challenge inequities that school perpetuate."[25] The Latinx students at Edgewood College included citizens, undocumented, DACAmented, asylum-seeking students, and students from mix-status families. The LIBRE project centered on the topic of immigration to support Latinx students and humanize the issues of immigration throughout the larger college community.[26]

Rehumanizing Education for Latinx Students

With the theme of immigration at its core, the LIBRE project was developed to focus on Latinx students' experience and participation. Only DACAmented students were selected to participate in the 2017 LIBRE trip, as a response to the fear that, after the 2016 election, DACAmented students would no longer have the opportunity to travel to the US-Mexico border. The project faculty were intentional about increasing the participation of these DACAmented students in the project.

In addition to the physical participation, the project aimed to highlight the topic of immigration as part of a field of Latino studies,[27] which the students could then continue to explore throughout their undergraduate careers. Many students had lived experiences related to immigration and the project sought to acknowledge those experiences as academic knowledge. Pérez Huber notes the "apartheid of knowledge in academia" as she critiques the ways in which knowledge production takes place.[28] She offers an important vision of *testimonio* as both theoretical framework and methodology, and we are indebted to her work. In validating their lived experience and connecting to academic fields, Latinx students were able to connect their learning with their intended majors including politics and immigration policies, multicultural counseling, education, and human services.

Another area where Latinx participation increased was in conducting research through the Undergraduate Student Research (USR) program. The faculty worked to develop a collaboration between the LIBRE program and the USR program to develop ways to scaffold research opportunities for students. The Latinx students were exposed to research methodologies in their early years in college and were able to use that for their research projects.

Rehumanizing Education for Non-Latinx Students

Three non-Latinx students participated in LIBRE's 2019 trip. For them, rehumanizing education was about experiencing the trip, processing their experiences, and being in community with the people we met at the US-Mexico border. Some of them had experience with migration in other countries and were able to compare and contrast those experiences. One reflected on how a border wall can have so many implications in how people are treated. Another explored the similarities and differences in the systems of oppression as they apply to the criminalization of people. All students who participated in the trip had learning experiences that are hard to recreate in a classroom.

The second goal of the program was to impact the larger Edgewood College community through the interactions that program participants would have on campus. In an interview with Anthony Rebora, Beverly Daniel Tatum points out that 75 percent of white adults in the United States have entirely white social networks.[29] She further states, "In my experience as an educator, a lot of young white people don't start thinking about racial issues until they get to college, because college is often the most diverse learning environment they've been in." In a PWI, students may not be familiar with issues around immigration, immigration status, and how people are impacted by policies. The LIBRE project helps to humanize the issues of immigration for students. The LIBRE participants were able to share their experiences and serve as a reference point for students (along with faculty and staff) discussing these topics. In doing so, the concept of immigration is humanized and brought home as these students see how people in Wisconsin, including their fellow students, are deeply impacted by immigration laws and policies.

Rehumanizing Education for Faculty and Staff

Edgewood College was founded by the Dominican Sisters of Sinsinawa. In 2013, the Dominican Sisters of Sinsinawa issued a corporate stance on immigration and reform where they outlined the moral call to welcome all immigrants.[30] Edgewood College's Dominican values include justice, compassion, and community and are embedded in the first year COR seminars (including one on immigration called Rethinking the Border), where students are prompted to ask themselves, "what is my role in building a more just and compassionate world?" The COR program stresses the importance of Edgewood faculty working to create a welcoming environment for all students. With that in mind, the faculty who participated in the LIBRE trip have provided professional development, discussion, and presentations about immigration and how that impacts students at Edgewood College. The hope is that faculty and staff, and Edgewood community at large, will understand more about immigration, how immigration policies impact many in our community, and what actions the Edgewood community can undertake to create a more welcoming environment for Latinx students at the college.

Methodology

The two authors of this chapter along with other faculty[31] in the School of Education developed the LIBRE trip as an action research opportunity for undergraduate students to learn about and experience how immigration policies and practices impact people living in the US-Mexico border. Six areas of focus relating to immigration were at the heart of the trip. The focus areas included (1) the US-Mexico border wall, (2) churches and the sanctuary movement, (3) The Tohono O'odham Nation and the border patrol agents, (4) Operation Streamline and the criminalization of immigrants, (5) immigration law and policy, and (6) DACAmented college students. Students explored each of these areas through different events and meetings with people and organizations, and used various technologies to document and process what they were learning. The ultimate goal of the project was to have students create digital stories of their learning. The website https://educatorsandimmigration.com/libre was created to archive the ongoing LIBRE project.

Roopika Risam, Justin Snow, and Susan Edwards draw attention to the gap that currently exists in undergraduate education in digital humanities with undergraduate programs receiving less attention and resources.[32] They presented the digital humanities initiatives at Salem State as an example of a program that can provide undergraduate students the opportunity to learn about digital humanities through collaboration between librarians, faculty, and students. The projects were housed in Salem State's library as a way to centralize the work. Furthermore, Risam explains the importance of decolonizing digital humanities, which "requires redress of the traces of colonialism that appear in digital scholarship, which has political and epistemological implications."[33] Risam explains the need to foreground the intersection of social identities including race, gender, sexuality, nationality, and disability, and to create spaces for the production of knowledge from these communities. Nicole N. Aljoe and colleagues (2015)[34] present the Early Caribbean Digital Archive as an example of how Caribbean slave narratives or testimonies can be used to present knowledge practices of resistance. Both articles state the importance of creating a space to house the counter-stories from our communities. It's important to have these digital spaces open to the public and to be intentional in working with undergraduate students in creating artifacts for these spaces.

Establishing and Funding LIBRE

As a non-HSI institution, Edgewood College is not eligible for federal grants or funding to serve Latinx students. Therefore, the faculty members who were involved with the LIBRE project had to develop partnerships, seek funding sources, and take charge of all project logistics. This process was similar to the cross-institutional collaboration that is described in this book by Martínez and Montelongo. With the faculty advocating for LIBRE, Edgewood College offered significant financial support for this project as it gave students a clearer path towards fulfilling the call of the college's COR program. The project received financial support from a number of campus entities, and additional fundraising, spearheaded by students, took place off campus. Faculty involved in the project were from the School of Education although the project was open to all Edgewood College students. Faculty were committed to having students at the project's center and setting up a structure through which they could fully engage with the resulting action research projects.

The project began in 2014 when three faculty members from the School of Education traveled to Arizona to build partnerships and understand the larger context of immigration. The first cohort of students, five DACAmented Latinx students, traveled to Arizona in January 2017. This trip emerged as a student initiative in the hours after the 2016 presidential election as DACA students were worried that they would be unable to travel after Trump's inauguration. The second cohort of students traveled to Arizona during the 2019 spring break. This trip was open to all students and students had to apply to participate. Five of the students were Latinx (from Mexico, Colombia, Venezuela, and Honduras), two were Black/African American, and one was white, and there were a range of immigration statuses among the students.

Ethical Considerations

Two ethical questions were important to consider in doing this research project. The first question revolves around immigrant student participants.

We had DACAmented[35] students as participants for both trips and their safety was our top priority. We worked with the students to make sure their documents were up-to-date, faculty members traveled with the students, and we had several consultation meetings with lawyers prior to leaving. We also requested letters from our institution and from our legislators that would identify the students as Edgewood College students. We went to all locations as a group and we flew back together.

The second ethical question revolves around how students interacted with the digital world. Mattson calls for educators to engage students in conversations about digital citizenship and digital ethics or dilemmas.[36] She proposes five ethical theories[37] and five steps[38] to support students in discussing the technology dilemmas. As the LIBRE project made use of several tools to document the trip, faculty and students discussed the implications—as both producers and consumers of digital media. For example, we discussed which pictures were going to be posted on social media, always with the goal of highlighting the organizations and people we were working with, as well as sharing information and resources. When we were doing service projects we did not take any pictures. Instead, we shared the important work that community-based organizations were doing. As a group, we engaged in metacognitive discussions about how we were using technology and the implications that it could have.

Six Research Focus Areas

As stated earlier, we identified six focus areas for the research topics. The faculty set up various meetings with individuals and organizations to learn more about each of the focus areas. In addition, the faculty planned activities and events to experience various aspects of each theme. The website https://educatorsandimmigration.com/libre provides more historical context for each of these areas, but we will provide a quick overview here.

The first focus area was immigration and the border wall. One of the major reasons for traveling to Arizona was for students to see the border wall, a markedly different experience from merely reading about it. About 580 miles of physical barrier exist along the nearly 2,000-mile border that goes from San Diego, California, to Brownsville, Texas.[39] Seeing this border wall is vastly different, and far more palpable, than learning about it from readings or movies. Jason De León explains the concept of "prevention through deterrence," describing how the US government, beginning with several initiatives under the Clinton administration, used the wall to shift migration patterns away from populated areas, forcing immigrants to suffer the life-threatening conditions in the Sonoran desert and other natural environments.[40] During the 2017 LIBRE trip, the group traveled to the border wall that divides Nogales, Arizona, from Nogales, Sonora, in Mexico. In 2019, LIBRE visited the wall dividing Douglas, Arizona, from Agua Prieta in Sonora. Both of these locations had border walls prior to the Trump administration. Between 2017 and 2019, the Trump administration deployed military troops to the border (including National Guard troops from Wisconsin) who added layers of barbed wire to the wall, creating an even harsher boundary. Being at the wall was a moving experience for all, and led to deep reflection on the ways in which a physical barrier can have such a huge impact on two communities that were historically able to "cross" with relative ease.

The second research focus area was churches and the sanctuary movement. One possible way to protect immigrants, and educate the larger public, is through sanctuary. The LIBRE trip offered us the opportunity to explore the work that the Southside Presbyterian Church and its pastor (Reverend Alison J. Harrington, who came to Southside after sanctuary founder Reverend John Fyfe retired) had done in terms of sanctuary. Beginning in 1982, Southside Presbyterian provided aid and temporary shelter to more than thirteen thousand Central Americans fleeing war, death squads, and torture.[41]

In another focus area, students learned about the Tohono O'odham Nation and how border patrol policies have impacted their community. We had the opportunity to meet with nation member Ofelia Rivas and learn about their territory that extends south to Sonora, Mexico, north to Central Arizona, west to the Gulf of California, and east to the San Pedro River.[42] Their homeland is located in the Sonora Desert between the United States and Mexico, with family members on both side of this political border. Members have to cross the border to visit family, attend traditional tribal ceremonies, and meet with the tribal council, and are routinely stopped, and often harassed by, the border patrol.[43] Meeting with Ofelia offered us the opportunity to learn about the important intersections between immigration and indigenous rights, including how US immigration policies affect the community and how the border patrol is using technology to surveil the Tohono O'odham Nation.

The fourth research area was experiencing Operation Streamline. Operation Streamline began in 2005 as an initiative of the Departments of Homeland Security and Justice as part of the establishment of "zero-tolerance" immigration enforcement zones along the US-Mexico border. According to No More Deaths, an activist group in Arizona, Operation Streamline costs $120 million annually in court proceedings, as well as more than $50 million in detention and incarceration costs.[44] Migrants who attempt to cross for the first time and are caught face prosecution for illegal entry (a misdemeanor) while those caught re-entering (illegal re-entry) face felony charges. The time-served sentence can vary between thirty and one hundred eighty days but may range up to twenty years with a criminal record. Up to seventy migrants, all shackled at the wrists, waist, and ankles are processed during a painfully fast court hearing that generally lasts between just sixty and ninety minutes. Witnessing Operation Streamline was one of the hardest things we did during the trip. It is a truly gut-wrenching experience and we worked to prepare the students before that experience by talking to local activists who explained both the process and their ongoing witness to that process. We also took time to reflect after leaving the courthouse, as everyone needed some time to absorb what we had just witnessed.

The fifth focus area was immigration law and policy. This was an ongoing research area as we met with various individuals and groups, including attorney Ray Ybarra Maldonado and Dr. Angeles Maldonado. Edgewood faculty developed a partnership with them during the 2014 trip, and shortly after that, attorney Ybarra Maldonado and Dr. Maldonado completed a residency at Edgewood College, examining current immigration laws and policies and how they were affecting people in Arizona. During our 2019 LIBRE trip, our group was able to visit and volunteer in two shelters working primarily with immigrants seeking asylum. When immigrants are seeking asylum, they must turn themselves in to border patrol agents to petition for asylum. They must then provide proof that they are being persecuted or have a well-founded fear of persecution based on race, religion, nationality, and membership in a particular social group and/or political opinion.[45] After that, these people must travel to where their US sponsor is located. Casa Alitas is a shelter where asylum seekers are sent after they are released by Immigration and Customs Enforcement (ICE)—all came with pending court dates, and a few had electronic ankle bracelets. Scores of volunteers support the migrants with medical attention, clothing needs, food, and transportation. The second shelter was Casa Mariposas, a shelter providing housing and support for LGBT immigrants who were released from prison and detention centers and who needed housing as they waited for their final hearings with ICE.

The last focus area was DACAmented college students. Participation in the 2017 LIBRE trip was limited to DACAmented students. As nobody knew if new travel restrictions would be put in place, or what the Trump administration would mean for the DACA program, the decision was made to offer the trip only to DACAmented students. In Arizona, we met with members of the Undocumented Students for Education Equity (USEE) and learned about the in-state tuition policies in Arizona. The resulting exchanges of information and history of state policies regarding in-state tuition were illuminating for both groups of students. In Wisconsin, AB 75 was approved in 2009 to extend in-state tuition to eligible undocumented students, but that was rescinded in 2011 with the passage of AB 40.[46] Similarly, Arizona had passed Proposition 300 in 2006 to prohibit public institutions from providing undocumented students with in-state tuition rates.[47] The students from USEE were fighting for in-state tuition for DACA students. This case went all the way to the Arizona Supreme Court, which ultimately denied in-state tuition for DACA students. The network between our DACA students and the DACA students from Arizona continued after the trip and several students began working at a national level with United We Dream, which works to provide a voice for undocumented students, develop leadership skills, and build organizing skills.

Research Technology Tools and Pedagogical Implications

The faculty developed an action research framework for the LIBRE trip as a way to explore immigration in the US-Mexico border. Action research projects are designed to explore an area of focus, reflect, and then act based on the findings.[48] The goal of the project was for students to deepen their understanding of the six focus areas through speaking with individuals and experiencing events during the trip, with the faculty always ensuring that students were processing what they were learning and experiencing. The group had debriefing meetings in the evening after they had learning activities through the day. Lastly, the group worked on various ways to share what they were learning and experiencing. The goal was to have the students' learning shared with others to help humanize immigration for other students and communities.

Digital Storytelling

One way to share the many facets of immigration that the students experienced is through digital storytelling. Digital storytelling helps students develop writing and digital skills, collaborate with peers, and publish their own stories.[49] LIBRE aimed to use digital storytelling as a way to have students tell their own story about their experiences by examining the intersection of immigration and immigration policies with various stakeholders. Using the manual from the American Friends Service Committee (AFSC), which focuses on immigrants and refugees,[50] we discussed the concept of digital storytelling prior to the trip. The Immigrant History Research Center (IHRC) at the University of Minnesota also provided many resources for creating digital storytelling with immigrants.[51] The goal of LIBRE was to create digital stories and *testimonios* and to create a website to share them with others.

To prepare the students to document their experience, we used several digital tools and strategies that can be digitized to help the students tell their stories. In terms of pedagogical implications, each strategy had two purposes: (1) a self-learning, self-processing, self-expression aspect and (2) implications for sharing with others thus impacting the learning of others around them. There were four research strategies that related to increasing the students' participation in digital citizenship including digital photography, social media, art creation, and digital resources. We selected a few artifacts to demonstrate how each of these was used. The LIBRE website will have more information and more examples from the project.

Digital Photography

Digital photographs are becoming more and more common as cell phones continue to develop more sophisticated cameras. Throughout the trips, LIBRE participants were taking photos of people, places, and symbols that related to what they were learning. One of the places where the photographs had the most impact was at the US-Mexico border wall. Marisol Clark-Ibáñez has documented how to use photo elicitation as a way to capture resilience, struggles, and activism.[52] Seeing the border wall, experiencing it, and touching the wall was one of the main motivations for the trip. Students took photographs and reflected on their meaning in how they understood themselves. For example, Lupe Salmeron took the picture below (figure 8.1).

Figure 8.1. Walking by the border wall. Courtesy of Lupe Salmeron.

> Walking along the border that has kept me from my family, culture, & dreams.
>
> —Lupe Salmeron

During the 2017 trip, the students were surprised when we arrived at the border wall separating Nogales, Arizona, and Nogales, Sonora. We were witnesses to two worlds isolated from each other by the wall. Looking through to the other side, students could see a school playground where an intense game of soccer was underway; vendors were on several streets—life going on as we watched through the wall. In addition to having the students process what it meant for them, the photographs also provided them with an opportunity to share their thinking with others. In the next example (figure 8.2), we see Zenab Nafid's photo of some clothing near the border wall along with her reflection on it.

Figure 8.2. Border wall. Courtesy of Zenab Nafid.

On March 21st, 2019, on a fairly warm and cloudy day, a small group visited a small partition between two areas of land. The fairly short, but incredibly long fence that separates the two drastically different areas of land seemed a lot shorter in person than it had sounded throughout the conversation of politics. Upon exiting the air-conditioned van and stepping into the sunlight, the colors seemed to pop on the other side of the fence, while it drained from the faces of my classmates. As I slowly walked up to the fence, carefully avoiding the barbed wire lined in spirals against its side, I felt an underwhelming sense of reality. My entire existence had imagined the barrier that separated lives, families, and tore hearts apart as something much more insidious than what it actually was. I noticed a graveyard not too far from the wall, and to my left a dirty pair of jeans, seemed to fit a child. Finally, I realized that it wasn't the wall itself that I found so insidious, but rather what it symbolized. It symbolized a "them versus us" narrative that divided my country. A 20 ft., low quality wall with so much power to its name. However, I understood that after seeing it was much more tangible and I felt a slightly greater sense of hope. Realizing that human beings put that wall there, and that it was much less insidious in person, gave me hope that it could be removed just as quickly as it was put there. It has only the power we gave to it (Zenab Nafid).

Zenab shared this reflection and picture with others as a way to understand further the complexity of the US-Mexico border wall. It should be noted that barbed wire was added to the wall between our 2017 trip and our 2019 trip, which changed how the students experienced the border wall. As students shared their photographs, one comment on one of their posts was from someone who said they had no idea that the border wall was already there (prior to Trump being elected). This allowed the student to provide further information on the border wall and background information for it. A photo blog that captures the border wall at various locations titled "The Border Wall that Already Exists" can be found at https://theweek.com/captured/683638/border-wall-that-already-exists.

Social Media

As noted, Edgewood College and its Undergraduate Student Research program provided funding for the 2019 trip. As we prepared for the trip, we were asked to use social media to post what we were doing as a way to share with the larger Edgewood College community. The goal was to publicize our experiences and connect those to Edgewood College's social media networks. We used the hashtag #LIBRE2019 on Facebook, Instagram, and Twitter to document our activities and the people we were meeting. Like the photographs, social media allowed students to share their thinking and processing. For example, Mindy Navarro posted the following poem after witnessing Operation Streamline. The poetry was one way of processing what we were witnessing. Social media allowed her to share her thinking and to share about this cruel process.

Operation Streamline

3/20 Day 5
I'm sitting in the back of
the William D. Browning
Special Proceedings
Courtroom to watch
hearings.
It's 1:30pm. It starts.
People who look like me
start to walk in the room
with chains in their hands
& feet.
I hear them.
My heart hurts.
The judge starts the
Stream Line process.
I hear the sentences.
My heart hurts more.
Mexicans, Guatemalans,
Hondurans, &
Ecuadorians.
4 women & the rest are
Men (teens and adults)
About 80 people got their
sentence today in Tucson,
Arizona.
Minimum of 30 days.
Maximum of 180 days.
The sentences are done.
The judge walks up to us
& says
"This is your government
In action."
My heart drops.
#Libre2019
Similarly, Vivi Velasquez shared her feelings.

Perspective

In the eye of the US
I know English
I have two legs
I have two arms
I am knowledgeable
Yet because I wasn't born here. I am not American
I am alone.
People don't deserve being in chains. No somos animales.
Dogs and cats are roaming freely
Kids are playing, in reach of this border that separates many families from achieving the
American Dream

Students posted about new information they were learning, cited books and other resources, and unpacked many aspects of immigration. Students also used social media to connect with other students and other organizations. For example, we met with Aliento (alientoaz.org), a non-profit advocacy organization led by DACA recipients to support individuals' well-being, emotional healing, and leadership development. It provides important information and updates for the immigrant community in Phoenix and throughout Arizona. When we met with them, we took a picture together that they posted on their social media, which we later reposted to our social media. In doing so, the students shared their experiences and created further networks of support and information. The students who participated in LIBRE used social media to expand their networks and collaborate with other students advocating for immigrants.

Art and Creations

As we were discussing heavy topics about immigration on a daily basis, it was important for the group to find a counterweight to some of that as we debriefed. Many of the participants had their own lived experiences with immigration. The topics, places, and activities were emotionally triggering as students thought about what their families had been through. Knowing

202 | Gerardo Mancilla and Donna Vukelich-Selva

the importance of attending to the students' social-emotional well-being, we decided to focus on art as it has often been used to heal and to express emotions. We also wanted to acknowledge the art movements that were part of the locations we were visiting. We explored local murals in Phoenix. The website https://www.phoenixmurals.com/phoenix-mural-map lists where the murals are located and has information about the muralists. Many of the murals we saw addressed historical events, celebrated culture, and delivered powerful messages. As our students were learning more about the realities of immigration, they were also learning about themselves and their identity. We decided to have an art night as a way to process our learning. That night, Jahdai Guerrero painted the following poster (figure 8.3).

Jahdai used the art creation as a way to reflect on who she is and what that means in our current times. The second pedagogical aspect of the art creation is sharing it with others. For example, Stephanie Florencio painted the following drawing (figure 8.4).

We had discussed the deportation process with various individuals, witnessed Operation Streamline, and experienced the border wall. The posters allowed the students to document what they were thinking and feeling. They also allowed them to share with others and to advocate for change. Our goal was to digitize these art creations to share with the larger Edgewood College community.

Figure 8.3. An immigrant made this. Courtesy of Jahdai Guerrero.

Figure 8.4. Families belong together poster. Courtesy of Stephanie Florencio.

Digital Resources

Another way that the LIBRE participants were impacted was by gaining digital resources that they continued to use and to continue to impact others. As mentioned before, attorney Ray Ybarra Maldonado and Dr. Angeles Maldonado have been integral parts of LIBRE since 2014. They are strong advocates and activists for the immigrant community in Arizona and beyond. They have worked to support individuals through Maricopa County Sheriff Joe Arpaio's raids in Arizona from 2008 to 2015. Their team produces video updates on immigration issues that are shared through their Facebook channel https://www.facebook.com/abogadoray. The LIBRE participants continue to watch these videos to stay up-to-date on issues about immigration, including changes in DACA policy, and they have also shared those videos with their own networks. Another example of how students were growing in their own knowledge through the many resources that they brought back includes a binder titled "What if I'm picked up by I.C.E.?" (figure.8.5).

The binder was developed by the Florence Immigrant & Refugee Rights Project (FIRRP).[53] It's available in English and Spanish and includes resources that families and community-based organizations can use to help families impacted by ICE raids. The binder includes a template of letters, information on creating a safety family plan, and how to prepare in case

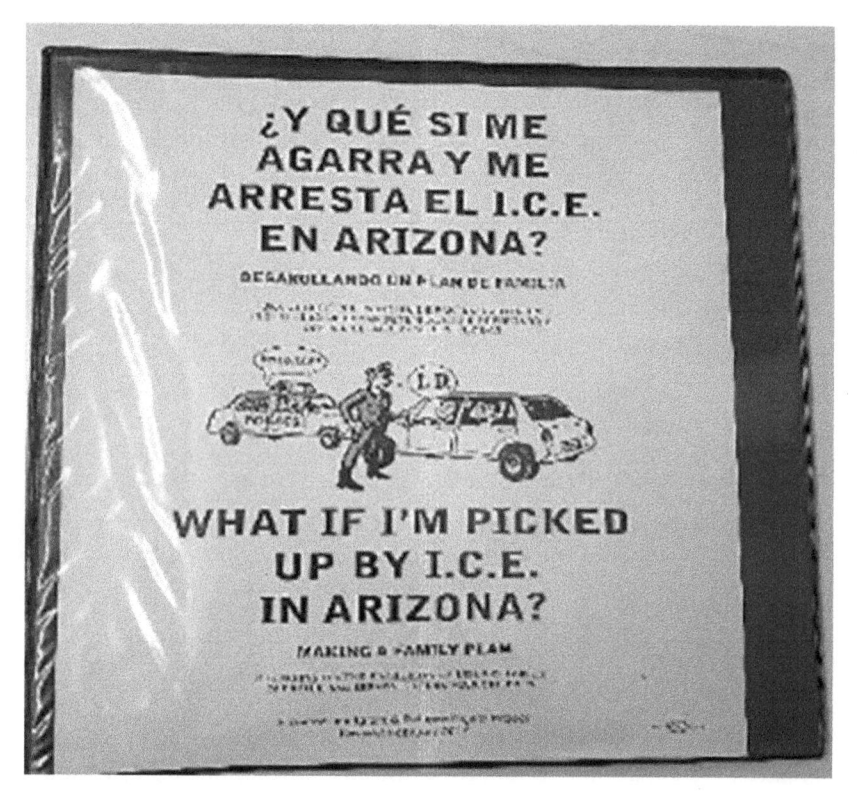

Figure 8.5. What if I'm picked up by I.C.E.? binder. Courtesy of the author.

there is an ICE raid. Although we received a physical copy of this binder, an electronic version can be found at https://firrp.org/resources/prose/parental-rights/. One of the LIBRE participants was working with a community-based organization so she presented the binder as a model of something that we could develop in our community. The digital resources that were shared helped the students learn more about various aspects of immigration. In addition, they provided resources that the students continued to use after our trip and impacted our larger community.

The four research tools that were used with the LIBRE participants served two purposes (1) they offered a self-learning, self-processing, and self-expression aspect and (2) provided paths for sharing with others and thus impacting the knowledge of those around them. Pedagogically, it was important for the students to engage in learning about the research areas, to process that learning, and to share their stories with others.

Results and Implications

LIBRE has established an important presence at Edgewood College and will continue to be a needed resource on immigration in the coming years. Digital storytelling became a useful tool to empower the LIBRE participants and to collect stories of immigration. The digital tools used as part of the action research project provided many additional ways to capture the impact on students as well as providing them with ways to share those experiences. The faculty members created the LIBRE website as an educational resource and a place to house digital projects emerging from the LIBRE experiences. The website serves as a resource for the Edgewood community and can be incorporated into course curricula, including the first-year immigration seminar. We plan to continue compiling *testimonios* in a digital archive that will serve as an ongoing, accessible resource for many within our community who may not be able to travel to the border but hope to learn about it. Part of this archive will also include digital stories and *testimonios* of students from the upcoming phase of LIBRE where we will focus on our local community and gather stories from immigrant students and their families, along with the stories of activists and others working for immigrant rights. The archive is envisioned as a living developing resource that will strengthen our work in the Edgewood community and beyond.

Sharing Their Stories

The LIBRE trips made a huge impact on each of us. Students returned energized to be change agents and to share their experiences, serving as guest speakers for undergraduate- and graduate-level classes and speaking to faculty and staff. They shared their stories, their experiences at the border, and how those connect to their lives as Edgewood College students. Some of the students were invited to area schools to talk about immigration. Others developed college-wide student-led discussions on immigration and the border. For some of the students, the trip solidified their passion for helping others and motivated them to pursue both volunteer opportunities and academic pathways related to immigration. Many of them are leading student organizations and volunteer programs that are supporting immigrant communities. One past participant is now a social worker working with the county's Immigration Affairs office and is a recognized activist in the community. Two others work with a non-profit organization that has been advocating for Latinx and immigrant rights in the Madison community for nearly thirty years. The trip has been tremendously valuable for both the students and the faculty involved.

The students who participated in the LIBRE research project have continued to conduct research in the focus areas and some were able to formally present their research at conferences. Upon their return, the 2019 participants presented at the Wisconsin Association of Independent College and Universities (WAICU) Student Diversity Conference and the 2019 Edgewood Engaged annual research conference. In addition, two of the students presented further research on the asylum-seeking process at the United States Hispanic Leadership Institute (USHLI) Conference.

Impacting the Edgewood College Community

The LIBRE trips have continued to impact the Edgewood community in rehumanizing the Latinx educational experience as well as rehumanizing immigration. The trips had a significant impact on the students who participated in the program. All five of the students who participated in the 2017 cohort have graduated. One student transferred from Edgewood College and graduated from another institution with a major in international political economy. As mentioned earlier, another participant is working as a social worker in the county's Immigration Affairs office. Two participants are working with a Latinx community-based organization supporting educational programs. The last participant is working supporting adults as a skills development specialist. The 2019 cohort had eight participants. Two participants have transferred to other four-year institutions and are finishing their educational programs. At Edgewood, we have two participants who will complete their bachelors' this year, one in elementary education and the other in political science. The remaining four participants have all graduated. One is an elementary education teacher, one is a site coordinator for the Boys and Girls Club, and the other two are applying for graduate programs in occupational therapy and in law school. They all continue to work with and support the immigrant community and pursued majors that allow them to support the immigrant community in their new professional lives. The trip helped center the issue of immigration in conversations at Edgewood and provided models on how to continue supporting the immigrant community. One of the students stated, "With the knowledge and insight from the many groups that we saw during the LIBRE trip, I was able to develop ways to form bonds and relationships in Madison and/or Edgewood to make people feel welcome and safe." Another student commented,

> LIBRE was what gave me a notion of what I truly wanted to do for my future. It gave me a sense of advocacy and passion for immigration and it also gave me the confidence to address the current issues within our social justice system. On a short-term basis, it allowed me to become more confident in myself and allowed me to figure out my passion in life. It also allowed me to embrace my identity in a different and stronger way while also showing me a different reality of the U.S. immigration system which is not released in the news.

The students' experiences and learning continue to impact the entire Edgewood community.

LIBRE also impacted non-Latinx students. One of the participants reflected, "I think about all of the beauty we saw along with the absolutely heartbreaking things we witnessed there. It gave me an entirely new perspective on life and my white privilege. On the trip, I received real time feedback on how to be a better ally to those who need me, and I am still using those tips to this day." The experiences of the LIBRE participants continue to impact others around them, in the classroom and around Edgewood College. The students hosted discussion workshops, educational presentations, and events for their peers. For example, one of the participants developed an "immigration simulation," which unpacked many myths about immigration and provided facts about immigrants. Many took on leadership roles across campus and used what they learned to inform events and ongoing conversations. Some have served as teaching assistants in courses focusing on immigration, while others work as resident assistants in student housing where they are able to plan informational events for their residents. Many expressed to the faculty that they felt more confident sharing facts about immigration and bringing up the topic in many of their class discussions. By sharing their experiences, the LIBRE participants also helped to humanize immigration for other students.

The faculty involved with LIBRE also continued to center the Latinx student experience and immigration through professional development. They presented information about the LIBRE trip as well as offering models of how to support undocumented and DACAmented students at the institution. They encouraged their peers to continue learning about immigration and to be aware of how things that are happening at the local, state, and national level may impact students. In 2022, the college offered three sections of the COR 1 class on Rethinking the Border. Both of the faculty involved with LIBRE are teaching a section of this course. In addition, they are proposing to co-teach a COR 2 class which will focus on bridging borders. The faculty are hoping to institutionalize the LIBRE learning experiences through the second course, which will include a trip to the US-Mexico border or travel to Mexico. They wanted to have another cohort of students during the spring 2022 semester but were supporting another learning opportunity trip for DACA students with Advance Parole.[54] In addition, the office of mission, values, and inclusion is planning a service-learning trip to the US-Mexico border in the near future.

Unfortunately, in September of 2018, ICE raids in Wisconsin resulted in the arrest of eighty-three immigrants, sparking much fear and uncertainty in the immigrant community. One of the 2017 LIBRE participants became one of the key community organizers providing support to the Latinx community on how to stay safe. As the college students returned to their classrooms after the ICE raids, which occurred over a weekend, it was important for faculty members to validate the fear and pain that Latinx students, as well as other communities, were feeling. One professor handled the situation by simply acknowledging the events at the beginning of class. She stated that she understood some students may have been impacted by the events and although she did not know much about immigration, she was available to help or to reach out to others who could provide assistance. In this way, that professor validated the immigration situation that had just occurred and rehumanized education for all students. Our goal is that by having more conversations about immigration with the faculty, we can continue to discuss best practices to support Latinx students at a predominantly white institution.

Conclusion

The Leadership Institute for Borderland Research and Education (LIBRE) program established at Edgewood College helped students explored the intersections of immigration, immigration policies, and the people affected by these policies in the Arizona borderlands. Students explored six major educational themes including (1) the US-Mexico border wall, (2) churches and the sanctuary movement, (3) Tohono O'odham Nation and conflicts with border patrol agents, (4) Operation Streamline and the criminalization of immigrants, (5) immigration law and policy, and (6) DACAmented college students. We used an action research framework to have the participants further explore these areas. The concept of digital storytelling guided the way the students captured their research, reflected on their experiences, and shared their knowledge. The digital tools included digital photographs, social media, art creation, and digital resources. The trip was a transformational experience for both students and faculty. After returning from the trip, the students were energized to create change in our community and to become active participants in issues around immigration in our city and state.

Future Possibilities

Our goal is to institutionalize the LIBRE trip at our college so that it can serve as an ongoing resource to more students. Both students and faculty have asked for a 2.0 version of the trip to be able to further explore the many issues around immigration. A possible 2.0 version of the trip could focus on doing similar projects with our local community, or travel to another location, making use of similar research strategies.

More and more students are interested in this kind of experience. We are currently exploring how to make this kind of learning experience available to a larger number of students. One possibility would be to embed it as a course where students would work the entire semester on learning more about immigration. The students would travel at some point during the semester and then return to create the digital stories as their final class projects.

A second possibility is to work with other educators, in both higher education and K-12 settings. There is significant interest from other faculty and staff at our college who hope to be involved with LIBRE. The focus on immigration, building relationships with students, and knowing what is happening is something many have mentioned that they hope to include in their curriculum. Given Edgewood's focus on teacher and administrator preparation, the topic is very relevant. Other educators in the K-12 educational settings have also asked if they can participate, as they want to engage with and know more about supporting immigrant students and their families. Lastly, we have engaged with students at other institutions of higher education who would also like to develop something similar for them at their respective institutions. As the students present about their experiences to other non-HSI institutions, we often hear what a great learning opportunity LIBRE offers. The opportunity to collaborate and develop partnership with other institutions is another possible way that this kind of learning could take place. Through active and ongoing collaboration with other institutions, this way of learning can help humanize Latinx education for multiple institutions and develop further networking opportunities.

Notes

1. Latinx (latin-ex) is a gender-neutral pronoun that is inclusive of all people of Latin America descent. It is an alternative to Latina or Latino. It addressed the intersections of gender, race, and class (Scharrón-Del Río and Aja, 2015). M. Scharrón del Rio and A. Aja (2015, December 5). The Case for Latinx: Why Intersectionality Is not a Choice. [Web log]. Retrieved from http://www.latinorebels.com/2015/12/05/the-case-for-latinx-why-intersectionality-is-not-a-choice/; Alternatively, people use the term Latine as another gender neutral term employing the *e* from the Spanish language (for example, *estudiante*). Vanesha McGee, "Latino, Latinx, Hispanic, or Latine? Which Term Should You Use?" Accessed August 11, 2022. https://www.bestcolleges.com/blog/hispanic-latino-latinx-latine/.

2. Excelencia in Education, "Degree Attainment for Latino Students (2015–16), United States," accessed May 28, 2020.

3. U.S. Department of Education, "Hispanic-Serving Institutions (HSIs)," last modified nd, https://sites.ed.gov/hispanic-initiative/hispanic-serving-institutions-hsis/.

4. Excelencia in Education, "Latino College Completion—Wisconsin," accessed May 28, 2020, https://www.edexcelencia.org/research/latino-college-completion/wisconsin.

5. Alverno College, "Alverno College First in Wisconsin to Be Named Hispanic-Serving Institution," last modified November 9, accessed December 2017, https://www.alverno.edu/newsroom/press-releases/hispanic-serving-institution.php.

6. Hispanic Association of Colleges and Universities, "HACU 2020–2021 Hispanic-Serving Institutions and Emerging HSIs: State Breakdown," accessed August 11, 2022, https://www.hacu.net/images/hacu/ResearchMenu/2022_HSIbyStateList.pdf.

7. J. Revel Sims, *Cuéntame Más: A Report on the Current State of Latinxs in Dane County, Wisconsin* (Madison, WI: Latino Consortium for Action, 2016). This report was a follow up to the *Cuéntame* report that the county had released in 2006.

8. United States Census Bureau, "Dane County, Wisconsin," accessed August 11, 2022, https://www.census.gov/quickfacts/fact/table/danecountywisconsin,US/PST045221.

Developing Action Research Projects for Latinx Students | 211

9. College Navigator, "National Center for Education Statistics: Edgewood College Fall 2021," https://nces.ed.gov/collegenavigator/?q=Edgewood+College&s=WI&id=238661#general.

10. Gina A. Garcia and Otgonjargal Okhidoi, "Culturally Relevant Practices," 345–57.

11. Gina A. Garcia, "Complicating a Latina/o-Serving," 120. It's useful to consider how a new and more complex understanding of race and identity can benefit all in the college community, including all students, faculty, and staff. How does being an HSI impact the college's identity and campus culture as a whole?

12. Django Paris and Maisha T. Winn, *Humanizing Research*, 2014. Too often student experience is marginalized and seen as not *academic* (and therefore, not legitimate). Centering those experiences leads to deeper and more complex knowledge.

13. Antonio Gramsci, *Selections from the Prison Notebooks*, ed. and trans. Quintin Hoare and Geoffrey Nowell Smith (New York, NY: International Publishers Co, 1971).

14. Tara J. Yosso, *Critical Race Counterstories*, 2006.

15. Gloria Ladson-Billings and William F. Tate, "Toward a Critical Race Theory of Education," 47–68.

16. Dolores Delgado Bernal, "Critical Race Theory, Latino Critical Theory, and Critical Raced-Gendered Epistemologies," 105–26; Tara J. Yosso, *Critical Race Counterstories*, 2006.

17. Daniel G. Solórzano and Dolores Delgado Bernal, "Examining Transformational Resistance through a Critical Race and LatCrit Theory Framework," 310. CRT and LatCrit have five important themes including "1. The centrality of race and racism and intersectionality with other forms of subordination. 2. The challenge to dominant ideology. 3. The commitment to social justice. 4. The centrality of experiential knowledge. 5. The interdisciplinary perspective." (312–14).

18. Gerardo Mancilla, "Latinx Youth Counterstories in a Court Diversion Program," 5.

19. Richard Delgado, "Storytelling for Oppositionists and Others," 2411–41.

20. Daniel G. Solórzano and Tara J. Yosso, "Critical Race Methodology," 23.

21. Donna Vukelich-Selva, *Immigrant Children Negotiate School*, 2014.

22. We use the term *DACAmented* for individuals who have DACA. Alternatively, people use DACA recipients or DACA beneficiaries.

23. Julián Jefferies, "Fear of Deportation in High School," 278–95.

24. María Pabón López and Gerardo R. López, *Persistent Inequality*, 2009.

25. Gloria Ladson-Billings, "Toward a Theory of Culturally Relevant Pedagogy," 469.

26. We are also aware that many immigrants at Edgewood College and in the larger community are not Latinx, and therefore humanizing the issue is really important for all in the community.

27. At Edgewood College, these programs have been part of Ethnic Studies. The particular name may vary across institutions.

28. Lindsay Pérez Huber, "Disrupting Apartheid of Knowledge," 639–54.

29. Anthony Rebora, "Widening the Lens," 32.

30. "Corporate Stance on Just Immigration Reform Stance," https://www.sinsinawa.org/peace-justice/sinsinawa-corp-stances.html. Many Dominican sisters have spoken up in support of immigrant families and comprehensive immigration reform. Their support and advocacy is an important institutional underpinning.

31. Donna Vukelich-Selva participated in the 2014 trip to help establish the partnership in Arizona. Gerardo Mancilla, joined Edgewood College in 2016, and started working on this initiative. Throughout the years, there were several other faculty members who were involved in the project.

32. Roopika Risam, Justin Snow, and Susan Edwards, "Building an Ethical Digital Humanities Community," 337–49.

33. Roopika Risam. "Decolonizing the Digital Humanities in Theory and Practice," 80.

34. Nicole N. Aljoe, Elizabeth Maddock Dillon, Benjamin J. Doyle, and Elizabeth Hopwood, "Obeah and the Early Caribbean Digital Archive," 258–66.

35. DACAmented students had their Wisconsin identification and their Edgewood College identification.

36. Kristen Mattson, *Ethics in a Digital World*, 2021.

37. The five ethical theories are (1) virtue ethics, which focus on an individual's character rather than a focus on society's rules, (2) nature law ethics, which focus on human nature towards being good, (3) social contract ethics, which focus on the social contract with society, (4) utilitarian ethics, which focus on results and consequences, and (5) deontological ethics, which focus on the motives of one's actions.

38. The five steps include (1) recognizing an ethical issue, (2) getting the facts, (3) exploring various options, (4) making a decision and testing it, and (5) reflecting on the outcomes.

39. Bianca Silva, "The Border Wall that Already Exists," last modified n.d., accessed January 2019, https://theweek.com/captured/683638/border-wall-that-already-exists.

40. Jason De León, *The Land of Open Graves*, 2015.

41. Southside Presbyterian, "The Sanctuary Movement," last modified n.d., accessed January 2017, http://www.southsidepresbyterian.org/the-sanctuary-movement.html. Madison was an integral part of the sanctuary movement in the 1980s, important history for our students to understand. In the initial trip to the borderlands in August of 2014, we met with Sanctuary founder, Reverend John Fyfe. In later trips, Reverend Alison Harrington met with our groups.

42. Jennifer Mendoza, "The Border Crossed Us," last modified May 15, accessed September 1, 2019, https://medium.com/race-law-a-critical-analysis/the-border-crossed-us-the-tohono-oodham-s-nation-divide-32c9260f1458. Students were able to begin to absorb the constructed reality of "borders" and how they have erased cultural identities in the interest of political boundaries.

43. Mendoza, 2019.
44. No More Deaths, *Fact Sheet*, 2012.
45. ARRC, "Community Navigator Training," 2017. This is an extremely difficult and drawn-out process, and there is no guarantee that any sort of status will be granted.
46. Higher Ed Immigration Portal, "Wisconsin," accessed August 11, 2022, https://www.higheredimmigrationportal.org/state/wisconsin/. Wisconsin previously offered in-state tuition at the University of Wisconsin (all campuses) to all residents, regardless of immigration status and all residents were able to obtain a driver's license. That changed when Scott Walker was elected as governor in the fall of 2010. Groups across the state continue to advocate for a return to those policies.
47. Higher Ed Immigration Portal, "Arizona," accessed August 11, 2022, https://www.higheredimmigrationportal.org/state/arizona/.
48. Ernest T. Stringer, *Action Research in Education*, 2008.
49. Wayne E. Wright, *Foundations for Teaching English Language Learners*, 2010.
50. AFSC, "How-to Manual for Digital Storytelling with Immigrants and Refugees!!" https://www.afsc.org/resource/how-manual-digital-storytelling-immigrants-and-refugees.
51. IHRC, "University of Minnesota Immigration History Research Center," https://cla.umn.edu/ihrc/immigrant-stories.
52. Marisol Clark-Ibáñez, *Undocumented Latino Youth*, 2015.
53. FIRRP, *What if I'm Picked Up by I.C.E. in Arizona?*, 2017.
54. The faculty, a LIBRE participant, and the director for Center for DREAMers started the Mexico International Study Opportunity for Learning (MISOL) program to provide a study abroad opportunity for DACA beneficiaries through the Advance Parole program. DACA beneficiaries can apply for advance parole for educational purposes. The participants will attend an educational program in partnership with the Universidad Nacional Autónoma de México (UNAM). https://dreamers.law.wisc.edu/misol/.

Digital Materials

AFSC Area Office of the Carolinas. "Storyology: Films." YouTube videos. https://www.youtube.com/user/afscnc/featured.
"Community Navigator Training and Resources." National Partnership for New Americans. https://partnershipfornewamericans.org/community-navigator-training-and-resources/.
"Hate Groups Map." Southern Poverty Law Center. https://www.splcenter.org/hate-map.
Higher Ed Immigration Portal. Presidents' Alliance on Higher Education and Immigration. 2021. https://www.higheredimmigrationportal.org/.

Immigrant Stories. Immigration History Research Center, University of Minnesota, Minneapolis, MN. 2013. https://cla.umn.edu/ihrc/immigrant-stories.

Khamala, Lori F., and Kali Ferguson. *Storyology: Digital Storytelling by Immigrants and Refugees*. American Friends Service Committee. October 2010. Digital Manual, https://www.afsc.org/sites/default/files/documents/STORYOLOGY%20HOW%20TO%20MANUAL%203.pdf.

Leadership Institute for Borderland Research and Education (LIBRE). Edgewood College, WI. https://educatorsandimmigration.com/libre/.

Phoenix Mural Project. Fractured Atlas. 2023. https://www.phoenixmurals.com/phoenix-mural-map.

Tohono O'odham Nation. "Tohono O'odham Nation Opposes a 'border wall.'" YouTube. February 19, 2017. Video, 6:22. https://www.youtube.com/watch?v=QChXZVXVLKo.

"United We Dream." United We Dream Network. 2018. https://unitedwedream.org/about/.

"What if I'm Picked up by ICE in Arizona?: Making a Family Plan." Florence Immigrant & Refugee Rights Project. 2017. https://firrp.org/resources/prose/parentalrights/.

Ybarra Maldonado Law Group (@abogadoray). "Ybarra Maldonado Law Group." Facebook, August 20, 2012. https://www.facebook.com/abogadoray.

Bibliography

AFSC. "How-to Manual for Digital Storytelling with Immigrants and Refugees!!" https://www.afsc.org/resource/how-manual-digital-storytelling-immigrants-and-refugees.

Aljoe, Nicole N., Elizabeth Maddock Dillon, Benjamin J. Doyle, and Elizabeth Hopwood. "Obeah and the Early Caribbean Digital Archive." *Atlantic Studies* 12, no. 2 (2015): 258–66.

Alverno College. "Alverno College First in Wisconsin to be Named Hispanic-Serving Institution." Accessed December 2017. https://www.alverno.edu/newsroom/press-releases/hispanic-serving-institution.php.

ARRC. "Community Navigator Training: Immigration 101." 2017.

Clark-Ibáñez, Marisol. *Undocumented Latino Youth: Navigating Their Worlds*. Boulder, CO: Lynne Rienner Publishers, 2015.

College Navigator. "National Center for Education Statistics: Edgewood College 2018–19." https://nces.ed.gov/collegenavigator/?q=Edgewood+College&s=WI&id=238561.

De León, Jason. *The Land of Open Graves: Living and Dying on the Migrant Trail*. Vol. 36, Oakland: University of California Press, 2015.

Delgado Bernal, Dolores. "Critical Race Theory, Latino Critical Theory, and Critical Raced-Gendered Epistemologies: Recognizing Students of Color as Holders and Creators of Knowledge." *Qualitative Inquiry* 8, no. 1 (2002): 105–26.

Delgado, Richard. "Storytelling for Oppositionists and Others: A Plea for Narrative." *Michigan Law Review* 87, no. 8 (1989): 2411–41.

Dominican Sisters of Sinsinawa. "Corporate Stance on Just Immigration Reform Stance." https://www.sinsinawa.org/peace-justice/corporate-stances/.

Excelencia in Education. "Degree Attainment for Latino Students (2015–16), United States." Accessed May 28, 2020.

Excelencia in Education. "Latino College Completion—Wisconsin." Accessed May 28, 2020. https://www.edexcelencia.org/research/latino-college-completion/wisconsin.

FIRRP. *What if I'm Picked Up by I.C.E. in Arizona?* Tucson, AZ: Gloo Factory, 2017.

Garcia, Gina A. "Complicating a Latina/O-Serving Identity at a Hispanic Serving Institution." *The Review of Higher Education* 40, no. 1 (2016): 117–43.

Garcia, Gina A., and Otgonjargal Okhidoi. "Culturally Relevant Practices that 'Serve' Students at a Hispanic Serving Institution." *Innovative Higher Education* 40, no. 4 (2015): 345–57.

Gramsci, Antonio *Selections from the Prison Notebooks*. Edited and translated by Quintin Hoare and Geoffrey Nowell Smith. New York, NY: International Publishers Co, 1971.

Higher Ed Immigration Portal. "Arizona." https://www.higheredimmigrationportal.org/state/arizona/.

Higher Ed Immigration Portal. "Wisconsin." Accessed August 11, 2022. https://www.higheredimmigrationportal.org/state/wisconsin/.

Hispanic Association of Colleges and Universities. "HACU 2020–2021 Hispanic-Serving Institutions and Emerging HSIs: State Breakdown." Accessed August 11, 2022. https://www.hacu.net/images/hacu/ResearchMenu/2022_HSIbyStateList.pdf.

IHRC. "University of Minnesota Immigration History Research Center: Immigrant Stories." https://cla.umn.edu/ihrc/immigrant-stories.

Jefferies, Julián. "Fear of Deportation in High School: Implications for Breaking the Circle of Silence Surrounding Migration Status." *Journal of Latinos and Education* 13, no. 4 (2014): 278–95.

Ladson-Billings, Gloria. "Toward a Theory of Culturally Relevant Pedagogy." *American Educational Research Journal* 32, no. 3 (1995): 465–91.

Ladson-Billings, Gloria, and William F. Tate. "Toward a Critical Race Theory of Education." *Teachers College Record* 97, no. 1 (1995): 47–68.

López, María Pabón, and Gerardo R. López. *Persistent Inequality: Contemporary Realities in the Education of Undocumented Latina/O Students*. New York, NY: Routledge, 2009.

Mancilla, Gerardo. "Latinx Youth Counterstories in a Court Diversion Program." *Taboo: The Journal of Culture and Education* 17, no. 4 (2018): 5.

Mattson, Kristen. *Ethics in a Digital World: Guiding Student through Society's Biggest Questions*. Washington, DC: International Society for Technology in Education, 2021.

McGee, Vanesha. "Latino, Latinx, Hispanic, or Latine? Which Term Should You Use?" Accessed August 11, 2022. https://www.bestcolleges.com/blog/hispanic-latino-latinx-latine/.

Mendoza, Jennifer. "The Border Crossed Us: The Tohono O'Odham Nation's Divide." Accessed September 1, 2019. https://medium.com/race-law-a-critical-analysis/the-border-crossed-us-the-tohono-oodham-s-nation-divide-32c9260f1458.

No More Deaths. *Fact Sheet: Operation Streamline*: No More Deaths, 2012.

Paris, Django, and Maisha T. Winn. *Humanizing Research: Decolonizing Qualitative Inquiry with Youth and Communities*. London, England: SAGE Publications, 2014.

Pérez Huber, Lindsay. "Disrupting Apartheid of Knowledge: Testimonio as Methodology in Latina/O Critical Race Research in Education." *International Journal of Qualitative Studies in Education* 22, no. 6 (2009): 639–54.

Rebora, Anthony. "Widening the Lens: A Conversation with Beverly Daniel Tatum." *Educational Leadership* 76, no. 7 (2019): 30–33.

Risam, Roopika. "Decolonizing the Digital Humanities in Theory and Practice." In *The Routledge Companion to Media Studies and Digital Humanities*, 78–86. New York, NY: Routledge, 2018.

Risam, Roopika, Justin Snow, and Susan Edwards. "Building an Ethical Digital Humanities Community: Librarian, Faculty, and Student Collaboration." *College & Undergraduate Libraries* 24, no. 2–4 (2017): 337–49.

Scharrón del Rio, M., and Aja, A. (2015, December 5). The Case for Latinx: Why Intersectionality Is not a Choice. [Web log]. Retrieved from https://www.latinorebels.com/2015/12/05/the-case-for-latinx-why-intersectionality-is-not-a-choice/. Silva, Bianca. "The Border Wall that Already Exists." Accessed January 2019. https://theweek.com/captured/683638/border-wall-that-already-exists.

Sims, J. Revel. *Cuéntame Más: A Report on the Current State of Latinxs in Dane County, Wisconsin*. Madison, WI: Latino Consortium for Action, 2016.

Solórzano, Daniel G., and Dolores Delgado Bernal. "Examining Transformational Resistance through a Critical Race and LatCrit Theory Framework: Chicana and Chicano Students in an Urban Context." *Urban education* 36, no. 3 (2001): 308–42.

Solórzano, Daniel G., and Tara J. Yosso. "Critical Race Methodology: Counter-Storytelling as an Analytical Framework for Education Research." *Qualitative inquiry* 8, no. 1 (2002): 23–44.

Southside Presbyterian. "The Sanctuary Movement." Accessed January 2017. http://www.southsidepresbyterian.org/the-sanctuary-movement.html.

Stringer, Ernest T. *Action Research in Education.* Upper Saddle River, NJ: Pearson Prentice Hall, 2008.
United States Census Bureau. "Dane County, Wisconsin." Accessed August 11, 2022. https://www.census.gov/quickfacts/fact/table/danecountywisconsin,US/PST045221.
U.S. Department of Education. "Hispanic-Serving Institutions (HSIs)." https://sites.ed.gov/hispanic-initiative/hispanic-serving-institutions-hsis/.
Vukelich-Selva, Donna. *Immigrant Children Negotiate School: The Border in Our Hearts (New Americans).* El Paso, TX: LFB Scholarly Publishing LLC, 2014.
Wright, Wayne E. *Foundations for Teaching English Language Learners: Research, Theory, Policy, and Practice.* Philadelphia, PA: Caslon Publishing, 2010.
Yosso, Tara J. *Critical Race Counterstories along the Chicana/Chicano Educational Pipeline.* New York, NY: Routledge, 2006.

Conclusion

Reimagining Digital Pedagogies in Hispanic-Serving Institutions and Beyond

Isabel Martínez and Irma Victoria Montelongo

Introduction

Three years after colleges and universities began to shut down due to COVID-19 and faculty began a messy and chaotic transition to emergency remote learning, we are still learning about the impacts that hurriedly developed digital pedagogies had on the teaching and learning of college students. We do already know that for undergraduate students, the digital divide, often hidden due to the ubiquity of computers on college campuses, is worse than previously understood.[1] We also know that this overreliance on technology negatively impacted Latinx students' mental health and, especially for students of color, their academic success.[2] Students, especially those attending Hispanic-Serving Institutions were often those who experienced the most disruptions to their learning, with campuses scrambling to support students at home and students most often compelled to take on additional responsibilities such as caretaking of younger siblings or older relatives at home or working, as well as facing the risk of and even contracting COVID-19 themselves.

Hastily thrown together and oftentimes not reflecting the demographic realities of their students, many summer faculty training sessions omitted much of this reality and instead shared superficial tips for using learning management systems and videoconferencing that are not designed for education.³ Rather than delving more deeply into critical digital pedagogies and/or engaging in *pedagogical alterity*, or questioning whether or not the pedagogies discussed were broadly applicable, these trainings were meant to be more of a Band-Aid, an emergency fix to get college educators through the pandemic.⁴ Some faculty and students, however, reported positive experiences with remote learning, and as a result there is little doubt that at least some level of expanded online teaching and learning will remain.⁵ In many cases, this reflects the extent of conversations about expanding digital pedagogies in Hispanic-Serving Institutions and other classrooms.

Although we conceptualized this project before colleges and universities were forced into remote teaching and learning, the discussions in this volume could not be timelier as we continue to make our way through multiple pandemics (COVID-19, structural racism, gun violence, climate change, hyper-capitalism) and to debate how technology should be utilized in college classrooms to best empower our students to challenge these persistent societal ills.⁶ Just as we did in 2017, after these past semesters utilizing digital tools to engage in online learning, we resume our pursuit to the question of how digital tools in Hispanic-Serving and Latinx Studies classrooms may be employed to challenge the dehumanization and digital injury enacted against Latinx communities. In this question, we pay special attention to probing underlying barriers that hinder access and invitations to engage with digital tools, and overall, guided and sustained critical teaching in order for students to experience transformative learning in their classrooms. Drawing from Rehn's 2017 framework that moves beyond basic digital engagement, we want for students to holistically harness the liberatory possibilities of technology and not only create robust digital projects and scholarship, but to also engage in more authentic and deeper connections by exploring and manipulating the technology in dialogue with each other. In these ways, students can experience more meaningful learning and knowledge and skill development. We also renew our call to use technology to critically enhance students' understandings of heterogeneous Latinx knowledges and subjectivities that span across space.⁷ Recognizing that technology and its use in classrooms is never a neutral act, we argue that the inequities that we overcome in our classrooms are rooted in white supremacy and hinder our Latinx students' abilities to fully actualize and realize "digital well-being" as well as more critical understandings of themselves and others.⁸ In order to disrupt continued marginalization, as well as excessive homogenization and division, of Latinx communities, we must ensure that Latinx students achieve *full* digital citizenship.

We come to these tasks with great urgency. As the second largest racial/ethnic group and the largest minority in the United States, Latinxs comprise approximately 18 percent of the US population, and before the pandemic they were also the fastest growing population enrolling in college.[9] Between 1996 and 2016, the share of Latinxs in colleges and universities grew from 8–19 percent.[10] In spite of this rapid growth, in 2021 Latinx students continued to lag behind other racial groups in terms of completion; at the two-year level, 33 percent of Latinxs and 38 percent of whites obtained an associate's degree while at the four-year level, the gap is larger: 52 percent of Latinxs compared to 65 percent of whites.[11] The pandemic widened these gaps as we saw steep drops in Latinx student enrollment in community colleges and drops, albeit less severe in four-year colleges in 2020.[12] In spring 2020, Latinx student enrollment dropped over 7 percent, with enrollment in community colleges the hardest hit at 13.7 percent.[13]

These gaps existed prior to and were exacerbated by the COVID-19 pandemic and will persist due to structural and systemic racism that, at the classroom level, manifests as colonizing practices and pedagogies. Flores-Carmona reminds us that colleges and universities were never meant for Indigenous, Black, Latinx, and Asian students and are characterized by the "colonists' perspectives and ideologies" that are deficit in nature.[14] For purposes of this monograph, it serves us to remember that most Hispanic-Serving Institutions in particular, and the colleges from which our authors hail, specifically, began as predominantly white institutions whose student demographics shifted to reflect changes in the surrounding regions and, in fact, are better characterized as Hispanic-Enrolling, and/or that Latinx Studies departments were born of protest and struggle. In other words, spaces that, at a minimum, tolerate Latinx presence and at best, engage in humanistic, asset-based, antiracist, antisexist, anti-nativist, anti-ableist and anti-homophobic curriculum, policies, and practices, did not emerge voluntarily; they were compelled into existence.[15]

For these reasons, it is imperative that we demand that advocacy for Hispanic-Serving Institutions *and* colleges that possess Latinx and Chicanx Studies programs and departments include an emphasis on investing more into not only technology and digital tools on their campuses and in their programs and departments, but also into the training of faculty to not only effectively utilize these tools but also to do so in critical ways that counter dehumanizing epistemicide and center Latinx students as knowledge producers and theory-makers.[16] Moving away from neoliberal definitions of pedagogies that are operationalized in standards and learning outcomes that oftentimes reflect social stratification projects, with this volume, we assert that college administrators and faculty should reimagine digital pedagogies as decolonizing and as "deeply intellectual and theoretical projects" that possess the potential to transform and "rehumanize" Latinx higher education.[17]

Across colleges and universities, there is a lack of consensus about whether this transformation and rehumanization should occur and how it may manifest.[18] Differentiated by diverse curricular and programmatic commitments to changing student populations, as well as distance and regional racialization and migration histories, colleges including Hispanic-Serving Institutions have tended to neglect students' ethnic and racial identities or possibly, engage in trivial public relations programming but not more substantial curricular overhauls. If and when Latinx students are *served*, regional silos are reproduced: Southwest Hispanic-Serving Institutions and Latinx Studies programs and departments enroll and emphasize ethnic Mexican and Chicanx realities while Northeast Coast campuses remain rooted in the histories of Puerto Ricans and Dominicans with limited inclusion of the many hybrid cultures created through the mixing and meshing of Latinx identities. As such, the histories of Latinxs located in other regions may seem disconnected, distant, and irrelevant to the past and futures of the students found in locale-specific institutions and classrooms.

This edited manuscript addresses the challenges and discusses the ways that technology has/can be used in classrooms in more effective and inclusive ways not only to serve Latinx students and overcome participation gaps, but also to more critically challenge the one-size-fits-all regional approaches of Hispanic-Serving Institutions and Latinx Studies programs. Rather, we believe that a critical Latinx Digital Humanities agenda must consider the heterogeneity of our communities and our students. For that reason, this volume includes discussions of rehumanizing innovative pedagogies being enacted across the country: on the West Coast, on the Gulf Coast, on the East Coast and everywhere in between; in community college as well as senior college classrooms; and lastly, in public, as well as private college campuses.

Elaborated upon across nine chapters, educators in this volume are teaching technological proficiencies and literacies that move beyond basic engagement to include a) "digital creation, scholarship, and innovation, b) digital communication, collaboration, and participation, and c) digital learning and professional development," all in relation to interrogating the contentious concept of *Latinidad*.[19] Like Norton, the authors are and have been *doing* digital humanities, sometimes without realizing it.[20] Experimenting with tools such as the shared web platforms Ning and Digication as well as utilizing digital storytelling and archive-making, we, as professors at Hispanic-Serving Institutions and Chicanx and Latinx Studies programs and departments, draw upon critical digital humanities to meet our students at the digital edge and provide them with the pedagogical and digital tools so that they are further equipped to lead technological and other revolutions.[21] As educators, we believe that infusing our pedagogies and curriculum with technology opens up new possibilities for us and our students to become digital creators by developing and presenting authentic knowledge but also transforms how they could connect with others across hundreds of miles. We were intentional in using these pedagogies with our mostly Latinx students whom we knew were alumni of under-resourced K-12 schools that overemphasized surveillance and discipline rather than critical thinking and innovation. In short, we use technology to empower students to overcome power imbalances that have traditionally characterized their educations.

The chapters in this monograph highlight the liberatory possibilities that Latinx Digital Humanities possess, outcomes that Hispanic-Serving Institutions should pursue.[22] Moving beyond the initial discussions about digital humanities that focused on Research 1 universities and scholarship created among (mostly white) professors and graduate students, over time, these chapters highlight digital humanities pedagogies found in Hispanic-Serving Institutions and Latinx Studies classrooms that have the potential to *level the playing field* and provide first-generation Latinx students with opportunities to engage in knowledge production, to recover and/or uncover their own untold narratives, and, frankly, to disrupt the feedback loop that, according to María Cotera, reproduces Latinxs and other communities' marginalization in acts of historical recovery and storytelling.[23]

This volume achieves this across its chapters. Martínez, Nieves, and Tanks, as well as Natividad and Wise first lay down the groundwork for this volume by providing an overview of the ways in which the boundaries of digital humanities and Latinx Studies are being broadened in order to overlap and/or include each other. All argue for bringing these fields together to counter local but also global dehumanizing practices and processes to advance a rehumanization curricula. The chapters that follow demonstrate the ways in which Latinx Digital Humanities is occurring in community college and senior Hispanic-Serving Institution classrooms located in New York City, El Paso, Texas, and California. While Acosta Corniel discusses the ways in which she utilized digital tools such as Google Docs and the CUNY Dominican Studies Institute's First Blacks in the Americas digital archive to fulfill Eugenio María de Hostos's teaching philosophy of "building students' intellects . . . will to learn and to be(come) global citizens" on a campus that is nearly 41 percent Latinx, Martínez and Montelongo emphasize the ways in which technology can extend brick and mortar classroom boundaries to authentically interrogate and disrupt the ways in which regions are racialized and colonized differently to create diverse Latinx groups. Stacy, Ramos, and Correa demonstrate how podcasting provides opportunities for pre-service Teacher Education teachers to engage in translanguaging and capture more authentic and dynamic ways of thinking and theory-building, or developing and showcasing students' "epistemological pluralism."[24] By using technology to bring students together within and across classrooms as knowledge producers, not solely recipients, new, dynamic, and hybrid knowledges about Latinxs are created and they themselves are empowered.

Turning to archival work, the next chapters highlight the work of educators from the University of Houston's revolutionary Recovering the US Hispanic Literary Heritage program (Recovery Program). Baeza Ventura, Gauthereau, and Villarroel focus on ways that educators can teach undergraduate but also high school students to uncover, recover, and reanalyze existing archives in order to center and digitally showcase previously muted historical Latinx contributions. Fernández Quintanilla and Zapata, on the other hand, introduce readers to the construction of one specific archive, the Delis Negrón Digital Archive, illuminating transnational Puerto Rican newspaper editor, poet, writer, professor, and activist Delis Negrón and his life and labors in order to counter the nativist and national narratives that all too often shape understandings about Latinxs in the United States. In both chapters, the authors provide models for critical digital scholarship and digital pedagogies for other scholars and educators so that they may integrate these emancipatory practices into their own research and classrooms.

The last chapters take readers to the highly misunderstood and contested US-Mexico border. Horcasitas and Quintanilla adopt a Latinx futurism approach and challenge their students to reimagine the US-Mexico border in a distant future that is more equitable and sustainable. Drawing from speculative fiction and science fiction, as well as their own lives for inspiration, students use Twine to create choose-your-own adventure stories that reimagine the San Diego/Tijuana frontera. Alternatively, Mancilla and Vukelich-Selva highlight the ways in which digital storytelling and social media can be utilized by students to document violence but more importantly, resistance, enacted on the Arizona-Sonora border. Learning from various actors located on this border including activists, members of the Catholic Church, members of the Tohono O'odham Nation, etc., students deftly use these tools to make meaning of what they were witnessing.

It is evident that all of these projects draw from the students' own knowledge and braid them with new learning. This political act reverses and supports students' recovery from subtractive schooling that has been prevalent in their education prior and due to multiple pandemics.[25] Especially now, it is imperative that we expand these sorts of emancipatory, political, pedagogical acts in the classrooms and that universities and colleges more intentionally transform and rehumanize their curricula to provide Latinx students with opportunities not only to reverse losses but also to flourish. To do this on a broader level, we offer the following recommendations:

1. Echoing many other policymakers and scholars, more monies must be automatically and permanently appropriated to Hispanic-Serving Institutions.[26] The pandemic only exacerbated the structural racism that has informed gross underinvestment in these institutions, which educate over 60 percent of the Latinx college-going population. While there is temporary relief due to the influx of stimulus monies, these monies are being stretched to overcome preexisting inequities as well as the ones that were exacerbated by the COVID-19 pandemic. In addition, in the first round of CARES (Coronavirus Aid, Recovery and Economic Relief Act) monies, campuses with higher numbers of full-time students were privileged.[27] However, while stimulus monies are being received and spent, state disinvestment and rising costs continue unabated.[28] Because of this, appropriations that not only close previously existing funding gaps but also actually address the socioeconomic realities of students as well as the educational inequities and cumulative disadvantages that have plagued students of color who have attended under-resourced K-12 public schools should be guaranteed (not competitive), permanent, and equitable.[29] Special attention should be paid to community colleges where the majority of Latinx students begin their college careers and are overrepresented as part-time students.[30]

2. These monies (and/or other monies) must be earmarked to improve digital infrastructure for students attending Hispanic-Serving Institutions. According to a survey administered by the Minority-Serving Cyberinfrastructure Consortium (MSCC) in collaboration with Internet2, Minority-Serving

Institutions, including Hispanic-Serving Institutions, possess a great need for basic infrastructure support. Surveys completed by administrators, faculty, and staff from 144 HBCUs, TCUs, and HSIs, revealed that infrastructure and funding (57 percent), followed by staff and institutional support (17 percent) were the greatest obstacles to expanding digital initiatives across all disciplines.[31] Pre-pandemic, laws including the 2008 HEA Reauthorization Act focused on providing monies to Hispanic-Serving and Minority-Serving Institutions to improve and expand their digital infrastructure including computers and Wi-Fi on college campuses. These monies have both not been enough and, as we experienced in the pandemic, must extend beyond brick-and-mortar campuses and ensure that students have access to infrastructure so that they can complete coursework *in their homes*.

3. Investments in digital infrastructure and tools must also extend beyond supporting traditional and expanding STEM and security related majors and include humanities and social sciences. It is no secret that STEM and increasingly, majors related to foreign and domestic security, have been increasingly touted as essential for the United States to remain economically competitive and viable in a global arena and, as such, are funding priorities. It is apparent that as the college population becomes less white and has included more first-generation college-goers, actions to ensure a tighter coupling of the university with the labor market and focus on the either/or of career readiness or college for a job versus critical thinking or democratic citizenship are becoming more explicit. With hopes pinned on them to become socially mobile, especially for those who are the first in their families to graduate, first-generation college-goers experience significant pressure to complete majors that will translate to in-demand jobs right out of college and near immediate upward economic mobility. While we agree with the need for a college education to provide students with skills to obtain fruitful satisfying careers, nor do we discount the oft-immediate needs to obtain employment that automatically translates into economic mobility, we are also aware that demographic shifts and increasing higher educa-

tion stratification could, although positions and salaries may change, ensure that the future hierarchy of labor remain status quo, or that decision-makers/owners of production remain overwhelmingly elite and white.[32] If we have any chance to disrupt this, humanities and social sciences must also be equitably funded to adopt and utilize digital tools so that these graduates may not only be competitive as workers, but they can also critique persistent, dehumanizing, exploitative systems that maintain this organization. As the country finds itself in the midst of a racial reckoning, the reality is that the United States needs humanities and social sciences more than ever. Ensuring that curricula in these fields integrate digital tools and competencies will allow students to develop career readiness as well as develop into critical thinkers and engaged citizens.

4. Courses that utilize these digital tools and establish digital proficiencies into their learning objectives must be threaded and scaffolded throughout majors and minors beginning at the 100-level and culminating at the 400 level.[33] Integrating digital proficiencies throughout major and minor curricula intentionally will further fulfill the aforementioned objectives of career readiness, critical thinking, and developing an engaged citizenry.

5. Lastly, in order to do this, it is not nearly enough to simply fund more computer laboratories and digital tools with the idea that webinars and a few IT staff can adequately assist students in developing digital competencies. Monies must be used to support professors to integrate critical digital pedagogies in their curriculum.[34] This is a costly challenge as many current faculty currently do not possess the skills (or time) necessary to ensure that students are introduced to and master essential digital competencies at different course levels. Universities and colleges can facilitate this by hiring more instructional designers to work with faculty, but these are costly.[35] Some institutions such as Northeastern University utilized graduate students to support faculty in revamping their traditional assignments into ones that integrated critical digital material and skills.[36] In the cases of Hispanic-Serving

> Institutions that may not be able to invest in enough costly instructional designers to support all departments, utilizing students in meaningful ways to teach or support professors will assist in ensuring that more, if not all, students can graduate with critical digital proficiencies.

Conclusion

Throughout this edition, we have provided examples for how faculty members at two- and four-year universities and colleges, Hispanic-Serving Institutions, and Ethnic and Latinx Studies departments and programs, can incorporate humanizing innovative pedagogies into their curriculum. As the Latinx undergraduate student population continues to grow, it is imperative that institutions and individual faculty and staff expand on these ideas and reimagine not only how we teach Latinx students across the nation, but also how we implement twenty-first-century tools and theories to do so. This volume calls us to rethink the ways that Hispanic-Serving Institutions and Latinx Studies departments actually *serve* their students and how as institutions they too can reimagine what it means to *educate and prepare* their Latinx students to become critical workers and members of the citizenry. As we continue to face neoliberal forces that sustain and exacerbate marginalization of Latinx young people, in this case, by reproducing digital-learning inequities laid bare during the pandemic, we must invest monies to counter not only the losses experienced by Latinx students and communities during the pandemic, but also compensate for the structural shortcomings that existed prior to the pandemic that were already resulting in widening academic and digital disparities. Only then can we wholly implement curricula with the proper tools to rehumanize Latinx undergraduate education.

Notes

1. Lindsay McKenzie, "Students Want Online Learning Options Post-Pandemic," 2021.

2. Center for Collegiate Mental Health, "COVID-19's Impact on College Student Mental Health," 2021.

3. Nathan Holbert, Paolo Blikstein, Sonali Rajan, and Lalitha Vasudevan, "Resist the Lure of Zoom School," 2021.

4. Ruha Benjamin, "Foreword," 2021.
5. McKenzie, 2021.
6. Daniel Solórzano, "Foreword," 2021.
7. Andrea Rehn, "DigLibArts 2020," 2017; Cheryl Brown, Laura Czerniewicz, Cheng-Wen Huang, and Tabisa Mayisela, "Curriculum for Digital Education Leadership," 2016; S. Craig Watkins, "Digital Divide: Navigating the Digital Edge," 2012; Henry Jenkins, Katie Clinton, Ravi Purushotma, Alice J. Robison, and Margaret Weigel, "Confronting the Challenges of Participatory Culture," 2006.
8. Rehn, 2017.
9. Luis Noe-Bustamante, Mark Hugo Lopez, and Jens Manuel Krogstad, "US Hispanic Population Surpassed 60 Million in 2019 but Growth Has Slowed," 2020.
10. Kurt Bauman, "School Enrollment of the Hispanic Population," 2017.
11. Excelencia in Education, "Fact Sheet: Latino College Completion: United States," 2023.
12. National Student Research Clearinghouse, "Summer 2020 Enrollment Report," 2020.
13. National Student Research Clearinghouse, "Overview: Spring 2021 Enrollment Estimates," 2021.
14. Judith Flores-Carmona, "Dime con quién andas y te diré quién eres," 2021.
15. Flores-Carmona, 2021; Solórzano, 2021.
16. Boaventura de Sousa Santos, "Beyond Abyssal Thinking: From Global Lines to Ecologies of Knowledge," 2007.
17. Carmen Kynard, "Anti-Racism and Racial Justice in the Teaching of Writing," 2021.
18. Gina A. García, "Complicating a Latina/o Serving Identity at a Hispanic-Serving Institution," 2016.
19. Rehn, 2017; Felice León, "Black and Indigenous Millennials are Canceling Latinidad. Here's Why," 2019.
20. David Jack Norton, "Making Time: Workflow and Learning Outcomes in DH Assignments," 2019.
21. Watkins, 2012.
22. Gina A. García, "Is Liberation a Viable Outcome for Students Who Attend College?" 2020.
23. Gwendolyn Beetham, "The Academic Feminist: Summer at the Archives with Chicana Por Mi Raza," 2013.
24. Vanessa Andreotti, Cash Ahenakew, and Garrick Cooper, "Epistemological Pluralism: Ethical and Pedagogical Challenges in Higher Education," 2011.
25. Angela Valenzuela, *Subtractive Schooling: US-Mexican Youth and the Politics of Caring*, 1999.
26. Viviann Anguiano and Janette Martinez, "Ensuring an Equitable Recovery for Latinos," 2021; Viviann Anguiano and Marissa Alayna Navarro, "Hispanic-Serving Institutions Need $1 Billion More in Federal Funding," 2020.

27. Kery Murakami, "Racial Equity in Funding for Higher Education," 2020.

28. Madeline St. Amour, "Looming Budget Cuts Threaten Proven Program," 2020.

29. Aaron M. Pallas and Jennifer L. Jennings, "Cumulative Knowledge about Cumulative Advantage," 2009; Patricia Gándara and Frances Contreras, "The Latino Education Crisis: The Consequences of Failed Social Policies," 2010.

30. Anne-Marie Nuñez, Jessica Rivera, Jennifer Valdez, and Victoria Barbosa Olivo, "Centering Hispanic-Serving Institutions' Strategies to Develop Talent in Computing Fields," 2021; Murakami, 2020.

31. Minority-Serving CyberInfrastructure Consortium, "Connecting the Dots: Using Campus IT Infrastructure Survey Data to Support Your Institutions' Research Goals," 2021.

32. Michael N. Bastedo and Ozan Jaquette, "Running in Place: Low-Income Students and the Dynamics of Higher Education Stratification," 2017; Samuel Bowles and Herbert Gintis, *Schooling in Capitalist America*, 1976.

33. Michael Anft, "Expanding the Digital Curriculum," 2020.

34. Steven Mintz, "Reimagining the Academic Experience," 2017; Nuñez et al., 2021.

35. Joshua Kim, "$12 Billion, Community Colleges and Online Learning Infrastructure," 2021.

36. Anft, 2020.

Bibliography

America Counts. Number of Hispanic Students More Than Double in 20 Years. Washington, DC: US Census, 2017. https://www.census.gov/library/stories/2017/10/hispanic-enrollment.html.

Andreotti, Vanessa, Cash Ahenakew, and Garrick Cooper. "Epistemological Pluralism: Ethical and Pedagogical Challenges in Higher Education." AlterNative: An International Journal of Indigenous Peoples 7, no. 1 (2011): 40–50. DOI:10.1177/117718011100700104.

Anft, Michael. "Expanding the Digital Curriculum: How Colleges Are Embedding High-Tech Skills to Prepare Students for Tomorrow's Jobs." The Chronicle of Higher Education, 2020. https://www.emich.edu/facdev/documents/expanding-digital-curriculum.pdf.

Anguiano, Viviann, and Janette Martinez. "Ensuring an Equitable Recovery for Latinos." Inside Higher Education, March 9, 2021. https://www.insidehighered.com/views/2021/03/09/federal-government-should-increase-support-hispanic-serving-institutions-given (Accessed March 14, 2021).

———, and Marissa Alayna Navarro. "Hispanic-Serving Institutions Need $1 Billion More in Federal Funding." Center for American Progress, December

8, 2020. https://www.americanprogress.org/issues/education-postsecondary/news/2020/12/08/492883/hispanic-serving-institutions-need-1-billion-federal-funding/ (Accessed March 14, 2021).

Bastedo, Michael N., and Ozan Jaquette. "Running in Place: Low-Income Students and the Dynamics of Higher Education Stratification," Educational Evaluation and Policy Analysis 33, no. 3 (2017): 318–39. https://doi.org/10.3102/0162373711406718.

Bauman, Kurt. School Enrollment of the Hispanic Population: Two Decades of Growth. Washington, DC: US Census Bureau, 2017. https://www.census.gov/newsroom/blogs/random-samplings/2017/08/school_enrollmentof.html.

Beetham, Gwendolyn. "The Academic Feminist: Summer at the Archives with Chicana Por Mi Raza." Feministing, September 4, 2013, http://feministing.com/2013/09/04/the-academic-feminist-summer-at-the-archives-with-chicana-por-mi-raza/ (Accessed March 21, 2021).

Benjamin, Ruha. "Foreword," In Critical Digital Pedagogy, edited by Jesse Stommel, Chris Friend, and Sean Michael Morris. Washington, DC: Hybrid Pedagogy, Inc., 2021.

Brown, Cheryl, Laura Czerniewicz, Cheng-Wen Huang, and Tabisa Mayisela. "Curriculum for Digital Education Leadership: A Concept Paper." 2016. http://oasis.col.org/bitstream/handle/11599/2442/2016_Brown-Czerniewicz-Huang-Mayisela_Curriculum-Digital-Education-Leadership.pdf?sequence=4&isAllowed=y (Accessed March 20, 2021).

Center for Collegiate Mental Health. "Part 1 of 5: COVID-19's Impact on College Student Mental Health," CCMH COVID-19 Blog Series, entry posted February 2, 2021, https://ccmh.psu.edu/index.php?option=com_dailyplanetblog&view=entry&year=2021&month=02&day=01&id=9:part-1-of-5-covid-19-s-impact-on-college-student-mental-health (Accessed March 14, 2021).

de Sousa Santos, Boaventura. "Beyond Abyssal Thinking: From Global Lines to Ecologies of Knowledge." Review 30, no. 1 (2007): 45–89. http://www.jstor.org/stable/40241677 (Accessed July 12, 2021).

Excelencia in Education. "Fact Sheet: Latino College Completion: United States." 2023. https://www.edexcelencia.org/lcc2023-usa-factsheet (Accessed January 12, 2024).

Flores Carmona, Judith. "'Dime con quién andas y te dire quién eres': Theories and Methodologies That Center Latinx/a/o Epistemologies and Pedagogies." In Studying Latinx/a/o Students in Higher Education: A Critical Analysis of Concepts, Theory, and Methodologies edited by Nicole M. Garcia, Cristobal Salinas, Jr., and Jesus Cisneros. New York, NY: Routledge, 2021.

Gándara, Patricia, and Frances Contreras, F. The Latino Education Crisis: The Consequences of Failed Social Policies. Boston, MA: Harvard University Press, 2010.

García, Gina Ann. "Is Liberation a Viable Outcome for Students Who Attend College?" Higher Ed Jobs, May 28, 2020, https://www.higheredjobs.com/blog/postDisplay.cfm?post=2256&blog=28 (Accessed July 14, 2020).

García, Gina Ann. "Complicating a Latina/o-Serving Identity at a Hispanic-Serving Institution." The Review of Higher Education 40, no 1(2016): 117–43. https://doi.org/10.1353/rhe.2016.0040.

Holbert, Nathan, Paolo Blikstein, Sonali Rajan, and Lalitha Vasudevan. "Resist the Lure of Zoom School." New York Daily News, June 2, 2021, https://www.nydailynews.com/opinion/ny-oped-beware-the-lure-of-zoom-school-20210602-beutvtagurcwljj6crtshhpbwy-story.html (Accessed July 13, 2021).

Jenkins, Henry, Katie Clinton, Ravi Purushotma, Alice J. Robison, and Margaret Weigel. Confronting the Challenges of Participatory Culture: Media Education for the 21st Century. The John D. and Catherine T. MacArthur Foundation. 2006. https://files.eric.ed.gov/fulltext/ED536086.pdf.

Kim, Joshua. "$12 Billion, Community Colleges and Online Learning Infrastructure." Inside Higher Education, April 5, 2021, https://www.insidehighered.com/blogs/learning-innovation/12-billion-community-colleges-and-online-learning-infrastructure (Accessed July 10, 2021).

Kynard, Carmen. "Anti-Racism and Racial Justice in the Teaching of Writing." Columbia University, Department of English and Comparative Literature, Pedagogy Colloquium. January 22, 2021.

Léon, Felice. "Black and Indigenous Millennials are Canceling Latinidad. Here's Why." The Root, September 26, 2019. https://www.theroot.com/black-and-indigenous-millennials-are-canceling-latinida-1838489077 (Accessed March 15, 2021).

McKenzie, Lindsay. "Students Want Online Learning Options Post-Pandemic." Inside Higher Education. April 27, 2021, https://www.insidehighered.com/news/2021/04/27/survey-reveals-positive-outlook-online-instruction-post-pandemic (Accessed July 16, 2021).

Minority-Serving CyberInfrastructure Consortium. "Connecting the Dots: Using Campus IT Infrastructure Survey Data to Support Your Institutions' Research Goals," March 18, 2021. https://internet2.hosted.panopto.com/Panopto/Pages/Viewer.aspx?id=959abd2c-3890-4174-b748-acef014fd62d (Accessed July 16, 2021).

Mintz, Steven. "Reimagining the Academic Experience." Inside Higher Education, February 28, 2017. https://www.insidehighered.com/blogs/higher-ed-gamma/reimagining-academic-experience (Accessed March 17, 2021).

Murakami, Kery. "Racial Equity in Funding for Higher Ed." Inside Higher Education, October 29, 2020, https://www.insidehighered.com/news/2020/10/29/racial-disparities-higher-education-funding-could-widen-during-economic-downturn (Accessed July 14, 2021).

National Student Research Clearinghouse. "Overview: Spring 2021 Enrollment Estimates." Current Term Enrollment Estimates, spring 2021. https://nscresearchcenter.org/wp-content/uploads/CTEE_Report_Spring_2021.pdf.

Noe-Bustamante, Luis, Mark Hugo Lopez, and Jens Manuel Krogstad. "U.S. Hispanic Population Surpassed 60 Million in 2019, but Growth Has Slowed." Pew Research Center. July 7, 2020. https://www.pewresearch.org/fact-tank/2020/07/07/u-s-hispanic-population-surpassed-60-million-in-2019-but-growth-has-slowed/.

Norton, David Jack. "Making Time: Workflow and Learning Outcomes in DH Assignments." In Debates in Digital Humanities edited by Matthew K. Gold and Lauren F. Klein. Minneapolis: University of Minnesota Press, 2019.

Nuñez, Anne-Marie, Jessica Rivera, Jennifer Valdez, and Victoria Barbosa Olivo, "Centering Hispanic-Serving Institutions' Strategies to Develop Talent in Computing Fields." Tapuya: Latin American Science, Technology and Society 4, no. 1 (2021), https://doi.org/10.1080/25729861.2020.1842582.

Pallas, Aaron M., and Jennifer L. Jennings. "Cumulative Knowledge about Cumulative Advantage." Swiss Journal of Sociology 35, no. 2 (2009): 211–29. https://doi.org/10.5169/seals-815047.

Rehn, Andrea. DigLibArts 2020: Digital Well-Being for the Liberal Arts. February 20, 2017, https://diglibarts.whittier.edu/digital-well-being-for-the-liberal-arts/ (Accessed March 15, 2021).

Solórzano, Daniel G. "Foreword." In Studying Latinx/a/o Students in Higher Education: A Critical Analysis of Concepts, Theory, and Methodologies edited by Nichole M. Garcia, Cristobal Salinas, Jr., and Jesus Cisneros, New York, NY: Routledge, 2021.

St. Amour, Madeline. "Looming Budget Cuts Threaten Proven Program." Inside Higher Education, June 30, 2020, https://www.insidehighered.com/news/2020/06/30/experts-worry-proposed-cuts-cuny-asap-foreshadow-trend-higher-ed (Accessed March 15, 2021).

US Department of Education. Education in a Pandemic: The Disparate Impacts of COVID-19 on America's Students, June 8, 2021. https://www2.ed.gov/about/offices/list/ocr/docs/20210608-impacts-of-covid19.pdf.

Valenzuela, Angela. Subtractive Schooling: US Mexican Youth and the Politics of Caring. Albany: State University of New York Press, 1999.

Watkins, S. Craig. "Digital Divide: Navigating the Digital Edge." *International Journal of Learning and Media* 3, no. 2 (2012): 1–12. https://doi.org/10.1162/ijlm_a_00072.

Contributors

Dr. Lissette Acosta Corniel is an assistant professor in the Ethnic and Race Studies Department at the Borough of Manhattan Community College (BMCC), City University of New York (CUNY). Her scholarship has focused on feminisms in the Dominican Republic and includes the articles "Juana Gelofa Pelona: An Enslaved but Insubordinate Witness in Santo Domingo (1549–1555)" (*PerspectivasAfro, PerspectivasAfro ½*, 2022) and "Elena: Running to Dance and Other Defects in Colonial Santo Domingo (1771–73)" (*Women, Gender, and Families of Color,* 2021*)*.

Dr. Gabriela Baeza Ventura is an associate professor of US Latino literature at the University of Houston. She is the author of *La imagen de la mujer en la crónica del México de Afuera* (2006), *US Latino Literature Today* (2004), and the co-authored chapter "A US Latinx Digital Humanities Manifesto" (w/Cotera, García Merchant, Gauthereau, and Villarroel, *Debates in the Digital Humanities*, 2023).

Adriana Correa is a teacher at the Gil Garcetti Learning Academy in the Los Angeles Unified School District. She is a proud graduate of California State University, Dominguez Hills.

Dr. Sylvia Fernández Quintanilla is an assistant professor in public and digital humanities in the Department of Languages and Literature at The University of Texas at San Antonio. Her digital and other published works include *The Urarina Digital Heritage Project* https://idrhku.org/urarina/ (w/Dean, Rosenblum, and Fabiano, 2022), and the articles "Transborder Knowledge-Making: Accessing, Reclaiming and Creating Digital Archives" (w/Alvarez, *Archeologies*, 2022) and "*United Fronteras* como tercer espacio:

Modelo transfronterizo a través de las humanidades digitales poscoloniales y la computación mínima" (w/de Luna and Zapata, *Digital Humanities Quarterly*, 2022).

Dr. Lorena Gauthereau is the digital programs manager at the US Latino Digital Humanities Center at the University of Houston. She is a Chicana literary studies scholar who received her PhD in English from Rice University and has published extensively on digital humanities and Chicanx literature including the journal articles "Recovering the US Hispanic Literary Heritage: A Case Study on US Latina/o Archives and Digital Humanities" (w/Baeza Ventura and Villarroel, *Preservation, Digital Technology & Culture*, 2019) and "Chasing Miss Jimenez: Rereading the Chicana Vendida through Colonial Affect-Culture" (*Frontiers: A Journal of Women Studies*, 2020) and was the guest editor on the "Special Issue: Documenting Transborder Latinidades: Archives, Libraries, and Digital Humanities" (w/Ramirez, *The International Journal of Information, Diversity, & Inclusion*, 2022).

Dr. Jeanelle Horcasitas earned her PhD in literature and cultural studies from the University of California-San Diego. She has published several chapters and journal articles on the topic of digital humanities including the co-authored chapters "Rewriting Graduate Digital Futures through Mentorship and Multi-Institutional Support" (forthcoming, w/Quintanilla, *Digital Futures of Graduate Study in the Humanities*), "A Call to Research Action: Transnational Solidarity for Digital Humanists" (w/Quintanilla, *Debates in the Digital Humanities*, 2023), and "Shedding Light on Migrant Prisoner Histories in Jessica Ordaz's 'The Shadow of El Centro: A History of Migrant Incarceration and Solidarity'" (*Society for US Intellectual History*, 2022)

Dr. Gerardo Mancilla is an associate professor of elementary education at Edgewood College. He has published and spoken extensively about undocumented college students and Latinx youths including in the chapter "Supporting Undocumented Students through Pre-College, College, and Post-College Transitions" (forthcoming, w/Jach, Corral, and Hansen, *Supporting College Students of Immigrant Origins: New Insights from Research, Policy, and Practice*), the journal article "Latinx Youths and Counterstories in a Court Diversion Program" (*Taboo: The Journal of Culture and Education*, 2018), and as the host of the podcast *Educators and Immigration* (www.educatorsandimmigration.com/podcast).

Dr. Isabel Martínez is an associate professor in the Department of Sociology and Anthropology and the Department of Cultures, Societies, and Global Studies, and the director of Latinx, Latin American, and Caribbean Studies at Northeastern University. Her primary scholarship has focused on unaccompanied minors and undocumented youths including her single-author monograph *Becoming Transnational Youth Workers: Independent Mexican Youths and Survival and Social Mobility* (2019), the coedited monograph, *Navegar por terrenos disputados: casos etnográficos de la vida migrante* (w/Marroni, 2023), and the journal article "Developing the Language to Immigrate: Immigration Discourses in the Lives of Mexican Immigrant Youths" (*Journal of Adolescent and Adult Literacy*, 2020).

Dr. Irma Victoria Montelongo is an associate professor of instruction and the director of the Chicano Studies program at The University of Texas at El Paso. She received her PhD in borderlands history from The University of Texas at El Paso. Her fields of study include gender and sexuality, Latin-American history, US history with a subfield in immigration studies, and borderlands history with a subfield in race and ethnic studies. Her research and teaching interests focus on race, class, gender, sexuality, and criminology on the US-Mexico border. Dr. Montelongo also serves as the online program coordinator for the Chicana/o Studies program. In 2018, she received the Border Hero Award from Las Americas Immigrant Advocacy Center as well as the Regents Outstanding Teaching Award from The University of Texas System.

Dr. Nicholas Daniel Natividad is an associate professor in the Department of Criminal Justice at New Mexico State University. He has published extensively on human rights and Hispanic-Serving Institutions including the chapters and journal articles "Understanding Human Rights along the US-Mexico Border through a Decolonial Lens" (*Decolonizing Approaches in Human Rights and Social Work*, 2023), "Lucha Libre and Cultural Icons: Successful College Transition Programs at Hispanic-Serving Institutions" (*New Directions for Higher Education*, 2015), and the article "Decolonizing Leadership: Towards Equity and Justice at Hispanic-Serving Institutions and Emerging HSIs (eHSIs)" (w/ Garcia, *Journal of Transformative Leadership and Policy Studies*, 2018).

Dr. Ángel David Nieves was dean's professor of public and digital humanities and director of the Humanities Center at Northeastern University. He was also professor of Africana studies and history and was an affiliate professor in the Department of English and in the School of Public Policy and Urban Affairs. He was the author of *An Architecture of Education: African American Women Design the New South* (2018/2020) and coeditor of *"We Shall Independent Be": African American Place Making and the Struggle to Claim Space in the U.S.* (w/Alexander, 2008). He coedited a volume in the Debates in the Digital Humanities Series, *People, Practice, Power: Digital Humanities Outside the Center* (w/Senier and McGrail, December 2021).

Dr. Olivia Quintanilla is a professor in the Department of Ethnic Studies at MiraCosta Community College. She is also a University of California president's postdoctoral fellow at the University of California-Santa Barbara.

Mildred Ramos is a teacher at 93rd Street School in the Los Angeles Unified School District. She is a proud graduate of California State University, Dominguez Hills.

Dr. Jen Stacy is an associate professor in the College of Education at California State University, Dominguez Hills. Her scholarship has focused primarily on literacy and culture in educational studies and has published the following chapters: "Deconstructing the Presentation of Self: Collaborative Intersectionality in Researcher-Participant Relations at a Hispanic-Serving Institution" (*Doing Fieldwork at Home: The Ethnography of Education in Familiar Contexts*, 2021), "Performing Neoliberalism: A Synecdochic Case of Kurdish Mothers' English Learning in a Nebraska Family Literacy Program" (*Refugee Education across the Lifespan: Mapping Experiences of Language Learning and Use*, 2021), and the article "Centering Language, Culture, and Power in Dual Language Teacher Preparation" (w/Fernandez and Reyes McGovern, *Journal of Culture and Values in Education*, 2020).

Cassie Tanks, MSLS, is an archivist, aspiring historian, and first-generation student originally from San Diego, California. She is pursuing a PhD in world history at Northeastern University, has an MSLS from the University of North Carolina at Chapel Hill, and a BA in history from San Diego State University. Tanks is developing the collaborative public digital history project "After the War," contributes to the Reckonings Project and *Apartheid Heritage(s)* at Northeastern University, developed the UNC Story Archive and "Queerolina: A spatial Exploration of LGBTQiA+ Experiences through Oral History" at UNC Chapel Hill, and is experienced in connecting students, community, and faculty with digital humanities skills.

Dr. Carolina Villarroel is the Brown Foundation director of research at the US Latino Digital Humanities Center at the University of Houston. She has published extensively on issues related to Latinx Digital Humanities including "Recovering the US Hispanic Literary Heritage: A Case Study on US Latina/o Archives and Digital Humanities" (w Baeza Ventura and Gauthereau, *Preservation, Digital Technology & Culture*, 2019) and the forthcoming "US Latinx Digital Humanities Manifesto" (w/ Baeza Ventura, Cotera, García Merchant, and Gauthereau, *Debates in Digital Humanities*, 2023) and is the coeditor of the forthcoming volume *The Penguin Book of Latina Writings* (w/ Baeza Ventura, 2024).

Dr. Donna Vukelich-Selva is an associate professor in the division of education at Edgewood College. She piloted and continues to teach a freshman seminar on immigration, Rethinking the Border, and is active in the Madison community. Her research interests include critical race theory, immigration, bilingual education, and restorative justice, and she has several publications in these areas including "We Are Trayvon's Teachers: Disrupting Racial Profiling in Schools" (*Trayvon Martin, Race, and American Justice: Writing Wrong*, 2015) and *Immigrant Children Negotiate School: The Border in Our Hearts* (2014).

Dr. Cynthia Wise is a postdoctoral fellow in the Borderlands and Ethnic Studies program at New Mexico State University. Her research interests focus on critical raza theory, educational equity, and ethnic studies.

Annette M. Zapata, MA, is a lecturer in the Department of Spanish at Lone Star College. She is currently completing her PhD at the University of Houston, and her focus is on Latinx literature, feminist studies, and digital humanities.

Index

Note: References in *italic* refer to figures.
References followed by "n" refer to endnotes.

access doctrine, 9, 14
Acevedo, Elizabeth, 90
Adler, Mortimor J., 105
African-Americans, 4, 191; conflict with Dominicans, 88; students, 3. *See also* Blacks
Afro-Latin American Research Institute, 70n3
Afro-Latin American studies, 59
Afro-Latinx, 88; communities/peoples, 20; cultural actors, 18; diaspora, 15; students, 50, 56
AFSC. *See* American Friends Service Committee
Aliento, 201
Aljoe, Nicole N., 190
Alternative Historiographies of the Digital Humanities (Kim and Koh), 13
Althusser, Louis, 38
Alverno College in Milwaukee, 183–84
American Dream, 67, 72n41
American Friends Service Committee (AFSC), 196
Andrews, Dorinda Carter, 104
Andrew W. Mellon Foundation, 18, 129, 179

anti-Asian racism, 11
Anzaldúa, Gloria, 14, 33, 36, 149
Aparicio, Frances, 154
APPDigital, 128, 139n7
Aquino-Bermúdez, Federico, 3
ArcGIS, 176
archipelago/a journal of Caribbean digital praxis, 18
Arizmendi, Elena, 130
Arriaga, Eduard, 13, 15
art and creations, 201–2, *203*
Arte Público Press (APP), 19, 128, 138n5, 152
Arthur Clarke Center for Human Imagination, 170, 178
assignment(s): classroom, 174–77; First Blacks (*see* First Blacks in Americas research assignment); immigrant obituary, poem assignment, 64–68; podcast (*see* podcast assignment); scaffolded, 132–34; space and place, memory, and place attachment assignment, 59–64
Association of Latina/o Students (AL@S), 185
Atlantic slave trade, 49, 56, 59
authenticity, 84, 89, 168

242 | Index

Aztlán, 2

banking, 86
Barrio Logan, 2
Benedict, Ruth, 80
Benjamin, Walter, 147
Bentley, Courtney C., 69
bhabha, homi, 149
Big Tent, 12–13
bilingualism, 21, 107, 110
BIPOC (Black, Indigenous, and people of color), 12, 13, 23; community groups, 24, 25; faculty, 23–24; students, 8
Blackboard, 20
Blackboard Discussion Board, 53–54, 59, 60, 61
Blacks: enslaved, 49–50, 56, 59; free, 49–50, 56; in Santo Domingo, 49; in Spain and Brazil, 49. *See also* African-Americans; First Blacks in Americas research assignment
BMCC. *See* Borough of Manhattan Community College
bootstrapping, 9, 14
Borderlands/La Frontera (Anzaldúa), 33
"Border Wars," 12
Borough of Manhattan Community College (BMCC), 20, 53, 69
Bracero History Archive, 131
Bracero Program, 10–11
Brady, Mary Pat, 10
Brown Beret Mario Solis, 2
Bucholtz, Mary, 102

California community college (CCC), 164–66; Latinx students in, 164–66
California State University (CSU), 164
California State University Dominguez Hills (CSUDH), 97, 98; Latinx pre-service teachers, 100–101; teacher education program, 98, 101–2, 108

California State University System's Retirement Fund, 18
Campos, Isis, 150
Candy Torres Collection, 134
Capetillo, Luisa, 130
care: in Latinx Studies classrooms, 82–86; relationship with trust, 92
CARES (Coronavirus Aid, Recovery and Economic Relief Act), 225
Caribbean Digital Scholarship Collective (CDSC), 18, 169
Carter, Bryan W., 80
Casa Alitas (shelter), 194
Casa Mariposas (shelter), 194
Casillas, Dolores Inés, 102
Caswell, Michelle, 128
CCC. *See* California community college
CDSC. *See* Caribbean Digital Scholarship Collective
Censer, Jack R., 11
Center for Puerto Rican Studies (Centro de Estudios Puertorriqueños), 78
Chavez, Leo R., 34
Chicana/o Studies programs, 9, 77, 82, 165, 184, 221, 223: New Mexico State University, 40; University of Texas at El Paso, 20
Chicana por mi Raza Digital Memory project (CPMR), 10, 130
Chicano Movement, 3
Chicano Park, 2–3
Chicano Studies Research Center, 165
Chung, Tiffany, 175
Cifor, Marika, 128
citizen, 34–35
City University of New York (CUNY), 3, 4, 68; Borough of Manhattan Community College, 20, 53, 69; Dominican Studies Institute, 49, 223–24

Clark, Christine, 54
Clark-Ibáñez, Marisol, 196
classroom(s): assignments and projects (case study), 174–77; cultural deficit models in, 82; culture of *confianza*, 82–86; digital technology in, 50; excitement in, 50–51; Hispanic-serving, 81–82, 220; open educational resource in, 50; texts and teaching, 93n13; undergraduate, Omeka in, 131–32; via videoconferences, 92
Clinton, Bill, 193
Colored Conventions Project, 131
Comic-Con, 171
community digital archives: future of, 155–56; practices in, 147–50. *See also* familial digital archive
"Community Digital Stories" assignment, 85
confianza, 82–86
consciousness: critical, 84, 86–89, 93n13; differential, 37; oppositional, 20, 35, 37
ContraVR, 170, 171
COR Program, 184, 189, 191, 208
Cotera, María, 1, 10, 130, 148, 223
counter-storytelling, 37–38, 40
COVID-19 pandemic, 117, 163, 219, 221; CARES, 225; digital divide and, 39; lack of access to technology devices during, 52–53; reimagining of education during, 41
CPMR. *See* Chicana por mi Raza Digital Memory project
Craig, Eva, 3
critical consciousness, 84, 86–89, 93n13; about US-Mexico border, 88; developing, 92
Critical Race Counterstories along the Chicana/ Chicano Educational Pipeline (Yosso), 164

critical race theory (CRT), 37, 185–86
Critical Refugee Studies Collective (CRSC), 169; repository for, 175–76; story maps with, 175–76
Cro, Melinda A., 103
CRSC. *See* Critical Refugee Studies Collective
CSUDH. *See* California State University Dominguez Hills
CUNY. *See* City University of New York

DACA. *See* Deferred Action for Childhood Arrivals
Dane County, 184
de Burton, María Amparo Ruiz, 130
DEFCon. *See* Digital Ethnic Futures Consortium
Deferred Action for Childhood Arrivals (DACA), 208; DACAmented students, 187, 188, 190, 192, 194–95, 207, 209; policy, 203; recipients, 201
deficit-based thinking, 165–66
dehumanization, 19–20, 220; immigrant threats and, 34; of Latinx, 34, 76, 77; of Mexican workers, 41; practice of, 33, 35; rehumanization *vs.*, 36; as tool of racism, 33
De León, Jason, 192–93
Delgado Bernal, Dolores, 186
Delis Negrón Digital Archive, 145–58, 224; creation of, 150–52; engagement with Latinx communities as HSI, 152–55; future of, 155–56; initial curation of, 158n2; overview, 145–47; practices in, 147–50
deontological ethics, 212n37
Detainee Allies project, 18
DeVos, Betsy, 11, 12

Dewey, John, 38
DHNow, 24
Digication, 68, 79, 81
digital age: rehumanization in, 38–41; students of, 38, 40
digital archives. *See* community digital archives
digital citizenship, 192, 196, 220
digital cultural record, 147, 149, 155; historical representations in, 158; in *New Digital Worlds,* 146; postcolonial, 147, 148
digital divide, 11, 12, 39
digital ethics, 192
Digital Ethnic Futures Consortium (DEFCon), 179
Digital Ethnic Studies: blueprint for, 179; community-based (case studies), 169–79; curriculum, 178, 179; practitioners, 179
digital humanities (DH), 9–15, 18, 20, 23–25, 136, 221–23; community projects, 157; definition, 5–8; initiatives, 18, 153, 190; interdisciplinary, 103; and new literacies, 103–4; postcolonial, 146, 149, 151, 154, 157; practice in, 20; problem of poverty, 8–9; scholarship, 149; training, 136; US Latinx Digital Humanities Center (USLDH), 21, 128, 129, 131–132, 137
digital photography, 196–99
digital resources, 203–4
digital storytelling, 81, 83, 85, 88, 104, 195–96, 223, 224; platforms, 22, 172; practices, 146, 147; projects, 146, 151, 152, 155; software, 79; techniques, 41
digital text, marking up, 6, 7
digital tools, 6, 9, 12, 15, 25, 53–55, 79–81, 90, 91, 223; for authentic teaching and learning, 91–92; Blackboard Discussion Board, 53–54, 59, 60, 61; Flipgrid, 63–64; Google Docs, 20, 53–54, 64, 65; Google Slides, 59–60; investments in, 226; Mapillary, 58; project-based learning, 135–36; to support learning, 80, 81, 88; used in immigrant obituary, poem assignment, 64; used in space and place, memory, and place attachment assignment, 59; use in classrooms, 90, *90–91*; videoconferencing, 79–80; Zoom, 63
Dinsman, Melissa, 13
Doherty, Mary Kate, 58
Dominicans, 78, 221; conflict with African-Americans, 88; cultural practices of, 104; in New York City, 78–79; Northeast Coast campuses, 222
Dominican Studies, 9, 59
DREAM Act, 187
DRSOJ project, 169, 177–79
Dublin Core, 133, 158n27; metadata, 132; standards, 135
Duran, Paola, 67

EBSCO database, 138n6
Edgewood College, 184–85, 192, 194, 208, 211n27; community, 189–90, 199, 202, 205, 206; COR Program, 184, 189, 191; funding to serve Latinx students, 191; LIBRE project (*see* Leadership Institute for Borderland Research and Education); student participation gap at, 186–87; Undergraduate Student Research program, 199
Educational Opportunity Program (EOP), 184
Edward, Susan, 190

El Paso Art Museum, 41
El Plan Espiritual de Aztlán, 2
Empire Zinc Mining strike, 41
encuentro, 1, 130
English Learners (ELs), 99
EOP. *See* Educational Opportunity Program
epistemological pluralism, 106, 111, 224
ethical theories, 192, 212n37
The Ethics of Care: Personal, Political, Global (Held), 133
Eugenio María de Hostos Community College, 4, 9
Every Student Succeeds Act of 2015, 119n11
Excelencia in Education, 183

Facebook, 39, 199; mobilizing Arab youth, 40
FaceTime, 80
face-to-face class, 51, 61, 79
familial digital archive: creation of, 150–52; engagement with Latinx communities as HSI, 152–55; future of, 155–56; practices in, 147–50. *See also* community digital archives
Feminismo Internacional (Arizmendi), 130, 134, 139n10
feminist pedagogy, 128; developing, 129–31
FIRRP. *See* Florence Immigrant & Refugee Rights Project
First Blacks in Americas research assignment, 20, 49, 50, 51; assessment, 55–56; digital tool used, 55; learning objectives, 55; method, 55; rehumanizes Latinx education, 56–58; teaching, future possibilities for, 58–59
Flipgrid, 63–64
Florence Immigrant & Refugee Rights Project (FIRRP), 203

Floyd, George, 11, 88
Fraìnquiz, Maria E., 100, 102
Freire, Paulo, 39, 51, 99, 100, 135
Friedrich, Markus, 147, 148
fronteras, 1–2, 4, 12, 22, 170
Front|eras: case study, 170–73; future of, 177; imagines San Diego, 170–71; re-imagine education through science fiction lens, 172–73

Gachago, Daniela, 69
Garcia, Gina A., 14, 184
García, Ofelia, 102
García-Peña, Lorgia, 88
Garcia-Torres, Julietta A., 3
Garza, María Luisa, 130
Gil, Alex, 13, 15, 18
Glover, Kaiama, 15, 18
Golumbia, David, 13
Gonzalez, Corky, 2
Google Docs, 20, 53–54, 64, 65, 223
Google Earth, 59
Google Slides, 59–60
Gorski, Paul, 54
Gran Colombia, 67, 71n36
Greene, Dan, 9
group e-portfolio, 89, 90, *90, 91*
Guadalupe Triptych, 3
Guatemalan immigrants, 62
Guerrero, Jahdai, 202, *202*

Haaland, Deb, 40
HACU. *See* Hispanic Association of Colleges & University
Halpern, Jodi, 84–85
Harney, Stefano, 1
HEA Reauthorization Act of 2008, 226
Held, Virginia, 133
Heppler, Jason, 6
Hernandez, Daisy, 90
Hispanic Association of Colleges & University (HACU), 184

Hispanic Periodicals in the United States (Kanellos and Martell), 139n13
Hispanic-Serving Institutions (HSIs), 4, 14, 81–82, 116–17, 131, 183, 219–22, 228; advocacy for, 221; Alverno College as, 184; approaches of, 23; BMCC, 22, 53; cases of, 227–28; classrooms, 223; contributions of, 146; CSUDH (*see* California State University Dominguez Hills); DH's place in, 9, 25; engagement with Latinx communities as, 152–55; humanizing pedagogy at, 100; key innovators at, 23; rehumanizing course, designing, 77–79; reimagine practices, 39; San Diego State University, 18; teacher education programs, 98, 117; teacher preparation programs, 98; in Wisconsin, 184
H-Net, 24
Hockey, Susan, 7
hooks, bell, 10, 50, 51
Hostos, Eugenio Maria de, 50, 223. *See also* Eugenio María de Hostos Community College
Humanities Commons, 24
humanizing pedagogy, 98–100, 103; critical consciousness, 86; educational settings, 82; at HSI, 100; skills, 104; in teacher education, 98, 100, 117; translanguaging as, 101–3. *See also* rehumanizing education

ICE. *See* Immigration and Customs Enforcement
ideological state apparatus (ISA), 38
Immigrant History Research Center (IHRC), 196
"Immigrant Obituary" (Pietri), 66, 69, 72n38

immigrant(s), 33, 59, 88, 207; Dominican, 78; Guatemalan, 62; LGBT, 194; Mexican, 88; perpetual immigrant, 35, 42
immigrant obituary, poem assignment: assessment, 64–65; digital tool used, 64; instructions, 65–66; learning objectives, 64; rehumanizes Latinx education, 66–68; teaching, future possibilities for, 68
immigration, 201, 205, 206, 208; for freshman and sophomore students, 184; historical patterns, 34; illegal, 34, 87; legal, 87; LIBRE project and, 187, 188; in predominantly white institutions, 22; rehumanizing education and, 187; restrictive policies, 41. *See also* migration
Immigration and Customs Enforcement (ICE), 194, 203–4, *204*, 208, 218
iMovie, 68, 79
Instagram, 39, 199
International Business Machines (IBM), 6
International DH Conference (Mexico City), 18
ISA. *See* ideological state apparatus

John Jay College of Criminal Justice, 68, 75; First Center for Puerto Rican Studies, 78; commuter campus, 79; Digication, 68, 79, 81; Department of Latin American and Latina/o Studies, 78; student population, 78; students, 80, 83, 84
John Jay Global Learning Community, 68, 75, 77, 80
Johnson, Jessica Marie, 13, 15
Jones, James, 40
Jones, Rodney H., 108, 109

Kanellos, Nicolás, 127, 139n13
Kearns, Sara K., 103
Kellner, Douglas, 38
Kendi, Ibram X., 13
Kim, Dorothy, 13
Kim, Gooyong, 38
kindness, 168
Kymlicka, Will, 38–39

Ladson-Billings, Gloria, 187
Lara-Bonilla, Inmaculada, 4
Las Mujeres Muralistas, 3
Latina/o critical theory (LatCrit), 185, 186
Latinidad, 76, 77, 78, 83, 84, 89, 90, 92, 222
Latino cARTographies project, 18
The Latino Threat: Constructing Immigrants, Citizens, and the Nation (Chavez), 34
"Latino Threat Narrative," 34, 42
Lazo, Rodrigo, 128, 155
LCSH. *See* Library of Congress Subject Headings
Leadership Institute for Borderland Research and Education (LIBRE), 185–210; art and creations, 201–2, *203*; collaboration with USR program, 188; digital photography, 196–99; digital resources, 203–4; digital storytelling, 195–96; Edgewood College Community, impact on, 206–8, 191; immigration and, 187, 188; Latinx students, rehumanizing education for, 188; non-Latinx students, rehumanizing education for, 188–89; LIBRE trip, 188–90, 193–95, 205–7, 209; participants, 196, 204, 207, 208; pedagogical implications, 195; research project, 206; research technology tools, 195; results and implications of, 205; social media, 199–201
learning, 224; humanizing, 100; online, 220; pre-service teachers, 104; project-based, 135–36; transformative, 82, 89, 220
learning management systems, 219–20
learning objectives, 52, 76, 227; courses, 50; of First Blacks in Americas research assignment, 55; immigrant obituary, poem assignment, 64; space and place, memory, and place attachment assignment, 59
Lee, Jin Sook, 102
Leonor Villegas de Magnón Collection, 134
LGBT immigrants, 194
liberatory pedagogy, 167
Library of Congress Subject Headings (LCSH), 133, 135
LIBRE. *See* Leadership Institute for Borderland Research and Education
literacy practices, 103–4
Lopez, Yolanda, 3
Lortie, Dan, 99
Lucero-Montano, Alfredo, 147

Madison community, 206
Maldonado, Angeles, 194, 203
Maldonado, Ray Ybarra, 194, 203
Mapillary, 58
map makers, 22
markup languages, 6–7
Martell, Helvetia, 139n13
Mattson, Kristen, 192
MAYA. *See* Mexican American Youth Association
McDade, Tony, 88
McGee, Patricia, 80
McPherson, Tara, 172
McWilliam, Carey, 138n4

MEChA. *See* Movimiento Estudiantil Chicano de Aztlán
Mexican-American: culture and politics, 147; population, 88; student, 16; Studies courses, 140n19. *See also* US-Mexico border
Mexican American Youth Association (MAYA), 16, 17
Microsoft Moviemaker, 68, 79
migration, 34, 35; global patterns, 39; in Guatemala, 62; Puerto Rican, 155. *See also* immigration
Minority-Serving Cyberinfrastructure Consortium (MSCC), 225–26
Minority-Serving Institutions, 226
mission, values, and inclusion (MVI), 185
Moodle, 54
Moraga, Cherrie, 149
Moral Social (Hostos), 70n6
Moreno, Victoria, 150
Moten, Fred, 1, 10
Movimiento Estudiantil Chicano de Aztlán (MEChA), 2
Mubarak, Hosni, 40
My Space, 85

Nafid, Zenab, 197, *198*, 199
narrative storytelling, 104, 105
National Endowment for the Humanities (NEH), 10
nature law ethics, 212n37
Navarro, Mindy, 199
Negrón, Delis, 21–22. *See also* Delis Negrón Digital Archive
NEH. *See* National Endowment for the Humanities
New Mexico State University (NMSU), 40–41
New York City: Dominicans in, 78–79; rapid gentrification, 84; students in, 91; undocumented students in, 86–87
No Child Left Behind Act of 2002, 119n11
Norton, Nadjwa E. L., 69

Obama, Barack, 76
Office of Student Inclusion and Involvement, 184–85
Okhidoi, Otgonjargal, 184
Olmos, Ana María Guzmán, 7
Omeka, 131–36; community outreach, 136–37; Latinx feminist praxis, 136; metadata field, 132; scaffolded assignment, 132–34; in undergraduate classroom, 131–32
ontological plurality, 116
Operation Streamline, 193–94, 200, 202, 209
Otay Mesa Detention Center, 18
Otheguy, Ricardo, 102, 112
othering, 33

Pai, Ajit, 11
Pakistani students, 52
PATH. *See* Preparing Accomplished Transfers to the Humanities
Paulino, Emmanuel, 63
PBL. *See* project-based learning
pedagogical alterity, 220
pedagogy: applying methodologies to, 168–69; approaches and methods, 166–68; colonizing, 221; digital, 49–69, 127–37; homeland, 69; humanizing (*see* humanizing pedagogy); innovative, 228; liberatory, 167; sentipensante, 167
Pérez, Emma, 76
perpetual immigrant, 35, 42
Pietri, Pedro, 52, 66–67
Planned Parenthood Collection, 134

Pluriversity Imagination Collective, 41
podcast: definition, 104; development, 105; resources for, 122
podcast assignment, 97–98, 104–5; culture, 109–13; culture as practice, exploring, 113–16; interlocuters in, *110*
postcolonial digital humanities, 146, 149, 151, 154, 157
Powell, Adam Clayton, 3
Preparing Accomplished Transfers to the Humanities (PATH), 178
pre-service teachers, 98, 99, 104; at CSUDH, 100–101; learning, 104; teachers, 224; training, 117
project-based learning (PBL), 135–36
"Puerto Rican Obituary" (Pietri), 52, 66
Puerto Ricans, 66, 155, 221; cultural and literary production of, 154; heritage, 145; migrants, 78, 158n5; Northeast Coast campuses, 222; students, 52

Quinametzin, 2
Quiroz, Pamela Ann, 18

Rabb.it, 90
racism: anti-Asian, 11; dehumanization as tool of, 33; institutionalized, 168; institutional power and, 37; structural and systemic, 221
Ramírez, Mario H., 128
Ramírez, Sarah Estela, 130
Recovery Program, 21, 137, 138n5, 150; collections, 131; at Hispanic-Serving Institution, 128; marginalized archive housed at, 132; mission, 129; US Hispanic Literary Heritage, 127, 145
regional myopia, 76–77

rehumanizing education, 77–79, 81–82, 102, 172; in California community college, 164–66; curriculum of, 20, 33, 35, 42; definition, 35–38; in digital age, 38–41; for faculty and staff, 189–90; First Blacks in Americas research assignment, 56–58; immigrant obituary, poem assignment, 66–68; for non-Latinx students, 188–89; practices, 99, 105, 116–18; space and place, memory, and place attachment assignment, 61–63; in teacher education, 99–101; and theoretical framework, 185–87; trust and, 85
Reid, Wallis, 102
Rendón, Laura I., 167
research technology tools, 195
respeto mutua, 83
Reyes III, Reynaldo, 102
Risam, Roopika, 18, 146, 148, 149, 190
Rivera, Lysa, 168
Robinson, Cecil, 138n4
Rockefeller Foundation, 127
Rodriguez, Laura, 2
Rosenzweig, Roy, 11
Ruiz, Marisol, 38
Ruiz, Vicki, 10, 148

Saisó, Ernesto Priani, 7
Salazar, Maria del Carmen, 82, 100, 102
Salinas City Elementary School District, 11
Salinas Valley of California, 11–12
Salmeron, Lupe, 196, 197, *197*
Same Boats, 18
San Diego: downtown waterfront, 174; Front|eras imagines, 170–71; Futures

San Diego *(continued)*
  Foundation, 178; re-imagining and creating future waterfront, 174–77
San Diego Community College District, 169
San Diego State College (SDSC), 2, 3, 9, 16
San Diego State University (SDSU), 18
Sandoval, Chela, 35, 36
scaffolded assignment, 132–34
Scalar project, 177
Scheinfeldt, Tom, 11
science fiction (SF), 172–73, 176–77
Scollon, Ron, 108, 109
Scollon, Suzanne Wong, 108, 109
SDSC. *See* San Diego State College
SDSU. *See* San Diego State University
Shabazz, Betty, 3
Shellenberg, Theodore R., 138n4
Sing Down the Moon, 39
Sixteenth-Century La Española, 49
Skype, 80, 90
slavery: in Americas, 49, 57, 58; in Latin America, 58; in Santo Domingo, 56–57, 59
Smith, Martha Nell, 13
Snow, Justin, 190
social contract ethics, 212n37
social identity, 34, 42, 98, 99, 100, 102, 116
social media, 199–201, 224; sites, 39–40
Soja, Edward, 10
Solórzano, Daniel G., 186
Southside Presbyterian Church, 193
Spanish Paleography Digital Teaching and Learning Tool, 55, 56
speculative tools of knowledge, 164, 167–68
Spivak, Gayatri, 149
STEM, 226
Stevens-Acevedo, Anthony, 49

Stewart, Kristian, 69
story map/mapping, *173*, 175–76
StoryMaps, 22
super-diversity, 88
Svensson, Patrik, 12

Take Back the Archive, 132
The Tattooed Soldier (Tobar), 52, 59, 60, 63
Taylor, Brionna, 88
teacher education: courses, 103; HSI programs, 117; humanizing, 104, 118; humanizing pedagogies in, 98, 100, 117; pre-service teachers, 224; programs, 21; rehumanizing Latinx education in, 99–101; undergraduate program at CSUDH, 98, 101, 108
technology, 40–41, 224; access to, 12, 15, 25, 52–53, 54; devices, 52; digital, 6, 9, 50, 146, 176, 185; mobile, 103; use at US-Mexico border, 41. *See also* individual entries
testimonios, 186, 188, 196, 205
Text Encoding Initiative (TEI), 7–8
TikTok, 39
Tobar, Hector, 52
Tohono O'odham Nation, 190, 193, 209, 224
Torn Apart/Separados, 18
Torre, Cecilia de la, 3
Torre, Rosa de la, 3
Torres, Carmelita, 40–41
transformative learning, 82, 89, 220
transfronterizeros, 171
translanguaging, 98, 100, 102, 105–6; definition, 102; as humanizing pedagogy, 101–3; moments, 108–16; with multilingual students, 102; in multiple facets of learning, 103; podcast through, 105, 108–16; power of, 113; resources for, 122; students, 116

Trump, Donald, 11, 76, 187, 191
trust, 85, 92, 93n13
trust-building: "Community Digital Stories" assignment, 85; and videoconferencing, 83
Twine, 22, 172, *173*, 177, 224
Twitter, 40, 199

UCLA. *See* University of California, Los Angeles
Uncaged Art, 41
undocumented students, 86–87, 187, 195, 207
Undocumented Students for Education Equity (USEE), 195
United Fruit Company, 51, 62
Universidad Nacional Autónoma de México, 7
University of California (UC), 164
University of California, Los Angeles (UCLA)
University of California San Diego, 169, 178; Arthur Clarke Center for Human Imagination, 170, 178; School of Global Policy and Strategy, 170; students of color at, 178
University of Houston (UH), 127, 129, 131, 145; Latino cARTographies project, 18; Special Collections, 128, 132
University of Texas, El Paso (UTEP), 68, 75, 83–84, 86, 87, 91; heterogeneity in, 77–78; local needs and, 78
Urban and Ethnic Studies (UES), 3
USEE. *See* Undocumented Students for Education Equity
US Hispanic Literary Heritage, 127, 145, 152, 224

US Latinx Digital Humanities Center (USLDH), 21, 128, 129, 131–132, 137
US-Mexico border, 4, 89, 145, 157, 187; critical consciousness about, 88; documenting counter-stories about, 22; human rights violations, 41; immigration policies and practices, 190, 195; messages about, 84; migrant laborers at, 41; service-learning trip to, 208; state-sanctioned violence, 87; wall, 196–99, *197*, *198*; weaponized technologies utilized at, 5
UTEP. *See* University of Texas, El Paso
utilitarian ethics, 212n37

Van Doren, Charles, 105
videoconferencing, 20, 79–80, 83, 86, 88, 219–20; classroom culture of *confianza* live via, 84; for communication, 80
virtue ethics, 212n37
Vygotsky, Lev S., 38

Wargo, Jon, 103
web-based applications, 68, 79
Weinstein, Harvey M., 84–85
Whitman, Walt, 68
Wisconsin Association of Independent College and Universities (WAICU), 206
Wix, 151, 152, 158n26

Yosso, Tara J., 164
YouTube, 39, 41

Zarnow, Leandra, 140n24
Zoom, 63